Hippy Days, Arabian Nights

From life in the bush to love on the Nile

KATHERINE BOLAND

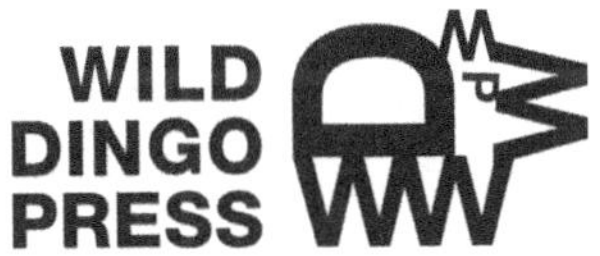

Published by Wild Dingo Press
Melbourne, Australia
books@wilddingopress.com.au
www.wilddingopress.com.au

First published by Wild Dingo Press 2017

Cover design: Gisela Beer, Mihirini De Zoysa Lewis and Emma Statham
Typesetting: Midland Typesetters, Australia
Editors: Katia Ariel and Catherine Lewis
Printer: Markono Print Media

National Library of Australia
Cataloguing-in-Publications Data

Boland, Katherine F, 1957-

Hippy days. Arabian nights: from life in the bush
to love on the Nile / Katherine Boland.

ISBN: 9780987381323 (paperback)

Boland, Katherine F.
Artists—Victoria—Melbourne—Biography.
Hippies—New South Wales—Biography.

Praise for *Hippy Days, Arabian Nights*

Katherine Boland's motto: 'Feel the fear and do it anyway', perfectly describes her absorbing story of courageous lifestyle choices. Told with exquisitely crafted prose and a whimsical sense of humour, the captivating imagery – which takes you from the uniqueness of the Australian bush to the exoticism of faraway Egypt – will have you wishing you lived in Katherine's shoes! A gripping story of true love with an admirable resolution. This should be read by many!

—Cheryl Koenig OAM, author,
2009 NSW Woman of the Year

This sparkling memoir will take you deeply into the lives of back-to-the-earth, self-sustaining hippies of the 70s, 80s and 90s and a passionate relationship between a feminist free-thinker and an Egyptian man twenty-seven years her junior. Artist Katherine Boland lived on the edge of social mores that most of us cling to. She tells her extraordinary story with humour, insight and a painterly eye.

—Jill Sanguinetti, educator and author

Make sure you read Katherine Boland's memoir, though fair warning, you won't want to put it down! Funny, wry, heartbreaking at times but always utterly absorbing, this is a must-read. Katherine has lived her life heart first; and her quest to collect experiences has been successful, to say the least. They say a life lived in fear is a life half lived, but Katherine felt the fear and did it anyway, living her life to the full. Katherine will charm readers with her self-deprecating humour and engaging frankness.

—Rebecca Barber,
Australian National University Library

To the mothership

Disclaimer

Every care has been taken to verify names, dates and details throughout this book but, as much is reliant on memory, some unintentional errors may have occurred. On occasions, real names have been replaced with substitute names to protect the privacy of those people.

The Publisher assumes no legal liability or responsibility for inaccuracies; they do, however, welcome any information that will redress them.

I've been absolutely terrified every moment of my life –
and I've never let it keep me from doing a single thing
I wanted to do.

—Georgia O'Keeffe

PART ONE

Hippy Days

We must cultivate our garden.
—Voltaire

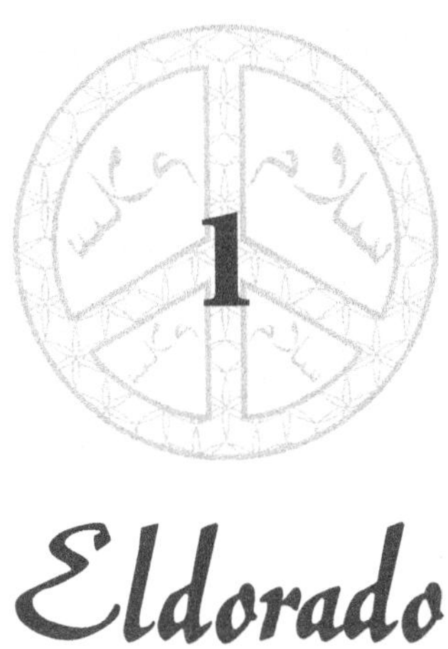

1

Eldorado

The Space Age Bookshop on Swanston Street adjacent to the Royal Melbourne Institute of Technology was a mecca for many an aspiring hippy living in Melbourne in the seventies. Once a week, I'd skip a life drawing class or a lecture on art theory and cross the road to check out the latest additions to their impressive collection of alternative lifestyle literature. Stepping through the sticky-taped and poster-plastered door, I'd enter a muted and bountiful world, far removed from the clamour and hubbub on the other side of the plate glass window. Amidst the haze of smouldering Nag Champa incense, to the dulcet strains of Pink Floyd, I'd scan the room; before me shelf upon shelf lined with books on every topic imaginable—from companion planting to building yurts, from Bach flower remedies to beekeeping, from kundalini yoga to curing bacon. After selecting a glossy-covered volume, I'd join the other long-haired, patchouli-scented, flared-jean wearing youths to sit cross-legged on the sea grass matting scouring its pages. As poverty-stricken students, we could rarely afford to buy a book but the staff at Space Age were cool, man; they never dreamt of throwing us free-loading undergraduates out on the street.

One day, I managed to scrape enough coins together to purchase a copy of *Earth Garden Magazine*, a quarterly publication featuring articles from hippies all over the country already living 'the good life': growing veggies, preserving fruit, milking goats, spinning wool and puddling mud into bricks. Itching to show it to my boyfriend John, I stuffed the journal into my tapestry shoulder bag and caught the Number 16 tram back to our flat in St Kilda.

'Check this out! This is *it*! This is what we have to do!' I announced as I burst through the back door brandishing the magazine; a cigarette paper and some fragments of marijuana bud wafting off the kitchen table onto the lino. Grinning at me adoringly in greeting, John bent to retrieve the leaf of Tally-ho and as I pulled my chair up beside him, spreading the journal before us, he finished rolling his joint.

Prior to my arrival on the scene, John and my high school sweetheart Shaun shared a grimy, sparsely furnished flat in a lane off Spencer Street in the city. When Shaun ditched me for a blonde and leggy Swedish exchange student, John, with his hazel eyes and spiky Rod Stewart haircut, stayed at home, offering me his shoulder to cry on. The 'angry young man'[1] who'd been dux, school captain and best but never the fairest on the footy ground at Wangaratta Primary had completed his HSC at night school after being expelled from no less than three secondary colleges, including the prestigious Haileybury College, for a pathological disregard for authority. Over the course of the next few months, John bided his time, trusting I'd get over Shaun and hoping I'd fall in love with him.

We had a lot in common. For one thing, we looked alike—

---

1 Used during the mid-20th century to describe young writers, intellectuals and artists who were disillusioned by traditional social norms and society in general.

resembling a pair of brushtail possums with our diminutive stature, fine features and brown hair and eyes. Clad in the regulation unisex garb of the time—denim jackets, bell-bottom jeans and clunky platform shoes, we were often mistaken for brother and sister. We both grew up in rural Victoria, John in the north of the state, me in the south. Like many country kids our age, desperate to escape a stultifying existence in a small country town, we'd left home and our families as soon as possible, keen to embark on an exciting life in the city and eager to launch our brilliant careers. Possessing a similar sense of humour, we shared an interest in Eastern philosophy, preferred dolmades and samosas over 'meat and three veg' and would rather have died than vote for the Libs. We liked the same music—Jackson Browne, Joni Mitchell, Neil Young and read the same books—Huxley, Kafka and Gabriel Garcia Marquez; and agreed that *Midnight Cowboy* and *Nashville* were two of the best films ever made.

Wrestling like bear cubs under the blankets, we'd spend the whole day in bed, kissing, canoodling and discussing everything that mattered, only leaving the flat as the sun set over a glassy Port Phillip Bay. Then laughing and scattering seagulls, we'd race to the end of St Kilda pier and wait in the luminous lilac light for the colony of fairy penguins to come home and roost in the rocks. On cornflower-blue-sky Sundays, we'd take a picnic basket into the Royal Melbourne Botanic Gardens and park ourselves on a tartan rug under a sprawling Moreton Bay fig, squabbling families of yellow-crested cockatoos screeching in the branches above. Nibbling at my chicken wings, I'd listen with rapt attention as my impassioned and gesticulating boyfriend (who could have really done with a soapbox) waxed lyrical about Lenin, Marx and revolutionary socialism.

'The way to crush the bourgeoisie is to grind them between the millstones of taxation and inflation,' John declaimed, quoting Lenin one afternoon.

'Man is born free and everywhere is in chains,' I countered, citing Rousseau's *Social Contract,* trying to get a word in edgeways and add my two-cents-worth to the conversation as I licked the soy-honey marinade from my fingers.

By the end of the year, inseparable and indisputably soulmates, John and I found our own flat to rent and moved in together.

Like half the globe, we'd read Schumacher's *Small Is Beautiful* which denounced the dehumanisation of people by the methods of mass production and advocated a global, small-scale approach to the manufacture of food, goods and services. Rampant materialism was destroying the earth, the renowned author claimed; a seductive thesis that appealed to our blossoming idealism and Arcadian sensibilities. John and I were in agreement—the impending threat of nuclear war notwithstanding, we needed to take a stand, get back to nature and save the planet from toxic pollution. Not only that but the thought of 'working for the man', being chewed up and spat out by the capitalist machine, was becoming an imminently terrifying prospect.

So, it was settled. Despite the fact that Labour Prime Minister, Mr Whitlam, was providing us with a never-to-be-repeated free university education, I'd drop out of art school and John would defer his political science degree at Monash; escaping to the country, we'd grow our own food and become totally self-sufficient. As the plane trees shed their brown-paper leaves and the mustard light, like looking through a glass of pale cider, slanted across the street, we packed our beat-up HR Holden station wagon with wood crates filled with rice, flour and tins of sardines, a two-man tent, a kerosene-fuelled lantern, a cast iron frying pan, a camping stove bought from the army disposal store in Russell Street and our prized possession, a recent purchase from The Space Age Bookshop: *The Vegetable Gardening and Animal Husbandry Handbook.* Young, in love, courageous or just plain foolhardy, with no strong ties, family or anyone significant to bid farewell in Melbourne, we left the city in search of a new life.

Up the Hume Highway, deep into Kelly Country, we arrived around dusk on the outskirts of Eldorado, a hamlet nestled in the Woolshed Valley that, in the 1850s, was the epicentre of the richest goldfields in Victoria.

John grew up on a sheep and wheat farm in the district; his father, Frank was a soldier settler and had been granted a large holding of land as a reward for his services in Papua New Guinea. The farm, spread across a flat and bleak expanse of terrain that had lain fallow for years, was punctuated by stands of limb-dropping river red gums and the odd murky-watered dam when Frank arrived in the parish of Boorhaman in 1951. The returned digger installed his petite and plucky new bride, Annie (whom he'd met in a dance hall in the city on his leave from the Air Force) in a weatherboard cottage set on the front boundary of the isolated property. Before her marriage, Annie was a dancer in the chorus line: four evenings a week she'd fix a victory roll in her hair, don her polka-dot frock, slip on her peep-toe pumps, dab a little *Vol de Nuit* behind her ears, put on some lipstick and rouge, then take her place on stage at the Palais Theatre in St Kilda. Saturdays, she'd play social tennis at the club in Port Melbourne, meet up with friends for a swim at the Sea Baths or go for a stroll along The Esplanade, more often than not dropping by the popular Polish cake shop, Monarch's in Acland Street for a French vanilla slice or chocolate éclair. On Sunday afternoons, she'd catch the tram up Chapel Street to see Fred Astaire and Ginger Rogers in the matinee movie at The Astor. One can only assume that Annie fell deeply for the shy, tall and handsome war veteran in uniform to give up the high life in the Big Smoke for 1000 acres of dirt. Or, perhaps she just didn't think it through.

Frank became an expert at breeding sheep, sowing grain and reaping a harvest from wheat. But when it came to his own seed, the bastards refused to germinate. In the spring of 1956, the nursery painted and decorated in their brand new three-bedroom house, Frank and Annie bundled their two-year-old adopted daughter Kay into the FX Holden and with quiet excitement and nervous anticipation, drove down the Hume to the Sisters of St Joseph's orphanage in Carlton.

Under the stark fluorescent lights, the air saturated with the scent of Pine O Cleen hospital grade disinfectant, a recess bell ringing in a school yard in the distance, the middle-aged couple were led along a row of cribs containing the bathed, talced and tightly swaddled infants; stooping in turn to inspect the sad little parcels of life asleep on their ticking stripe mattresses. John was consigned to a cot at the end of the row and as she looked down upon his wee, worried face, his rosebud lips working as if to suckle, Annie felt a profound and distinct tug inside. Is this what motherly love feels like she wondered? Her heart ached for the tiny forsaken soul, this newborn with a scruffy thatch of tawny hair, yellowish skin and the gaunt features of a drowned rat.

Lifting the puny package from his crib, Annie placed a light-as-a-feather kiss on John's corrugated brow and turned to her husband. Frank, nodding, signalled to Matron.

'We want this one, please,' he said with firm resolve.

John was eleven when Frank took him aside to ask if he wanted to stay on the farm when he grew up. But having watched his father work like a dog, day-in, day-out, year after year, John rejected the offer, horrified by the prospect. The ambitious lad had a grander and more illustrious future in mind. One day he'd be a scientist or like his hero, Olympic athlete Ron Clarke, a long-distance runner. Disappointed but resigned to his son's lack of interest, Frank sold the farm and retired comfortably 'off the sheep's back', buying a triple-fronted brick veneer house on a quarter-acre block in

Wangaratta. A decade later John was working day-in, day-out, on his own property; the irony not wasted on the sheep farmer's son from Boorhaman; and probably not on his father, either.

⛌ ⛌ ⛌

On that first night, like the bushrangers who roamed the Woolshed Valley a hundred years earlier, John and I holed up in a well-hidden spot on the banks of a running creek amongst the undergrowth, grey box and wattles—our home until we found a farmhouse to rent. In the fast fading light, we unloaded our camping gear and pitched the tent. John built a fire with the abundant twigs and branches scattered under the trees; I cooked a lentil and potato stew, boiling the billy just as the gully plummeted into inky darkness.

In our private open-air theatre-restaurant, illuminated by firelight and flying sparks, a backdrop of gum trees swooshing and swaying in the wind, we drew our deck chairs up to the campfire, ate our smoky meal and drank our sweetened tea—enthralled by Mother Nature's dramatic performance and in awe of the life we were on the precipice of living.

A choir of warbling magpies and highly amused kookaburras woke us at dawn. Stretching and yawning, we clambered out of the clammy, airless tent into a fresh and fragrant day to begin, what was to become our unhurried and orderly morning ritual. Together, we collected twigs and broken boughs, lit the fire, cooked breakfast and heated some water in a saucepan; the echoes of our banter accompanied by metal clinking on metal reverberating through the trees as we rinsed our tin mugs and plates in the chipped enamel basin. To a stranger passing by we could've been mistaken for that young couple in McCubbin's triptych, *Pioneer*. On numerous excursions to the National Gallery as a student, I'd sat in reverie before that masterpiece of Australian art, the artist's romantic depiction of the landscape never failing to capture my young and impressionable heart—my hippy heart.

Housing was our first priority. Most days, we'd wipe our faces and 'pink bits' with a warm, wet cloth, dress as neatly as we could, considering our primitive living conditions and head into Wangaratta to make the rounds of the real estate agents; once a week stopping off at the laundromat to do a load of washing before heading back to camp. But as days turned to weeks with the bush becoming a wonderland of crunchy white frost and still with no place to live, the idyll began to lose its gloss. Nights were the worst. Huddled inside the tent lit by a flickering Tilley lamp, we'd toast our be-socked feet on a sooty cast iron pot chocked with red hot coals, and share, for medicinal purposes only, slugs of Jack Daniels straight from the bottle, whilst taking turns to read out loud the only works of fiction we owned— Sartre's mind-numbingly depressing, *Nausea* or Voltaire's comical *Candide,* a battered, second-hand volume I'd kept since studying 18th Century History in Year 12. Sometimes, as much to ward off the bone-chilling cold as to satisfy our youthful urges, we'd try to have sex. Rugged in multiple layers of clothing, looking like a pair of fornicating Michelin Men, we'd awkwardly make love; afterwards, clutching each other for warmth in our tiny refrigerated tomb. Overnight, icy stalactites formed on the tent's ceiling and each morning we'd be woken by a freezing drop of water on an exposed forehead or cheek.

And then it started to rain. Whether it was a hard and merciless downpour or a relentless, insidious drizzle, the rain didn't stop. The campsite became a quagmire. Our sleeping bags, perpetually damp and growing a ghostly film of patchwork mould, began to smell like the dingo enclosure at the Melbourne Zoo. Defecating was a miserable exercise involving a raincoat, a shovel, an umbrella, gumboots and a damp roll of toilet paper. Unable to light a fire outside, we'd be confined to the tent, heating up baked beans on our little butane stove.

There were tears. All of them mine.

'When are we going to find somewhere to live?' I'd snivel, my stiff upper lip giving way to the wobbly lower one.

Staving off mutiny, John would pack me into the station wagon, turn the heater on full blast and take me for a drive. Motoring at a snail's pace through the streets of Eldorado we'd kill time with nowhere particular to be, hoping to come across a 'House to Rent' sign; envious of the lucky inhabitants inside their brightly lit houses, their televisions blinking and smoke curling from chimneys and flues. With my nose pressed against the foggy glass, I'd stare out of the car window and yearn for a home of my own.

✗✗✗

Thankfully, it wasn't too long before we struck gold—a weather-beaten, two-bedroom, unfurnished asbestos-clad shack sat in an ocean of wheat stubble in the sparsely populated farming community of Tarrawingee. On our first night in our luxurious new abode, basking in the sauna-like conditions, we slept on the blow-up mattress *au naturale* in front of a roaring log fire. We decorated the place with bits and pieces gleaned from the local tip and stuff we found by the side of the road. The second-hand shop in town gave us a good deal on a wrought-iron bed, a large pine table, four Bentwood chairs and a jarrah spinning wheel. At a clearance sale on the property next door, we won bids on a leather, horse-hair-stuffed couch, a Fowler's Bottling Kit, a hand-grinding flour mill and a box of mismatched crockery and cutlery.

We were officially ready to become 'alternative life stylers'. In the months that followed, my respect for the early settlers, especially the pioneering women, grew as I came to realise what being self-sufficient entailed. We ground grain into flour and baked crusty loaves of wholemeal bread in our temperamental wood-burning stove. I taught myself to sew, spin wool, knit and crochet. With the help of *The Vegetable Gardening and Animal Husbandry Handbook* we established a thriving veggie garden, cultivating everything from asparagus spears to zucchini flowers. Meanwhile, John became proficient with his burgeoning collection of tools. Armed with the rudimentary skills he'd picked up as a youngster on the farm at Boorhaman, supplemented when necessary with an appropriate reference book, he repaired the house paddock fence, fixed the water pump and built a chicken coop. We raised chickens, bottled fruit, made jam, sauces and pickles from our excess produce. The wizened goat-breeding lady next door showed me how to milk our goat Ellie-Mae and I discovered the instructions for fermenting yoghurt and curdling cottage cheese in a *Grass Roots* magazine.

When our tasks for the day were done, we'd cast off our clothes, spread a patchwork quilt on the ground and practise Hatha Yoga under the gnarled old gum in the backyard—a warm breeze fanning our naked bodies as the sun dropped like a newly minted penny behind the paddock of bleached-blonde wheat.

'*Get off!* This is *serious*. I'm trying to do the downward dog,' I'd say, bum in the air and laughing as John pounced on my lithe, brown-as-a-berry body from behind.

Evenings were reserved for study—Ramacharaka's *Fourteen Lessons in Yogi Philosophy and Oriental Occultism*, *A Guide to the Woodbutcher's Art* and *The Natural Health Book* by the renowned Australian herbalist, Dorothy Hall. Many nights we'd sit around the kitchen table sketching floor plans and elevations of the house we dreamed of building one day.

Yet despite living mostly off the land, and our determination to live outside the mainstream economy, we still needed money—after all, we couldn't barter for rent, petrol or what had become our weekly treat—a king-size block of Cadbury's fruit n' nut chocolate! We found some seasonal work in an apple orchard nearby, so at first light, we'd be on the road to Beechworth, whizzing past paddocks air-brushed in titanium white, steam rising from the ground like a writhing exodus of bushranger's ghosts. There wasn't a great deal to learn about apple picking. First, you strap a large canvas bag to the front of your torso. Next, you position a three-pronged metal ladder under a laden tree. With your fingers sticking to the freezing steel frame and vapour streaming from your dripping nostrils, you climb the icy contraption and pick the fruit.

All day long, we'd sample the produce—Red and Golden Delicious, Gravenstein, Jonathon, Cox, Granny Smith and the ultimate delicacy: the tiny, snowy-fleshed Roman Beauty—rivulets of the sweet-tart juice cascading down our chins with each crispy bite. By lunch time the mist would lift to reveal a sparkling sunny day and lying prone on our hand-spun crocheted rug, we'd eat our scrumptious home-grown bounty: hunks of crusty wholemeal bread, goat cheese, olives and freshly picked cherry tomatoes, washed down with a strong brew of Russian Caravan tea. Apart from the plump, tortoiseshell cats roaming the grounds on the lookout for parrots to kill, we had the orchard to ourselves. But one afternoon, just as John was struggling to zip up his fly, the boss appeared on the horizon. A moment earlier and the elderly and straight-laced Mrs Christensen, would have witnessed a sight to behold—her lusty young employees locked in an amorous embrace, rolling in the grass beneath the boughs of a Golden Delicious.

⚎⚎⚎

Eighteen months had come and gone and we knew what we had to do. Peter Gabriel's lyrics, 'You've got to get in to get out' felt like a personal message. We needed to find a way to make some serious money and buy our own block of land. 'Working for the man' we agreed, with Machiavelli's logic, was a necessary evil, a temporary means to an end.

Another apple-picker mentioned there were jobs going in Western Australia. You could earn big money on the prawn boats, he'd heard. Breaking our lease on the little farmhouse in Tarrawingee, we gave or threw away our motley collection of furniture and most of our belongings and loaded the rest under the ancient wooden canopy in the back of our EH Holden ute. To the blaring of Neil Young and Crazy Horse on the cassette player we headed west; Rael Imperial Aerosol Kid, our recently acquired Siamese kitten named after the hero in Genesis's concept album *A Lamb Lies Down on Broadway*, coming along for the ride.

✗ ✗ ✗

'*Far out!* What's with the trees?' John exclaimed as we came upon a curious spectacle on the outskirts of Geraldton. Neither of us had ever seen anything like it. As far as the eye could see, giant eucalypts stood permanently bent at the waist, their branches spread-eagled all over the ground.

'Salvador Dali would've been rapt,' I joked as, oblivious to what caused the Surrealist landscape, we drove through the avenue of 'liquefied' gums. That evening, we pitched the tent in a clearing in a grove of flowering, camphor-scented melaleuca, the grass carpeted with white petal confetti, but just as we were collecting twigs for a fire, a strong gust of wind (no doubt similar to the one that had subjugated the trees we'd seen earlier that day) snatched up our lightweight shelter and dumped it in a crumpled heap where it stood on the ground. Painstakingly, we unloaded our crates of food and equipment from the back of the ute, wolfed down a meagre and hastily prepared meal and crawled inside the wood canopy to sleep.

Next day, we headed into town to find the local branch of the Commonwealth Employment Service. We'd arranged for our dole payments to coincide with our arrival in Geraldton so at least we'd have some income until we began making our fortune on the prawn boats. However, as John and I stood expectantly at the reception counter, it became clear the C.E.S. had no record of any such arrangement. The best they could do was to issue us with a ten-dollar food voucher which was only redeemable at the local supermarket. Undeterred, we made our way down to the small fleet of fishing boats moored in the harbour.

Figuring this was men's business, John strode purposefully to the far end of the wharf to ask about work and negotiate the terms of our employment. As I sat on shore, teasing Rael with a desiccated ribbon of seaweed, the whiff of fish guts on the strengthening breeze, I could see, in the distance, my boyfriend and a brawny fisherman engaged in a heated argument. Curiously, every so often the two men would turn to look in my direction and a few minutes later, a furious John marched back up the jetty.

'Well that's that,' he announced angrily, reaching my side.

'Why?' I asked. 'What happened?'

'They can give us a job alright,' he said, seething. 'I can work on deck and you can cook down below. But there's a catch. As part of the deal, you have to have sex with the crew.'

So that, definitely, was that. Homeless and practically broke, we used most of the remaining credit on our food voucher to buy tins of cat food for our ravenous kitten. Fortunately, we had enough tinned tomatoes and sardines, dried pulses, rice, tea, sugar, muesli and powdered milk to keep us from starving to death.

For the next few days, we hung out at the beach with the local Aboriginal community, before deciding on a plan of action.

I would go to Sydney, stay with my mother and look for work; John, along with the Royal Siamese, would head north to Mount Tom Price up in the Pilbara. Rumour had it that there were plenty of well-paid jobs for unskilled builder's labourers up in the mines.

'It'll only be for a few months, max,' John assured me when he saw the tears well in my eyes. 'Until we've saved enough money for a deposit on some land.'

For now, though, we didn't even have the funds to buy a train ticket to take me back across the Nullarbor Plain and up to my mother's flat in Vaucluse. We made a beeline for the post office to make a reverse charge call to John's father, hoping he'd cough up for the fare. As John parked the car, I noticed the file of youths, dressed like us in peasant tops, flowing skirts, waistcoats and flares, waiting to use the public phones. Joining the queue, I caught snippets of dialogue as, one by one, the young people made their calls.

'Mum, it's me. Yeah, I'm fine. Listen. Yes, Mum. Listen, Mum. *Mum, listen!* Can you send us some money?' I heard one scruffy desperado beg. Obviously, reports of a 'gold rush' had spread far and wide and it seemed that we weren't the only ones in a precarious predicament.

Eventually, a young man with a ponytail and goatee, possibly a model for one of those Sunday school paintings of an Anglicised, flaxen-haired Jesus, gestured John over to his cubicle; ever so gently placing his receiver down before delicately picking it up again.

'Now you can use it and it won't cost a cent,' he said smiling like an angel as he climbed onto his bicycle.

That morning, someone had super-glued a twenty-cent piece into the slot of the pay phone and numerous mercy calls were made that day.

'Peace,' our young saviour said as, giving us the two-fingered hippy salute, he peddled off down the road.

Our separation lasted all but six weeks. Pining and weepy, unable to bear being apart any longer, I begged John to come back to me. It took my love-sick boyfriend five days driving virtually non-stop from one side of the continent to the other, to reach my mother's door. But by now, John was an experienced brickies labourer; we had a passport to realising our dreams.

John soon found work on a Sydney construction site and we applied for a live-in-maid and gardener/chauffeur position in the salubrious North Shore suburb of Mosman. Lady Hooker, widow of deceased real estate tycoon Sir Leslie Hooker, ushered John and me into her living room overlooking a glittering Middle Harbour. We were barely twenty years old. Although John had tried to conceal his long plait down the back of his shirt and I was wearing a smart and conservative dress bought from the Salvos especially for the occasion, we did *not* look like the usual hired help. However, perhaps softened by the recent death of her husband, Lady Hooker must have taken pity on the babes from the bush perched nervously on the edge of her Herman Miller couch. The kindly old woman with the lavender-tinted, Dame Edna bouffant, agreed to give us and our yowling Siamese cat a three-month trial.

The following day we moved into the servant's quarters, a compact one bedroom flat tucked under the post-modern, Mondrian inspired mansion in Hopetoun Ave—the street recently voted Sydney's Number One by the Australian Financial Review. Greeting us at the top of the garden stairs, Lady Hooker handed John a remote control so he could park our car in the garage next to her shiny silver BMW.

'Is that your car dear?' she asked me, gesturing towards to a late model Golf on the other side of the road.

'No, Lady Hooker. It's that one,' I replied, pointing to the trusty old ute still wearing its dilapidated wooden canopy and covered in red bull dust from the desert.

'Oh my goodness!' she said scanning the street for neighbours. 'Quickly, dear. Put it in the garage.'

That afternoon, John and I grabbed our swimmers and beach towels and raced down the steep flight of sandstone steps, past the hot pink and orange flowering azaleas, hibiscus, bougainvillea and a bronze plaque inscribed with the words, *'Here Lies L J Hooker Kt. who loved this place, this land and especially its people'*, to the water's edge.

Sir Leslie hadn't always lived on the North Shore. Of Chinese heritage, he was orphaned at eight and by thirteen had left school to work as a clerk. At the age of sixteen the ambitious and tenacious young man owned his first property and, after marrying a store-keeper's daughter, Madeline Adella (Delzie) Price and surviving the Depression, his real estate business flourished.

The Depression had obviously left a lasting impression on Delzie Hooker, evident in her passion for recycling. Instructed to wash and dry used bits of Glad Wrap and aluminium foil, I was also directed to scour butter and yoghurt containers before stacking them in toppling towers in the walk-in pantry for re-use as storage containers. Every twelve weeks the three of us would pile into the BMW and head to one of those bulk warehouses to stock up on cut-price washing powder, toilet paper and cleaning products. 'Waste not, want not' extended to such utilities as electricity: John and I scolded if we left the lights on.

In those days, with her husband the largest pastoral landholder in Australia, Lady Hooker was the wealthiest woman in the country and could have well afforded to hire caterers for her Christmas parties. Instead, she and I did the preparations for her guests ourselves. I'd polish the silverware, buff wine glasses and decorate the living room and together we made hundreds of tiny meringues and mini toasted breads smeared with caviar or Camembert. Trussed uncomfortably in pressed trousers, a black satin cumber band and a starched white shirt, John was the waiter: his task to mingle inconspicuously with the guests and refresh their champagne glasses as required. But as I loaded the dishwasher in the kitchen, I could hear John's voice rise above the subdued conversations in the voluminous living room as he launched into a diatribe against the director of the AMA or some other establishment institution: the words 'fat cats', 'corporate greed' and 'come the revolution' standing out in particular.

One day, Lady Hooker asked if I'd like to accompany her to the ballet at Sydney Opera House. Lady Fairfax had bailed at the last minute and she had a spare ticket. Having never been to so much as a poetry recital at the iconic venue, I was beside myself with excitement. As our chauffeur for the evening, John drove the BMW up to the grand entrance, jumped out of the car, opened my door and with a wink and a grin, bowed as, turning heads in my classic vintage op shop ensemble, I stepped onto the pavement like a Logie nominee on award night. I followed Lady Hooker up the burgundy carpeted staircase to the foyer and after finishing our champagne we joined the smartly dressed throng as they made their way into the auditorium. It was half way through the first act when I turned to Lady Hooker to comment on the grace and beauty of the prima ballerina only to find my elderly employer, eyes closed and head lolled to one side, snoring softly in her seat.

The post-modern, Mondrian-inspired house boasted five bedrooms and three bathrooms but there was only so much mess one little old lady could make, so my cleaning duties were relatively light. To supplement our income, I worked three mornings a week as a checkout chick in a local fruit and veggie barn and Friday nights I washed dishes at pancake parlour on Military Road. Every so often

Lady Hooker would take off on one of her Women's Weekly World Cruises, sometimes for weeks at a time. With little to do and the whole of upstairs to ourselves, John and I could take it easy. On glorious Sunday afternoons, we'd sit on the balcony overlooking Brett Whiteley's dazzling harbour, smoking joints, sipping the champagne we'd appropriated from Lady Hooker's well-stocked wine cellar and, pretending we were rich and famous, waving to the binocular-wielding Japanese tourists on the tour boats if we happened to hear a loud-speaker point out the Hooker house on the right.

XXX

After two-and-a-half years of domestic servitude we'd saved enough money to buy a hundred acres of bush on the Far South Coast of New South Wales. At the age of twenty-three, these uni dropout, anti-capitalists were landholders. Sir Leslie would have been tickled pink.

It was time to say goodbye to 'The Hook', as we'd affectionately come to refer to our benevolent boss. She was sad to let us go, she said. I think her young, feral and just-married housekeepers had brought a little joy and a certain frisson of excitement into her life. For the next few years Lady Hooker sent me fifty dollars on my birthday and another fifty at Christmas.

But there was no time for sentiment. John and I had a dream to pursue. It was Easter, 1979. We packed the ute with the cat, a brand-new cement mixer, a Pittsburgh pot belly stove, a giant Stihl chainsaw, as well as a gleaming collection of the finest carpentry and gardening tools money could buy and headed south.

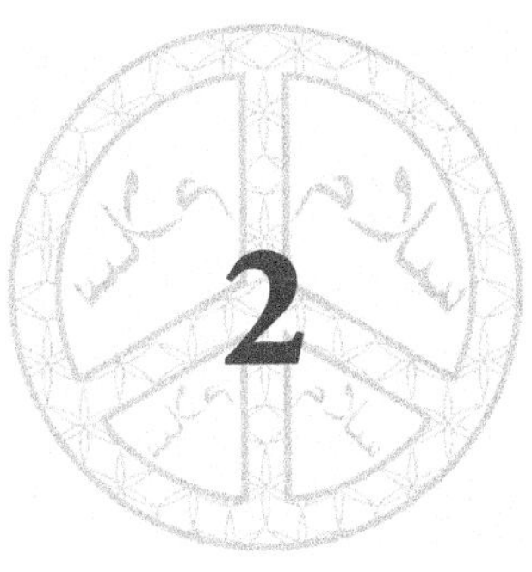

2

Fairsky

In 1957 on a cold, wet mid-summer's day, I was born in the wind-swept West Riding of Yorkshire, and promptly named Kathy after the Gothic heroine from Emily Bronte's *Wuthering Heights*. When I was four years old and my sister Lisa just two, fed up with the English weather and craving a better life in the sun, my parents made a momentous decision. Leaving the dolphin-grey skies and incessant rain behind, they emigrated to Australia. The *Fairsky*, formerly known as HMS Attacker during her commission with the British Royal Navy in World War II, bore her mainly working-class passengers across nine thousand nautical miles of ocean. Australians called us Ten Pound Poms. Under the provisions of the Assisted Migration Scheme, the Australian government required migrant workers to breed and build the economy, and introduced a nominal fare of only ten English pounds to entice thousands of Brits half way around the world.

Desperately seasick for the entire six weeks, I spent most of the voyage languishing in a cot in the ship's hospital, my mother tempting me with chicken broth or forcing spoonfuls of vile banana-flavoured medicine down my throat. Every so often, she'd carry me and my robust, chubby-cheeked sister up on deck to get some fresh air. With my pasty little face stuck between the railings, my bloodless fingers gripping the metal bars, I'd fix my eyes on the horizon, gulping at the wind like a fish out of water. Decades later, on becoming an artist, that horizontal line, having stamped itself so permanently on my subconscious, would appear over and over again in my work.

In England, my father, who'd quit his job as a qualified draftsman to become a professional photographer, hadn't exactly been shining in his new career. At thirty-two, he had dreams of making it big in the 'lucky country'. Soon after arriving in Melbourne, he got a job taking photographs for an Australian publishing house; a stranger in a strange land travelling into Central Australia and up to the Northern Territory to capture picture postcard images of the iconic red desert landscape, quaint Antipodeans and Aboriginal people 'in their natural habitat'; arriving home bearing presents—a bark painting, a boomerang or a pair of burnt clapping sticks. However, less than two years on, for reasons known only to himself, Dad bought a small-time photography business five hours drive away in the township of Bairnsdale in south-east Victoria. Negotiating a second loan with the bank, he purchased a house in nearby Eagle Point, a sleepy and unremarkable hamlet set on the rotten-egg-smelling, seaweed-strewn banks of the Gippsland Lakes.

'Your mummy is really pretty,' said my little classmates when she accompanied me to my first day at Bairnsdale Primary School.

With her flawless English complexion, trim figure, curly brunette bubble cut, up-to-the-minute attire and white framed cat eye sunglasses, my mother looked ten years younger than many of the drably dressed, sun-scorched and already lined mums in the playground.

Thanks to my young-at-heart and fun-loving mum and despite my father, my childhood was happy. There was water-skiing and sailing on Lake King, swimming in the Mitchell river, the Moondale Drive-in (*Chitty Chitty Bang Bang*, *The Sound of Music*, *Mary Poppins*) horse riding, panning for gold, rodeos, the Ashton's Circus, mini-golf, the Buchan Caves and tobogganing in the snow at Mount Hotham. Mum would take Lisa and me on shopping excursions to Melbourne—on one occasion we only got as far as Sale, 70 kilometres from Bairnsdale, when bits from underneath her Volkswagen Beetle began dropping onto the highway; Mum, desperate for some retail therapy, pushing on regardless until the engine eventually died and it was the end of the road for the little black bug.

Summers were spent on the Ninety Mile Beach at Lake Tyres or at the pool—my mother in her emerald green swimsuit, a plastic nose shield attached to the bridge of her sunglasses, one milky-white arm breast stroking wavelessly through the sun-dappled, turquoise water, her free hand holding a smouldering cigarette aloft. We owned a dog—an adorable floppy-eared Beagle named Hoover who'd spend all day, nose to the ground, hoovering up a smorgasbord of dog-delicious smells. I had lessons in ballet, piano and tennis and loads of friends for sleep-overs. Mum excelled at over-the-top birthday parties, Easter egg hunts and all-frills Christmases; Lisa and I always the best and most ingeniously dressed at costume parties and school plays.

Although I must have driven her to distraction, mum was always there to help me realise my fantastical creative visions, such as the design and construction of a three-storey doll's house, a playground-cum-learning centre for our cat's latest litter of kittens or a Disney-inspired cardboard maze. Likewise, she was there to console me when my ambitious artistic endeavours turned out to be nothing like what I'd seen in my mind's eye. On school holidays, in an effort to avoid all-out war, the frazzled mother would allow her squabbling daughters to black out the passageway in the centre of the house. Backlighting our heads with torch light, Lisa and I took turns tracing the outlines of our silhouettes on the sheets of butcher's paper we'd sticky-taped to the door at the end of the hall. Afterwards, peace descending on the household, we'd sit at the kitchen table filling in our crudely drawn profiles with India ink whilst Mum fixed herself a Bex before disappearing into the bedroom for a good lie-down.

One day, Mum came home with half a dozen glossy, rust-coloured pullets and I took on my most challenging project ever—a chook shed makeover. Inspired by Laura Ashley's interior design ideas, gleaned from the pages of a 'Home Beautiful' magazine, I roped Lisa in to help me paint the walls pink and stencil the laying boxes with chicken motifs; Mum ran up some gingham curtains on the Singer to hang at the tiny sash window. When, some years later, the hens stopped laying, my father couldn't bring himself to wring their necks or chop off their heads so the old-age pensioners remained in their prettily decorated premises before falling off their hand painted perch and dying from natural causes.

On rainy Sundays, my stir-crazy sister and I would upend the sewing basket and build cities out of cotton reels, buttons, a deck of cards, chess pieces and domino tiles or make tall and colourful towers with rods of Cuisenaire. When that ended in tears, as it invariably did, Mum would let us draw Texta weather maps on the living-room windows. Then, pointing out the concentric rings of high or low pressure with a knitting needle and enunciating our words with well-rounded vowels, we took turns being the ABC's Weather Girl from the Bureau of Meteorology. Hours could be spent on my bedroom floor designing outfits in an oversized sketch pad—culottes, hot pants and mini-skirts—whatever featured in the fashion pages of *Dolly Magazine* that month. Cutting out my groovy ensembles with the utmost precision, I'd hang them by their tiny shoulder tabs on my handmade paper mannequins.

In spring—if there wasn't a drought—the grass would become overgrown on our quarter-acre block and I'd fight my sister for the right to drive the ride-on mower.

'Do it properly,' Dad would sternly insist, throwing his bag of clubs in the boot of the car before taking off for the golf course in a cloud of dust.

But as soon as I was sitting astride the mower, barefoot and still wearing my apricot chiffon shorty nightie, the sweet smell of freshly cut grass mingling with the sulphurous odour of composting seaweed, my father's instructions to mow in a methodical grid forgotten, I'd give full rein to my creative impulses: by midmorning, the lawn would be a masterpiece of swirling crop circles and intricate geometric patterns.

Even when she was at work, mum was a good mum. Lisa and I would hang around the shop after school, waiting for our parents to knock off so we could all go home for dinner. Mum would be at her table re-touching the latest batch of my father's freshly developed black and white photographs. If I promised to keep still, she'd allow me to sit next to her and watch as she erased wrinkles, pimples, freckles and moles with a tiny brush and a razor-sharp blade. Dad would be out the back in the darkroom, developing images of plain looking brides in the acrid chemical-saturated air or jiggling a teddy bear in the studio, trying to coax a grizzly baby to smile, under the hot, glaring lights.

Unfortunately, my father didn't share my mother's *joie de vivre*. By the time I was ten years old, he had slowly but surely become a misery guts. Compared to life in lively Manchester, no doubt he found his existence in rural Victoria soul-destroying and dull. At the age of forty, disillusioned with how things had turned out,

Dad became increasingly depressed and maudlin, drowning himself in drink. Every Sunday, ensconced in his armchair in the living room, he'd hit the bottle. Smoking Benson and Hedges and quaffing Penfolds fortified wine, he'd gaze teary-eyed across the white-capped lake, dreaming about what could have been; instilling in me a life-long hatred for opera, as the whole family was forced to listen to the shrill, strident and interminable sounds of Wagner, Dvořák or Handel on the record player. Mum and I began to refer to him as 'the black cloud'.

Now my parents argued constantly: about money, work, Dad's drinking and I suspect, other women. There were loud, vitriolic outbursts, like the Richard Burton and Elizabeth Taylor fights in *Who's Afraid of Virginia Woolf?* My gentle, sweet-natured little sister, who just wanted everyone to be happy, was distraught. Plugging our fingers in our ears, Lisa and I would run to our bedrooms to sing *Mary had a Little Lamb* at the top of our voices as we waited for the storm to pass. Although, on one such occasion when I was eleven, angry and fearless, I flew from my room to defend my distressed and sobbing mother.

'*Leave her alone!*' I screamed, standing like a snarling Jack Russell terrier between my startled father and her. 'I hate you. I wish you were dead,' I yelled as I fled out the back door.

The line was drawn. Enlisted as my mother's champion, I went into battle, inuring my nascent and disenchanted heart against the male of the species until well into my adult life.

'I wish she'd leave him,' I said to Lisa later. 'We'd be better off on our own.'

'But what would Dad do?' she asked, her small brow furrowing with concern.

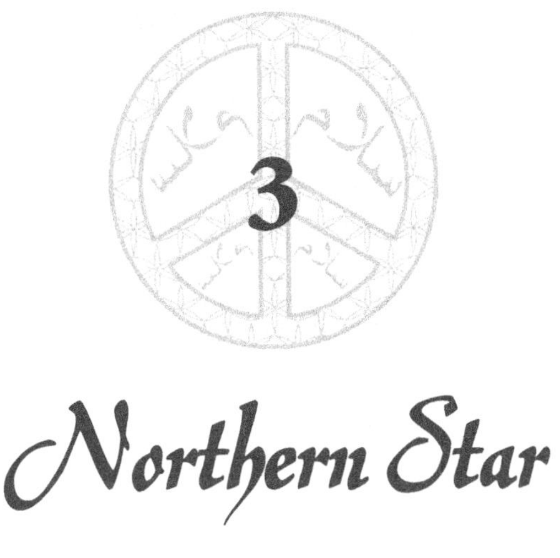

3

Northern Star

Despite my fervent wishes, my mother didn't leave. Like so many women of her generation, she believed she'd made her bed and therefore had to lie in it. In the early seventies, with no welfare services, income support or indeed family to fall back on and with two daughters to raise, she felt stuck. Where would she go? How would she feed and clothe her children? Having enjoyed the advantages of a middle-class existence and its trappings—nice clothes, expensive beauty products, vacations and hobnobbing with the Bairnsdale elite—doctors, solicitors and other local entrepreneurs—she couldn't face a life of financial hardship. There were women worse off than her, she thought. Maybe things will get better, she hoped. Meanwhile, unbeknown to my father, she was working on an exit plan. When Poseidon discovered vast nickel deposits in the Pilbara, creating the largest mineral boom the Australian Stock Exchange had ever seen, Mum, little by little, withdrew five hundred dollars from their joint bank account and purchased some shares. But she'd left her run too late. By the time she bought, the boom was ready to bust; her money swallowed up by a hole in the ground.

Ten years after settling in Eagle Point, their marriage a festering sore, Mum and Dad, along with many other migrants homesick for the Mother Country, decided to sell up and return to England. Putting their lake frontage property and photography business on the market, they packed all our belongings into thirty plywood tea chests and said farewell to their friends and the Australian way of life. For Lisa and me it was devastating to be ripped away from everything we knew and loved on the whim of our parents. As the *Northern Star* sailed out of Sydney Harbour, I felt my heart stretch across the widening gap from ship to shore. I was convinced I'd never see my beloved Australia again and sobbing with anger and grief, I fantasised about throwing myself overboard. At the same time, I was relishing the tremendous adventure and the intoxicating lure of the unknown. Drinking in the sight of the diminishing strip of land on the darkening skyline, I peered into the frothy wash, inhaling the briny spray as the seagulls' shrill cries chased us through The Heads and out into open water. When the sun finally disappeared beneath the horizon, my mother, concerned for her about-to-jump-ship daughter, came up on deck.

'Come on, love. You'll catch your death out here,' she said, putting her arm around my shuddering shoulders. 'You can always come back when you grow up,' she added reassuringly, shepherding me to our poky cabin below.

I spent the first three days of the journey vomiting into a toilet bowl. Thankfully, it wasn't long before I found my sea legs and was up and about. The *Northern Star* felt like a small country town. Two thousand people—passengers and crew—lived on board the run-down, sluggish liner for the lengthy voyage across the Pacific and Atlantic Oceans. It wasn't long before we all came to recognise each other by sight. The teenagers on board quickly discovered each other and soon had the run of the ship—staging midnight raids on the galley, playing on the one-armed bandits and sneaking down below to explore the off-limits engine room. Like a gang of hooligans, we'd race, hooting with laughter, from one end of the ship to the other to catch the first then the second sitting of morning tea, stuffing ourselves with cream cake and lemon meringue pie. Taking advantage of the murky maritime laws and the fact that our parents and younger siblings were nowhere in sight, we'd perch on barstools in the *Northern Star* Tavern, smoking Peter Stuyvesant cigarettes (our 'international passport to smoking pleasure') and ordering tumblers of Cinzano Rosso on ice from a bored and indifferent bartender.

Most mornings, we'd meet at the swimming pool and mess around for hours. But one day, in rough seas, we got into difficulty. At first it was fun, but as the ship began to pitch more violently to the stern, the water swept us with it, throwing our defenceless bodies against the wall at the other end of the pool. Before we had time to pull ourselves out of danger, the ship would pitch aft-wards, sweeping us back again. Tossed from one end of the pool to the other like tadpoles in a martini shaker we thought we were doomed until a burly deckhand, noticing our futile efforts, threw us some life buoys and dragged us, waterlogged and half-drowned, to safety.

✗✗✗

There's a whale on the starboard side! The ship's loudspeakers would proclaim. Springing from our deckchairs, we'd run to the right side of the ship. But by the time we got there the whale would have dived and was nowhere in sight.

There's a whale on the port side! The speakers would declare again, everyone running to the left side of the ship, only to be greeted by a flat expanse of nothing.

There's a whale on the starboard side! The ship's captain would bellow into the microphone once more. Yeah right, we'd think, going back to our game of deck quoits.

However, our captain's advice was worth taking when, after a few days at sea, he announced on the ship's intercom, the first sighting of land. It was 4 a.m. Still half asleep, Lisa and I climbed out of our bunks, clambering up on deck in our nylon quilted dressing gowns, hair unbrushed and faces unwashed, to witness the sun come up behind the islands of Moorea and Tahiti. In the pale, pastel light, steep-sided, dark green mountains, back-lit by a glowing sky-filling sphere of pink-gold, jutted majestically from the stainless-steel surface of the ocean.

'Smell *that*,' I said to Lisa as, chaperoned by a squawking white petrel above, the ship navigated its way into Papeete Harbour; canoes loaded with waist length raven-haired girls in grass skirts and bare-chested young men bearing trinkets and flower leis casting off from the beach to greet us. As I licked my salt-laced lips and breathed in the balmy scent of frangipani and jasmine blossom mingled with diesel fumes, enamel paint and the smell of the sea, the slow throbbing of the ship's engine underfoot, my pulse quickened at the prospect of going ashore.

Next, we forged on to Acapulco, down to Curacao and Barbados, through the Panama Canal, across the North Atlantic Ocean and on to Lisbon. The last leg to England over the notoriously perilous Bay of Biscay was an ordeal, all on board aware of the vulnerability of our tin can vessel on the wild and roiling ocean. Finally, having endured six weeks at sea, we stepped wide-eyed and shaken onto dry land in Southampton, relieved to see the stern of the *Northern Star* and grateful to be alive.

XXX

The return to England was a disaster for my parents. We moved into my grandfather's damp and camphor-smelling, old person's house—a semi-detached, double-storey building in a row of identical houses in Oldham, near Manchester. Granddad had already moved out before we arrived—gone to shack up with his middle-aged, gold-digging lady-friend (who after his death managed to acquire the bulk of his estate) in her council flat in Rochdale.

At the age of eleven, my grandfather and grandmother were sent to work in one of the many cotton mills operating in Lancashire at the time. Crawling on hands and knees under the thunderous industrial looms, it was their job to collect the drifts of lint building up on the factory floor; their hearing permanently impaired in the process. The appalling workplace conditions incensed my grandfather and, rising through the ranks of the union movement, he became head of the Cotton Mills Workers Union; subsequently presented to the Queen for his role in gaining compensation for employees afflicted with byssinosis, a fatal lung disease linked to the milling of cotton.

Mum grew up an only child in a household of elderly relatives and a sickly, asthmatic mother. Sharing a bedroom with her snoring Oliver Hardy-sized grandma and her wheezing Stan Laurel-proportioned aunt, she slept with her head under the covers to prevent an asphyxiating fart-related death. An octogenarian uncle lived under the stairs in the box room, a space not much bigger than a broom cupboard. On the first floor, her parents' bedroom overlooked its mirror image on the other side of the street. In the middle of the night, young Ruth would be woken by the light switched on by her gasping mother as she stood on the landing struggling for breath.

My grandfather believed in the 'nobility of poverty'; his interior decor clearly inspired by the theme. Huddled on the threadbare club lounge we'd struggle to feel the warmth emanating from the flickering gas heater set in the wall on the opposite side of the living room as we sat watching *The Goodies* or *The Top of the Pops*. Icicles grew from the bath taps in the pea-green and battleship-grey bathroom and that winter I drew patterns in the frost on 1930s 'sunburst design' stained-glass windows upstairs. As the months flew by, it became obvious that Dad wouldn't find work. Then he was gazumped on an offer he made on a flower farm business in Cornwall. After that, he stopped looking for employment altogether and began to drink port instead.

Meanwhile, Lisa and I were enrolled at Chadderton Grammar School, dodging ridicule and bullying by dropping our broad Aussie accents and adopting a passable Lancashire brogue. On the positive side, we were given cooked dinners at lunch time, on the negative, we were made to play hockey in a blizzard with large and violent grammar school girls. In the changing rooms following the match, we'd run naked and squealing along a row of shower heads which squirted freezing cold water on our blotchy, plucked chicken-like bodies. Our buxom and ruddy-cheeked PE teacher, Miss Randell, waiting—towel in hand—was only too eager to dry us off.

I fell in love with a boy from Cheshire. The son of Lisa's godparents, Patrick's resemblance to David Cassidy from the *Partridge Family* was uncanny. Two years my senior and studying for his O Levels, Patrick would catch the coach from Stockport to Oldham, turning up on my doorstep on a Saturday morning dressed in a calf-length, burgundy, fake-leather jacket, a black ribbed-knit turtleneck sweater and a silver 'ban the bomb' pendant. As I opened the door to greet him, I'd go weak at the knees. Banishing Lisa upstairs, I'd light the fire in the formal and seldom-used front room where Patrick and I would spend the day lip-locked and playing records—The Moody Blues, Queen, David Bowie, Rod Stewart, The Stones, T-rex, and by the time my groovy young suitor left to catch the last coach home, my chin would be covered in a weeping red rash.

In denial of his circumstances or possibly not knowing what else to do, Dad decided that we needed a holiday in sunny Spain and at the next school break we bundled our gear into our station wagon and headed south to board the ferry at Dover. Driving through

France and then down the Spanish coast to Catalonia, we came to a stop at Denia, a sleepy picturesque fishing village situated on the Costa Brava half way between Valencia and Alicante. My parents, seen as a breath of fresh air in the closeted enclave of wealthy, bored and alcoholic retirees, were quickly embraced by the ex-pat community, mainly the English, Germans and Dutch. For the next two weeks, there were parties and 'drinkies' every night. At the end of the holiday, Mum and Dad agreed it would be an excellent idea to move to Spain permanently. We returned to England to pack and make the arrangements. On the day of our departure, Mum drugged our beloved, slightly obese black and white cat, Howard, stuffed him, unconscious and camouflaged with her ash-blonde wig, into her shoulder bag, and smuggled him onto the plane.

In the spring of 1972, we moved into a white-washed hill-top villa surrounded by groves of flowering almonds and rows of budding citrus. A wide terracotta-tiled balcony overlooked the township of Denia; an imposing twelfth-century castle fortress dominating the headland. Beyond lay the azure Mediterranean Sea. Unable to speak a word of Spanish, Lisa and I were placed in school—a Catholic convent on the outskirts of town where, apart from a prim and proper Amish American girl, neither the nuns nor students spoke English. I'd just turned fifteen.

The school day commenced with religious instruction. Supervised by a pair of dour nuns in black habits, we'd spend the morning in the chapel circumnavigating a shrine of the Virgin Mary while reciting the names of an endless catalogue of saints.

'Santa María, Madre de Dios, ruega por nosotros, pecadores, ahora y en la hora de nuestra muerte. Amen,' nuns and pupils would chant as we walked in file around the Mother of God.

Each girl bore a candle in a brass holder, cupping the flame with her hand so as not to ignite the thick, oiled and highly flammable braids of the girl in front. But one day, one of the girls tripped and triggered a pile-up. In the chaos, an exposed flame caught my untamed locks and set them alight; a chorus of blood-curdling screams ricocheted off the stone chapel walls. Fortuitously, before I had the chance to cry *ay, caramba*, the host of Spanish angels swooped; flapping and slapping they extinguished their little Aussie classmate.

As Mum and Dad began to lose all direction, perpetually arguing and lurching from one alcohol-fuelled party to the next, my sister and I were left to our own devices. Cast adrift, we clung to each other, trying to keep afloat as best we could—wondering when and where we'd find a safe harbour.

'We should go back to Australia,' we'd whisper to one another in our bunk beds at night. 'Everything'd be okay if we went home.'

Mercifully, we were able to latch onto others. Lisa met a kind and dependable English boy who adored her. I found Domingo (meaning Sunday)—a twenty-year-old, wild-eyed, black-maned, aquiline-nosed Spaniard—a student at the Art Academy in Valencia. We'd come across each other during siesta, our eyes meeting across one of those soccer tables in a tapas bar in Denia. The tall, proud and cologne-drenched Catalan dressed in style: a knee-length indigo duffel coat, a pink cashmere sweater, blue jeans, a paisley cravat and Cuban-heeled boots; he looked like a modern-day Velázquez subject minus the whiskers. It wasn't hard to fall for the handsome, hot-blooded young man in denim and duffel. In the beginning, before I learned to speak Spanish, our conversation was unsurprisingly stilted, but fortunately Señor Sunday and I found a much more plea-surable way to communicate, embracing it with *mucho gusto*.

One siesta, having missed the school bus into town, I stood at the convent gates, picking paint off the iron bars and trying to decide if I should or shouldn't walk the two kilometres into Denia when, in the distance, I noticed a Kombi van careening headlong on the dirt road towards me. Moments later, the van, decorated with images of skulls and crossbones, coffins, cobwebs, bleeding hearts and crucifixes came to a halt at my side. As I approached the vehicle, the door slid open and out stepped three whiskered, long-haired, rangy youths in Levis, T-shirts and heavily embossed cowboy boots.

'Peace, man,' one of them said with the 'V' sign and an American accent. And then the roadies, on tour with *The Grateful Dead*, offered me a lift. Thirsty for adventure and thrilled at the prospect of hanging out with the groovy young men, I jumped into the front seat of the car with gleeful and naïve alacrity. For a while, we drove around the Spanish countryside, through the terraced olive plantations and past the odd herd of goats, eventually coming to a stop at a rocky outcrop overlooking the hazy, sapphire blue sea. The guys smoked a joint and played their guitars.

'Do you want to make out?' the one with the George Harrison handlebar moustache asked me.

'No thank you,' I said politely, not knowing what he meant, but, on some level, sensing his intent.

'That's cool, man. I can dig it,' he said as we climbed into the van before heading back to the convent. As I stood at the gates waving goodbye, watching the snaking trail of pale, orange dust wind its way down the hillside, I half-wished I could run away and join the circus, not realising how lucky I was to be unharmed and alive.

✕✕✕

One day, in a poorly thought-out attempt at uniting us as a family, Mum and Dad decided an outing was in order. The following morning, we piled into our tiny, cherry red Fiat 500 and headed into Denia to *la plaza de toros* to watch a local bullfight. I'd caught glimpses of world-class *corridas* on telly—huge, sleek, black, muscle-bound beasts rushing into a spectacular, filled-to-capacity arena looking for someone to gore and disembowel. But we lived in a small country town, *un pueblo pequeno*, and on arriving at the unremarkable, pocket-sized stadium, seating ourselves in its rickety uppermost tiers, I could tell this was going to be a very different affair. Heralded by trumpet, a young, scrawny, tan-coloured bull ran panicked and bewildered into the ring, followed by the sequin-clad matador. With a wide, straight-legged gait, satin slippered feet pointing like a prima ballerina, the slim, tight-bottomed man strode towards the little bull, taunting it with elegant flourishes of his large gold cape in order to test its courage. When the frightened bull trotted off in the opposite direction, the audience jeered; a sea of white handkerchiefs fluttering in the air—a sign of the people's disgust at its cowardly retreat.

The matador withdrew and two picadors on horseback and a pair of *banderilleros* brandishing barbs festooned with colourful crepe paper ribbons pranced proudly into the arena; sidling up to the wheeling bull and jabbing it in the neck with their decorated spears until the ill-fated creature, head hung and panting, resembled a giant, blood-drenched pin-cushion. Horrified, Mum and Dad had seen enough. In need of a *cerveza* or two they got up to leave; Lisa, grey with shock, behind them.

'Can I stay?' I asked. I was appalled and sickened by the carnage too but figuring this was something I'd never see again and curious to witness the dark side of humanity for myself, I felt I should sit it out. At my age, with few experiences to speak of, I was determined to collect as many of them as I could.

The matador re-entered the ring and approached the bull; the crowd hushing in anticipation; the exhausted and listing animal rooted to the ground, staring at its foe with a defeated expression, its long, pink tongue lolling from a mouth of froth. It knew, as did I, that the end was near and I fought an overwhelming urge to shut my eyes, stick my fingers in my ears and sing *Mary had a Little Lamb* at the top of my voice. With a graceful pass of his red cape, the matador stepped forward, then holding his sword straight out in front of him he stood high on his toes, plunging the steel blade deep between the bull's shoulders; the wretched beast teetering mid-air before toppling heavily to the ground amid a cloud of dust. Now the stadium erupted with cheers and applause. To the fanfare of a discordant brass band, the dead bull, its ears and tail lopped off and thrown by the triumphant matador as a prize to the prettiest señoritas within range, was dragged hog-tied to horses from the ring. Shaking, blinded by tears and traumatized for life, the nauseating, metallic scent of *la sangre de toro* rising on a warm updraft of wind from below, I stumbled outside to look for my parents.

That night, having lived in Spain just short of six months, my father announced that with the last of his dwindling savings he'd buy a yacht and take us sailing round the Greek Islands. *Gracias a Dios*, my mother had had enough and much to the delight of her homesick daughters, she put her foot down, demanding we return to Australia, this time minus Howard the Illegal Immigrant Cat.

Why my parents chose to go back to Eagle Point I don't know. Maybe they were at a complete loss and unable to think of what else to do. After leasing a bleak and ugly fibro-cement holiday shack right around the corner from the magnificent property they'd owned on the banks of Lake King, Lisa and I were sent back to Bairnsdale High. Dropping our Lancashire accents and seamlessly slotting in, we picked up where we'd left off only eighteen months before.

However, things rapidly deteriorated. Thinking he'd never grace Australian shores again, my father had signed a contract forbidding him, in perpetuity, from opening another photography business in the area. Mum found a job as a filing clerk with a solicitor's firm in

Bairnsdale and having no skills or experience in anything other than taking and developing pictures, Dad got a job laying carpets. Two weeks afterwards, he had a head-on collision with a gumtree.

'I won't be able to work now, will I,' he said to my mother in hospital as he adjusted the neck brace fitted to alleviate his whiplash. Mum was incensed. Dad, who'd probably been drinking, had written off our beautiful, leather upholstered Humber car. It was only later, when the police asked her if my father was prone to blackouts that she suspected he may have run off the road deliberately.

'It's strange,' the sergeant said. 'We usually see skid marks at the scene of an accident. But in this case, there was no evidence of any such thing.'

Dad came home and took to bed. Hardly eating and not washing, he'd stay, all day and night, like a hibernating bear, in his bedroom. On the brink of a break-down herself, Mum would get home from work and cook dinner; she, Lisa and I eating in front of the television and trying to ignore what was going on in the room at the end of the hall. We were living in hell; a place so awful that the only way to survive was to deny it was happening. Don't mention it, don't think about it, try not to feel, was our unspoken rule as we clung to our sanity by the skin of our teeth. Apart from my sweet sixteen-year-old boyfriend Shaun, no one at school knew what was taking place behind our closed doors.

'Should I contact Derick?' my mother asked Dad, thinking that her brother-in-law in Adelaide may be able to help. But my father was adamant. He did *not* want his successful younger sibling to know how low his mighty older brother had fallen.

During a spate of teacher strikes in 1973 (something to do with restructuring and changes to work practices) I was often home from school. As I sat at the kitchen table studying my Year 11 *Spanish by Correspondence*, Dad, crawling from his bedroom on hands and knees, would come crying and clawing at my side.

'Help me,' he'd beg, tugging at my T-shirt, his ravaged face streaked with tears.

But I was repulsed by my father's pathetic and disturbing behaviour, by his drinking and the way he'd treated my mother. I knew about his affairs, having once discovered his arty black and white photographs of half-naked women while searching for loose change in his wardrobe. Repelled and appalled I just wanted to get away from him. Yet, somehow, I'd manage to pick his wasted frame up off the floor, manoeuvre him down the passage, push him back into the dark, malodourous bedroom, shut the door and go back to my textbooks—tearing at the eczema that was sweeping like the plague across my body. It took eight weeks before a doctor arranged for Dad to be admitted into a psychiatric hospital.

A month passed and, looking more like his old self, Dad was back. Then one morning, when Lisa and I had left the house to catch the school bus and Mum had gone to work, he took his car, drove into bushland not far from home and parked among the eucalypts. He was well prepared. After hooking up a hose from the exhaust pipe to the car's interior, he got back into the vehicle and turned the key in the ignition. Amid the lethal fumes, Dad swigged from a flagon of port and swallowed the sleeping pills prescribed by a psychiatrist during his brief stint in the clinic.

Sometimes, I try to imagine Dad looking out at his feature-less surroundings, waiting for the end to come. Did he simply go to sleep? Did he gasp, choke or clutch at his throat? Was he reconciled and at peace? Maybe, at the last second, he changed his mind, trying but failing to escape his makeshift gas chamber. I wonder if he gave a thought to his daughters and how they would feel. I can only speculate on what was going through his mind. If Dad left a note, the police never passed it on.

'The Lord's my Shepherd, I shall not want, He maketh me to lie

down in green pastures,' I mumbled dry-eyed into my tatty *Book of Common Prayer* at the funeral. Sitting clench-fisted and rigid in the pew at the front of the church, I was, to all appearances, a pillar of stone. Yet deep inside, boiled a cauldron of rage. I was furious with my father for what he'd put us through—for his infidelities, drinking, his weakness and irresponsible behaviour. But at least he had someone to mourn his passing that day. Overcome with grief, Daddy's little girl Lisa was carried weeping in a heap from the chapel.

In the weeks that followed, Mum became the subject of speculation and gossip—some in the community blaming her for her husband's suicide. Fortunately, Gloria and Pete, owners of the local dry cleaners and friends with Mum and Dad for years, stuck by her. Once they'd taken care of the funeral arrangements, they quickly sold Dad's ignominiously tainted car and our family of three moved out of the gloomy house in Eagle Point and into a modern and comfortable two-bedroom flat in Bairnsdale. My boyfriend Shaun—a lifesaver, the young man with a maturity far beyond his years—stepped into the breach, packing my father's clothes and bits and pieces into cardboard boxes and hauling them off to the op shop. It wasn't long before my mother was offered further assistance. On the pretext of being concerned for her welfare, a couple of opportunistic married men in my parent's social circle came calling to see if the vulnerable widow needed help in the bedroom, only to be sent packing by my disgusted and disinterested mum.

To tell the truth, I felt nothing but relief. At last the horror was over, and I'd survived to tell the tale. Not that anyone wanted to hear it. Everyone at school knew what had happened, but in those days any mention of suicide made people uncomfortable— unable to look me in the eye, my teachers and classmates never once broached the subject. Grateful I didn't have to elaborate,

I threw myself into my studies. Lisa consoled herself with food and my mother, blocking out her guilt about not having done more to prevent my father's death, went back to work. Bonded by our horrendous ordeal forever, we'd wear the scars for the rest of our days. But I, for one, decided there and then I wasn't going to let anything stop me from living the remarkable life I intended to live.

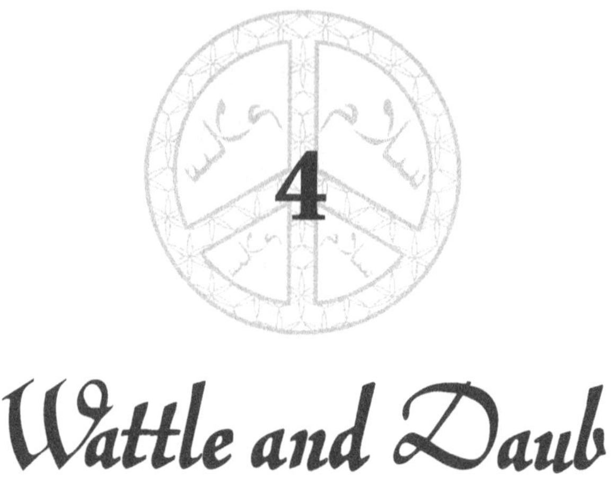

4

Wattle and Daub

Wading knee-deep through a sea of tussocks and dead bracken, the dusky purple profile of Mumbulla Mountain was barely visible through the dense layering of trees. The whip-crack call of an unseen bird rang in our ears. After so long in the city, the yearned-for scent of the bush was intoxicating. Here we were. Actually walking on our land. *Our land*, we'd say at every opportunity, like lovers who can't stop mentioning each other's name. Back in Hopetoun Avenue, John and I had sat up in bed talking into the night about what we'd do and how it would be when we moved to the country. It was hard to believe we'd made it; that this hundred acres of bush in the Bega Valley actually belonged to us.

We set to work within moments of arriving on the property, scraping back the undergrowth with our new tools, setting up the campsite and pitching the tent. This, we decided, was where we'd live until we constructed something more substantial further up the ridge. John connected the gas cooktop to its cylinder while I made up the bed and stocked our wood crates with canisters of tea, brown rice, lentils, oats, raw sugar and wholemeal flour. Our next priority was water and we filled four twenty-five litre plastic containers at the Brogo Dam, located a few minutes' drive down Warrigal Range Road, and carted them home in the back of the ute.

It was late afternoon when John built the campfire, our limbs pleasantly aching from our labours and our hearts full with a sense of achievement. As the sun set behind the stringy barks, casting slender shadows over our small clearing, I heated a saucepan of water on the flames. With my back to the chilly autumn breeze and shivering with cold, I stepped naked and goose-pimpled into the basin of warm water, giving my face, armpits and crotch a cursory wipe with a wet cloth before quickly dressing again.

By now, we were ravenously hungry.

'So hungry I could eat the arse out of a low flying duck,' John joked as he threw a gnarled wattle stump on the fire.

Dinner was a few blackened potatoes and burnt-beyond-recognition sausages. On that first night on our land, land that only two hundred years ago was occupied by the Dyiringanj people, we sat in silence in the dancing firelight, eating our food and sipping our tea, watching as darkness fell over our magnificent domain.

'We did it,' I said turning to John, my eyes shining with tears.

'Yes, we did,' he said softly, putting his arm around my shoulders and planting a kiss on my smudged, still-grubby brow.

Our next job was to clear the bush to make way for a house site, an orchard, the vegetable garden, a workshop and, more importantly, with winter coming, some kind of shelter. A bulldozer and operator could have cleared the area in a week. But bulldozers were an expense we couldn't afford and a gung-ho operator could wreak havoc in minutes. Our budget and ecological ideology demanded a thrifty and environmentally sensitive approach to land clearing. Blissfully unaware of what we were about to get ourselves into, we decided to undertake the mammoth task ourselves.

✕✕✕

The new Stihl chainsaw (christened Stephen after Stephen Stills from the '70s rock band Crosby, Stills, Nash and Young) sat squarely on the ground. Like a bullfighter facing his opponent, my husband circled it warily, preparing for the moment of truth. Finally, donning his ear muffs and goggles, John gave me a confident thumbs-up, picked up the lethal weapon and marched over to a young sapling on the perimeter of the house-site. With my fingers in my ears, I stood out of the way, willing the beast to start, watching as John failed in his fervent attempts to engage the engine. At last, Stephen sprang violently to life. John placed the whirring bar against the base of the tree. Instantly, with a surprisingly loud crash for such a small and spindly structure, the sapling toppled to the ground.

'Come and feel *this*!' John yelled above the din of the chainsaw and reaching his side, he placed my hand on his chest. Despite the thick woollen sweater, I could easily detect the wild thumping of his heart.

Suddenly, I was overcome with grief. We'd just killed our first tree; a tree that up until we'd arrived on the scene was looking forward to a long and healthy life in its pristine environment. I looked around at the hundreds of trees we'd be chopping down in the following weeks and wanted to cry.

'What's wrong?' my partner-in-crime asked when he saw my face. But when I told him how I was feeling, John just laughed.

'Don't worry,' he said, slapping me reassuringly on the back. 'I promise we'll make good use of the timber.'

For the next few months, John and I spent every day from sunrise to sunset clearing the land and in time, I became inured to the sight of toppling trees. My lumberjack partner quickly graduated from lopping reedy saplings to felling huge stringy barks, yellow box and red gums, the constant whine of Stephen dominating the previously peaceful bush. Once felled, John cut up the crown of the tree into sections light enough for us to drag to the nearest stack of superfluous branches at the edge of the clearing. Attaching one end of a steel chain to a bush pole, we'd wrap the other end round our waists and, like human beasts of burden, haul the log to the stockpile at the top of the ridge. With the canopy of a fallen tree often covering an area the size of a basketball court, it could take all day to clear the leafy debris from just one casualty.

Next, we'd turn our attention to the tree trunk. The *Skills of the Australian Bushman* advised removing the bark as quickly as possible. First, you bash the bark with the butt of an axe, then perforate it with the axe blade. Ramming the crowbar into the perforation you prise, with all your might, the bark away from the timber and if it's your lucky day, a miracle occurs. All of a sudden, the bark pops from the wood; before you lies an immaculate, virgin, ivory white pole, so beautiful you can't help but touch its damp, milky flesh or bend to smell its tannin perfume.

If left too long, however, moisture evaporates from the log and the bark fibres stick like glue to the timber. That's when the dreaded 'draw knife', a thirty-centimetre-long blade with handles at right angles on either end, came into its own. Standing astride the trunk, I'd hack the blade into the bark, then, drawing the knife towards me, strip it like giant curls of potato peel. It was a tedious and frustrating process and, as I was soon to discover, dangerous too.

One day, the draw knife jumped unexpectedly out of the bark and into my knee. Toppling sideways off the log onto my back, I clasped my wounded leg, rocking and howling on the saw-dust carpeted ground in agony. Once I realised I wasn't going to die, trembling and in shock I got up to inspect the damage—an inch-long, clean-cut tear in my overalls. I couldn't bring myself to roll up my trouser leg to see how seriously I was hurt but I could tell it was bad from the amount of ruby-red blood saturating my sock. This is going to need stiches, I thought. John was chain-sawing a log in the gully and hadn't heard my screams so I hobbled, whimpering and snivelling down the hill to place myself in his range of vision. As I stood flapping my arms like a fledgling wedge-tailed eagle, he caught sight of me and switched off his machine.

'I barked my knee,' I squawked pitifully.

'Shit,' he said when he saw my blood-soaked sock. 'Let's go and see Charlie. It'll take too long to get to the hospital.'

As luck would have it, we'd met the doctor from Sydney in the laundromat in Bega the week before. With a fervent desire to escape the city and get back to nature, Charlie had just moved with his young family into a run-down dairy on a neighbouring property. Clearing the breakfast dishes from the kitchen table when we turned up unexpectedly at his ramshackle residence, he asked his wife to fetch a needle and thread. As I lay on the table top, clenching a rolled-up tea towel between my teeth, the neighbourly medic dabbed my knee with Dettol, sutured the wound with a few rough stitches of black cotton and wrapped it with a muslin bandage. Charlie's wife made me a cup of chamomile tea while the men smoked a joint and then John and I drove home. That afternoon, albeit with a bit of a limp, I was stripping the bark from another stringybark log.

'You're a legend,' said John with a grin as he picked up the chainsaw and headed back into the bush, my feathers ruffling with pride.

Ripping out fence posts from a barked log takes skill. However, following a few aborted attempts that produced some weird and wonderful configurations, John was able to churn out straight and true specimens in rapid fire succession. Expertly, he'd score the length of a pole with the chainsaw, placing three or four large iron wedges along the groove. Wielding the sledge hammer, John would drive the wedges into the heart of the timber and in two or three strikes, you'd hear it—the satisfying crack of splintering wood. A beautiful new fence post was born.

A gruelling three months later, we'd cleared approximately two acres of bush, our immediate reward being a panoramic view of Mumbulla Mountain. But there was incriminating evidence all over the murder scene; a minefield of tree stumps contaminated the landscape. This was a job for Dynamite Man.

Ray Wheeler was one of those elderly, stocky, bow-legged blokes with chapped, sausage-fingered hands and a paunch belly.

'You've got some pretty big stumps here,' he declared, stating the bleeding obvious as he scanned the clearing.

Ray set about the delicate task of laying sticks of dynamite around the base of each stump, John trotting around behind him, picking the old-timer's brains about anything and everything to do with explosives. After a few hours of concentrated effort, it was time to blow things up. Ray directed us to take cover and, like a pair of excited little kids, John and I hid behind a stack of fence posts. The explosions were tremendous. Looking up, we watched as a shower of wood and earth particles rained down on the land, the caustic smell of gunpowder infusing the air. Ray gave us the thumbs-up and we stepped out to survey the considerably altered landscape. The dynamite had worked a treat. Where there'd been unsightly stumps protruding from the ground, now there were large craters pock-marking the slope.

⧓⧓⧓

Before we knew it, the winter of 1980 was upon us and we were cold and fed-up. In the blustering icy wind, the tent became a torture chamber of wildly writhing and flapping canvas. Some nights, to avoid our flimsy refuge being blown away altogether and ending up in the South Pacific Ocean, we'd tie back the window and door flaps to allow the ferocious squalls to pass through unobstructed. It was dark by five o'clock so we'd take to our bed by six, reading the appropriately titled, *Les Miserables*, to each other or trying to listen to Alistair Cooke's *Letters from America* on the ABC above the howling gale. We desperately needed shelter; we had six hundred dollars stashed in a battered Arnott's biscuit tin under the bed.

Not letting a trifling matter like poverty stand in the way of progress, we decided to build a mud hut. Wattle and daub, a construction method dating back to the Neolithic Period, involves daubing a lattice of wood stakes with a mixture of wet mud and straw. As a structure made of mud costs virtually nothing to build, it was a perfect choice for a pair of destitute, contemporary Stone-agers like ourselves. Without considering that we may need council approval, we drew up a floor plan and got to work on our mud humpy.

To start with, we dug a dozen deep holes in the ground. Once the bush poles were erected, we raised the plates and rafters; the tray in the back of the ute serving as a scaffold platform.

'*Hurry!* I'm going to drop it!' I'd scream, teetering on the top rung of the ladder, struggling to hold the unbearable weight of a lengthy, unseasoned pole as John made his fastidious measurements.

'Hang on,' John would calmly respond, ignoring my distress as he held up his ruler, marked the timber with a pencil, re-measured and re-marked before finally making his cut with the chainsaw. *Measure twice, cut once* was my husband's obsessive-compulsive motto and on numerous occasions it would almost be the death of me.

It was my job to collect the wattles. Setting out soon after breakfast, I'd tramp through the bespangled, dew-drenched bracken and native grasses in search of a stand of slender saplings—a truffle-like perfume of leaf mould issuing from the damp earth, the last wisps of grey mist diffusing into the ether; all around me, the ear-piercing, incessant chiming of bellbirds and the cackling of kookaburras cracking themselves up. With the wan wintery light filtering through the blue-green canopy of gum leaves above, I'd spend my day felling wattles with the bushman's saw and lopping off the extraneous branches with a hatchet. At smoko, I'd unwrap the apple and cinnamon pikelets made on the campfire the night before and pour myself a cuppa from the thermos. Then, sat on a lichen-speckled log, I'd sip my tea and listen to the faint tap-tap of John's mallet as he chiselled out a mortice in the distance. One day, alone in the gently rustling bush, it dawned on me: I was actually living *in* McCubbin's *Pioneer* triptych, the painting that had captured my young and impressionable heart as an art student in Melbourne and smiling quietly to myself, I drained my mug, polished off the last of the rubbery pancakes and got back to work.

By the end of the month, we had an impressive bundle of wattles stacked neatly onsite and John and I began to attach the stakes, one above the other, to the corner posts of the building. Next, we stretched chicken wire over the timber framework. Then came the 'daub': a combination of soil, straw and water agitated together in the cement mixer. Working side by side, we toiled through the afternoon, pressing our sticky wads of mud between the gaps in the saplings. However, as the sun's last rays crept from the valley, we watched in dismay as, before our eyes, the panel we'd just finished constructing, swayed and buckled before collapsing in a graceful faint at our feet—our mixture obviously far too wet.

Once the walls were up, we clad the roof with two hundred dollars' worth of brand-new, glinting-in-the-sun sheets of corrugated iron. Now we needed a low-cost solution for the floor. John had a brilliant idea. He cut some rounds of wood, like giant slices of salami from a red gum trunk in our stockpile, spread a layer of river sand on the ground, covered it with sheets of black plastic and placed the timber disks on top; me coming along behind, tamping a pungent paste of fresh cow manure and sawdust into the crevices between the disks. Over time, however, the mortar dried out and sank. Five years after it was laid, the floor became an obstacle course for our daughter as she was learning how to walk; her little foot getting lodged in a crack and pitching her head first onto the hard timber floor. Holding her screaming in my arms I watched as a purple lump, the size of a hard-boiled egg, sprouted on her forehead. From then on, until the cracks were refilled, my sensible toddler relegated her walking practice to carpeted surfaces and level ground.

In the beginning, our life in the lightly-populated dairy-farming parish of Brogo was hermetic; contact with our conservative National Party neighbours a rare and unlooked-for occurrence. As forerunners of the new settler community, it wasn't until months following our arrival in the valley that like-minded couples, like Charlie and his wife, began to flood in from either Sydney or Melbourne. Not that we minded or even noticed, so engrossed were we in pursuing our self-sufficiency agenda. But it *was* a treat to get a visitor, to have a conversation with another human being other than a mono-syllabic sales assistant in Bega or the pimply youth, good-natured but no intellectual giant, pumping petrol at the Caltex depot on the edge of town. Frank made a visit as did John's sister, Kay. Although they didn't say so, I think they were shocked by our primitive living conditions. Both born and bred in the country, they weren't sissies when it came to doing it tough but John and I had taken the concept to a whole new level.

There was still a bit to do to make our mud dwelling habitable but one day disaster struck and we had no choice but to move into the unfinished building overnight. In a nice surprise, my mother and Lisa dropped in for a visit. John and I were at a critical juncture installing the Pittsburgh pot-belly stove so offering to make us a cup of tea, Lisa wandered down the hill to boil the billy. Rather than go to the trouble of collecting twigs and lighting a fire from scratch, my sister decided to use the gas cooktop instead. But with the window and door flaps tied back and a Category 5 hurricane passing through the tent, each time she lit a match, a gale force wind would snuff it out. After releasing the ties and zipping up the flaps, Lisa bent again to light the stove. Nature grasped its opportunity; in the next gust it ripped the tent in two.

5

Back to the Garden

Our aim, of course, was to become entirely self-sufficient in the food production department. Once we'd settled in to our new home, we dug a massive vegetable patch and began cultivating tomatoes, beans, potatoes, lettuce, carrots and cucumbers, to name but a few. Next, came the orchard—along with citrus, vines and nut trees, we planted apples, plums, peaches and apricots; the bare-rooted stock, just twigs sticking out in a choppy, chocolate brown ocean of freshly ploughed soil. As youngsters, our fruit trees' needs were few—a sprinkle of water, a handful of fertiliser and a light prune in winter was all they required to blossom and grow. Like an excited mum who couldn't wait for her little one to walk or talk, I'd dream of the day I could pick the sun-ripened bounty from their branches. But patience is a virtue when it comes to dealing with nature. It'd be three or four years before the trees bore fruit.

Meanwhile, I was battling an outrageous glut of tomatoes. Apart from bottling and making tomato sauce and pickles, I needed to find a way to deal with the overwhelming surplus. In a second-hand bookshop in Bega, I came across a recipe for dehydrated tomato paste. Once the fruit was reduced to pulp, I dried it in shallow trays in the warming oven of our wood-burning stove; the flat sheets of crimson leather then cut into strips, rolled into balls the size of a Tom Bowler marble and stored in a wax paper-lined tin in the kitchen cupboard.

Like the tomato, the zucchini plant is a natural wonder. One day, you'd notice it had sprouted three or four cute little babies, all dressed up in their frilly, yellow flower bonnets, the following morning you'd discover that the brood had grown up overnight and were now the size of your arm. On the other hand, sweetcorn was a mean-spirited and greedy plant, gobbling up vast quantities of water, fertiliser and real estate and producing only one ear of corn— two if you were lucky. As per gardening folklore, I planted onion seedlings on the winter solstice, smiling at the end of the day when the garden bed resembled a green swath of transplanted hair. On the longest day of the year, I'd pull the fattened bulbs from the ground, plaiting them with twine into bunches to hang on the veranda with the posies of herbs, strings of waxy red chillies and braids of bulging garlic corms. I found a novel and efficient way to grow spuds. After stacking old car tyres one on top of the other, I filled the cavity with straw and seed potatoes; adding extra tyres and straw as the sprouting foliage grew skywards. Three months later, I'd dismantle the tall rubber towers; the immaculate white tubers tumbling like cut strands of large, luminous pearls to the ground.

With the garden and orchard well and truly established, John and I made an addition to the wattle and daub hut: a mud-brick workshop where we could make rustic furnishings—tables, bookshelves, rugs, and store our growing collection of tools and machinery. Against one wall sat a vintage treadle sewing machine, my jarrah spinning wheel, a hessian sack of lanolin-scented lamb's wool and a sturdy timber-framed loom. Across the other side of the room, John kept Stephen the Chainsaw in pride of place on an oiled hardwood bench.

On wet winter days, I'd stay indoors: sat at my spinning wheel beside the pot-belly stove or hunched over my loom weaving lengths of material I'd use to make clothes. When the weather cleared, I'd hike through the bush searching for sticks to whittle into king-sized knitting needles and knit a loose-knit vest in an afternoon. God knows what the local shopkeepers thought of us when we made our fortnightly pilgrimage to town for supplies—these crazy hippies in their hand-spun, hand-woven, hand-knitted garb laced with leather and buttoned with seashells or small disks of wood. But if they thought we were nutters, they kept it to themselves, realising I'm sure, that the influx of new settlers into the area was, apart from the haberdashers, extremely good for business.

By now, hippies had swelled the Brogo population and social gatherings were a regular occurrence. Dyeing Day became an annual, mid-winter event when the women in the community came together to dye their skeins of hand-spun wool. We built fires in the open and placed cauldrons of water to sit over the flames, submerging our muslin pouches of vegetable matter into the steaming hot depths—to one vessel lichen, to another onion skins or maybe some parsley. We experimented with walnut shells, tansy, chamomile and mulberries. All afternoon, the gaggle of hippy witches tended their simmering broth, adding their hanks of wool to the bitter brew; the surrounding bush draped in every colour of the rainbow as the yarn drip-dried in the breeze.

Encouraged by my success with all things woolly, I decided to try my hand at making rawhide leather to turn into a carpenter's nail-bag, a water pouch or maybe even a tambourine or a drum. In exchange for a day of John's labour, a cattle-farming neighbour gave us a freshly skinned cow-hide. Once the hair, fat and remnants of flesh are removed, the hide can be stretched over a timber frame to dry, the experienced cow cocky explained. I spread the giant pelt over an upturned forty-four-gallon drum and amid an annoyingly sticky cloud of blowflies, spent a couple of days scraping off the thick layer of coagulated fat and goo with the draw knife. Before I had a chance to finish the job, however, the skin began to reek. Consulting *Skills of the Australian Bushman*, I found the instructions, for what appeared to be a more effective way of tackling the task. According to the author, a hide could be weighted down in a flowing creek—after seven days, the hair, fat and flesh dislodged and washed away by the current. Somehow, I managed to convince John of the merits of this process and he rolled up the stinky skin, hoisted it over his shoulders and made his way down to our creek—a barely running trickle in the gully. A week passed. It was time to bring the hide home and my long-suffering husband set off on his odious quest.

I was standing at the kitchen sink when I smelt something unbelievably foul wafting in through the open door of the shed. Wiping my hands on a tea-towel, I went outside to see what it was. There was nothing or no one in sight but the dreadful odour seemed to be gathering strength. Trying to figure out from which direction the stench was coming, I noticed, in the distance, a stooped and shadowy figure appearing from out of the bush. It was John— schlepping his way through the paddock with the oozing and disintegrating hide on his back.

'*Get it out of here!*' I shrieked as he drew closer and closer to the shed. 'For God sake, take it *away!*'

Cursing both me and the *Skills of the Australia Bushman*, John, dry-retching in between holding his breath, bound the sorry mess of decomposing flesh with rope, tied it to the tow-bar at the back of the ute and dragged it unceremoniously to its final resting place on the far side of the property, leaving it to rot amongst the withered, rust-coloured bracken. That afternoon in a frenzy of scrubbing in the shower, John feared he'd never be rid of the grisly and ubiquitous smell of death.

My husband's queasy reaction notwithstanding, generally speaking the South Coast Hippy was a tougher breed than their northern counterpart. Compared to the south, the weather in northern New South Wales was mild. There was no urgency to build a shelter or do anything much at all. Tropical fruit dripped from the trees. Rainwater was in plentiful supply; plump marijuana seeds germinating where they fell on the moist and fertile soil. The North Coast Hippy could live comfortably in a bamboo-framed, plastic-sheet covered geodesic dome, playing the bongos, twirling fire-batons, gazing at their navel or making macramé plant hangers out of rainbow coloured twine. As far as we were concerned, those Nimbin nancies didn't know the meaning of hard work. We southerners were made of sterner stuff, taking our mission to achieve self-sufficiency seriously. On the Far South Coast of New South Wales, not only did it take an effort to reap a harvest from the land, we needed to protect ourselves from a harsh and unforgiving climate.

To the local council's dismay, there were all manner of non-compliant and illegal dwellings being erected throughout the district as everyone rushed to provide themselves with some kind of shelter. Few of us, however, were prepared to spend our limited finances on the building permit necessary to allow the legal construction of our temporary accommodation. Aerial surveys were conducted to gauge the extent of the problem as the authorities realised they were losing control of the situation. There were hippies everywhere in 'them thar hills'. The council was missing out not only on lucrative building permit fees but potentially would be liable if an under-engineered roof collapsed and killed or disabled an unsuspecting hippy; although I suspect some councillors may not have mourned too deeply. Barely three years after our arrival in the valley, there was a push to reign in and regulate the burgeoning rural sprawl. The Bega Valley Shire Council declared war on the new settler population, announcing that they'd bring in bulldozers to flatten our illegal structures unless we complied with building regulations.

Not to be handcuffed by red tape, an Owner Builders' Association was formed by the new settlers to fight what we considered to be draconian measures. On a regular basis, we met in a community hall or in someone's home to discuss strategy. It was a social occasion, with everyone bringing a plate, a few bottles of homebrew and a sample from their latest crop of marijuana. We'd share experiences and pass on recently acquired building knowledge and local gossip. Composing and submitting letters to the editor at the Bega District News, we'd defend our case, praising the logic of the early settlers who'd built bark huts and lived in temporary shelters until they established themselves on their undeveloped properties.

Then we hit on a strategy that forced the council to rethink their position. The district was inhabited with traditional families who'd been living and farming in the area for generations. These born-and-bred locals had, since time immemorial, erected sheds, outbuildings or extensions to their existing homes without ever applying for a permit or paying a fee. The Owner Builder's Association told council they'd be happy to meet their demands as long as all rate payers in the community complied with the regulations. Unsurprisingly, we never heard from them again. Despite the proliferation of illegal buildings in the shire, to my knowledge not a hair on a hippy's head was ever harmed nor a dollar paid to the Bega Valley Shire Council's Department of Planning.

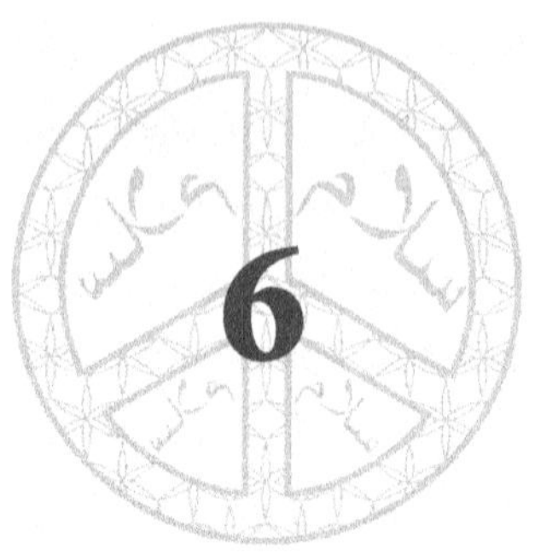

6

Honey

No self-respecting hippy household in the Bega Valley would have been seen dead without a goat. Like most goats, our goat Honey was smart. Having becoming acquainted with our two black sheep, JR and Sue-Ellen, I'd come to the conclusion that sheep were dunces by comparison. Love them or hate them you have to admire the goat. If Honey hadn't stuffed up her karma in a previous life she may have been reincarnated as the shrewd and quick-witted former British Prime Minister, Margaret Thatcher. Honey wasn't much to look at. Not a pretty brunette like the kohl-eyed, mascaraed Anglo-Nubian goat—the Audrey Hepburn of goats—nor refined like the statuesque blonde Saanens, unquestionably the Grace Kelly of the goat world. But what Honey lacked in looks, she made up for in goatish presence and brains.

Like the Iron Lady herself, Honey came from humble beginnings; and she lived her life with the same steely will. Honey's policy was to never waver in the pursuit of her goal, namely her relentless quest to fill her stomach. Unlike Margaret, Honey lived her life chained to a stake. Had she been free to roam she would have undoubtedly run off to find greener pastures which, in the mind of every goat, exist anywhere other than where they already are. But shackled to the spot, Honey did an excellent job of keeping down the weeds and blackberries as they tried their damnedest to sprout in our orchard.

Each morning, John would move the wily animal to a fresh patch of grass, making sure her water bucket was filled and not in a position where she could kick it over, a feat she nevertheless managed to accomplish at least once a day. Honey knew some sucker would come to replenish her water supply; she might strike it lucky, scoring a crust of bread, an apple core or even just a friendly scratch behind the ear. At the very least she'd get yelled at, which was better than nothing. If we left the property for any length of time, John would place Honey's stake well away from the branches of the fruit trees. But more often than not, on arriving home, we'd find that Honey had stripped one or more of the branches bare. Somehow, the hairy Houdini would have managed to stretch the chain, lengthen her body and elongate her neck like a periscope. Sticking out her flickering tongue, à la an anteater, Honey would have grasped a leaf at the tip of a branch, millimetre by millimetre pulling it in before devouring her prize.

xxx

In contrast to the sheep's woolly fleece, a goat's coat lacks water-resistant lanolin. Consequently, goats get soaked to the skin in the rain. Furthermore, in the baking hot summer, their short, fibrous hair provides little insulation from the sun. A responsible goat owner has a duty of care to provide their goat with some kind of shelter. These things I knew from my close study of *The Complete Herbal Handbook for Farm and Stable*, written by the renowned and no-nonsense Juliette de Bairacli Levy; her books essential reading for anyone interested in animal husbandry and becoming a proper hippy.

'*Stop the car!*' I shrieked one afternoon as John and I were driving home after picking up a load of fencing supplies in town. I'd seen a goat in the middle of a treeless paddock. It was a scorcher of a day and the poor thing looked as if it was about to keel over and die.

'What are you doing?' John asked cautiously as he pulled up beside a dilapidated, paint-peeled weatherboard house, its corrugated iron roof riddled with burnt orange rust.

'Wait here,' I commanded as I got out of the car and began marching towards the tumble-down building I assumed belonged to the owner of the suffering animal in the paddock. Once I'd squeezed through the corroded and seized half-open gate, I scaled a set of rickety front steps, strode across the veranda and rang the doorbell; sweltering in my bib and brace overalls and tie-dye singlet as I waited for someone to answer the door. I was on the verge of ringing again when the door creaked open—a stooped and shrunken old man with snowy flyaway hair, milky turtle eyes and a scrawny chin of sparse white stubble, teetering in the entrance. Despite the heat, the hoary fellow wore a darned and tattered bottle-green cardigan over a checked flannelette shirt, both stuffed unevenly into a pair of heavyweight wool-blend trousers. A sulphurous odour of broiling silverside and cabbage drifted up the hallway from the kitchen. I could hear a budgie chirping somewhere at the back of the house.

'Yes, dear?' the geriatric gent asked, blinking like an ancient tortoise in innocent expectation.

I took a deep breath.

'Do you realise that goats don't have lanolin in their coats?' I proclaimed. 'It is very cruel to leave them out in the sun,' I added.

And with that, I turned on my heels and stomped back to the car. Curiously, John had disappeared but when I opened the passenger door, I found him cowering in his seat, mortified by another one of my evangelistic crusades.

Rain or shine, every morning I'd pull on my gumboots, dress in whatever clothes came to hand and make my way to the goat shed to milk Honey; bleating, turning in circles and stamping her cloven hoof, the rapacious critter would be expecting me. Once I'd manhandled Honey into her stall, I'd give her a generous handful of lucerne hay before perching myself on the milking stool at her side. From that point on, the goat was oblivious to what was happening at the other end of her body—thinking of England no doubt. Placing my cheek against Honey's warm flank, I'd close my eyes as I squeezed the milk from her teats; the sound of contented munching and the bizarre inner workings of the ruminant's gastrointestinal tract in my ear.

Honey was a good milker: our buckets were quite literally running over with the stuff. Goat yoghurt, goat cheese and bottles of goat milk proliferated on the shelves in the dark and spooky recesses of our antiquated kerosene fridge. After breakfast, I'd strain the morning's yield through a square of cheesecloth to filter out the goat hair and specks of dirt before pouring it into a bottle to store in the fridge with the plethora of other dairy products. I'd leave milk in ceramic bowl by the wood-burning stove where, overnight, it would miraculously turn into yoghurt and make cottage cheese by adding the juice of a lemon to a saucepan of heated milk—the curds instantly separating to bob like fluffy white clouds in the straw-coloured whey.

According to *The Vegetable Gardening and Animal Husbandry Handbook,* once in a while you should allow your nanny goat to experience the joy of motherhood in order to keep the milk flowing. Fortunately, Honey, a fine figure of a woman like Margaret, had her admirers. King Brian, a randy, stinky old rascal who lived on a property in the next valley, spent his days rubbing his bony, ginger-haired frame up against fence posts or cocking his leg to piss on his own straggly, urine-drenched beard. When Honey's pink bits became all red, juicy and swollen, we knew it was time to bring in The King. Honestly, I don't know what she saw in him but from the moment he alighted statesman-like from his mini goat-float, Honey, becoming all girlie and skittish, was his.

✕✕✕

One morning, as I went to squeeze her teats, Honey jumped like a jack-in-a-box in the air. I got on my hands and knees to take a look under her belly and straightaway saw what was wrong. Honey's left teat was scarlet and oozing with pus. The goat had mastitis—an inflammation of the mammary gland. Wondering what Juliette prescribed for the ailment, I consulted *The Complete Herbal Handbook for Farm and Stable*. Garlic was the remedy. It's a natural antibiotic, the author claimed. Luckily, I had plenty on hand; using it, not just in cooking but to make a spray that eradicated the aphids on my broccoli plants. There were two plaited bunches of fat bulbs hanging above the Rayburn stove on the veranda.

Juliette suggested pushing a few cloves of garlic down the goat's throat, far enough so the crafty creature couldn't spit them out. The procedure went without a hitch for a couple of days. However, on the third morning, as I shoved the medicine down her gullet, without warning, Honey clamped her mouth shut like one of those giant clams on the Great Barrier Reef. Letting out a scream that could have woken the dead grocer's daughter herself, I tried to pull my hand from the teeth of what felt like a steel-jawed rabbit trap. But I could see the crazed, serial-killer look in Honey's eyes. She had no intention of letting go. This is revenge for chaining me to a stake, I could have sworn she was thinking. Hearing the commotion,

John came running, and immediately assessing the situation, he grabbed Honey in a headlock and tried to pry her mouth open with his hands. The recalcitrant refused to budge. By now, I was thrashing around on the ground, kicking, screaming, crying and begging for release, my arm elevated in a contorted Nazi salute, attached at its extremity to the 'jaws of death'.

'*Hurry up*! *Get her off me*!' I screamed hysterically.

Like Anthony Mundine at the World Championships, John began to punch Honey with a volley of body blows to her side. But he faced a formidable opponent. Holding steadfast in the face of adversity, the barnyard embodiment of Thatcherism would not stand down. There was only one thing left to do. John raised his fist and, with a powerful king-hit to the head, he knocked Honey out; my punctured hand falling free as she dropped like a stone to the floor.

✕✕✕

With the thirty-acre Big Paddock finally constructed, we set Honey loose to hang out with the other members of our dynasty: our dim-witted but adorable sheep, JR and Sue-Ellen and our Jerusalem donkeys, Jamaica and Jemima. At dusk, I'd stand on the veranda and call her home and eventually, when she deigned to make an appearance, I'd lead her to her night quarters. But one evening when I called, Honey didn't materialise. For more than an hour I trudged around the paddock hollering her name until, just as I was about to give up, I spotted her. There she was, lying on her back in a patch of bracken, spindly legs rigid and pointing to the heavens, her eyes rolling in their sockets and a frothy white foam bubbling from her mouth.

John and I loaded the dying goat into the car and set off for the vet; me driving and John cradling Honey's head in his arms in the back seat. We were half way to town when John put his hand on my shoulder.

'I think she's dead,' he said.

I stepped on the gas, speeding down the highway like a hippy after a hash cookie when, in the rear-view mirror I noticed that John was doing something to Honey's lifeless body.

'What's happening? What are you *doing*?' I cried. John didn't answer. Suddenly it dawned on me. My husband was giving our dead goat mouth-to-mouth resuscitation. As Honey spluttered into life, I planted my foot on the accelerator.

'What's wrong with her?' I asked the nice young vet as Honey lay prone and barely breathing on the stainless-steel table.

'I think she's got bracken poisoning,' the vet said. 'It causes extreme Vitamin B deficiency. To be honest with you, her chances aren't good. I can give her a massive dose of Vitamin B to see if that'll revive her but I should warn you, if she does live, she might be blind.'

The vet injected the antidote. Within an instant, Honey perked up but, as predicted, she couldn't see. We took her home and kept her indoors where she'd spend the day stumbling around, bumping into walls. The poor animal's life was a misery and John and I, distraught and at a loss as to what else to do, decided to put her down. On the morning of Honey's execution, I made the mournful trek to the Goat Shed to give her her last supper. Imagine my surprise when I entered the shed to discover that the invincible goat had regained her sight. Jumping to her feet and bounding like Bambi across the room to greet me, she stamped her hoof, turning in circles and demanding I give her breakfast. The Iron Lady was back!

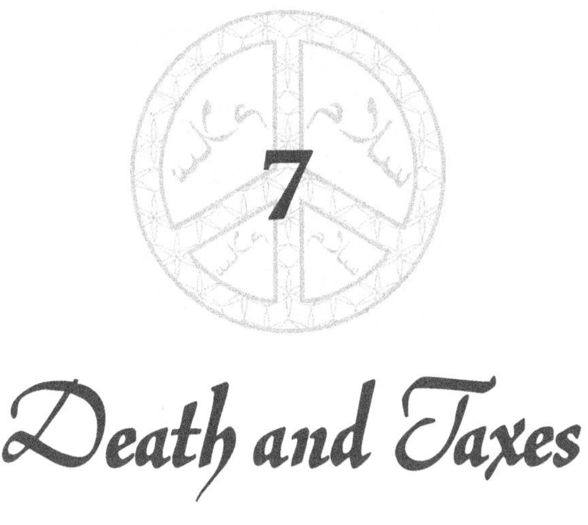

7

Death and Taxes

Our Jerusalem donkey, Jemima, didn't share Honey's good fortune. Up until the winter of '82 she and her best friend Jamaica, had lived two carefree years on our property—foraging for tender green shoots and succulent young thistles, basking in the sun, rolling in the dust, having their coats brushed and bellies tickled by humans and eeyawing whenever the spirit moved them. Yet, that year, as the days grew short and icy, for some reason Jemima's hair began to fall out. Once again, I consulted *The Complete Herbal Handbook for Farm and Stable* but found nothing in its pages relating to the donkey's symptoms. The results of a biopsy left us none the wiser. The vet had no idea why Jemima was moulting so severely but she wasn't going to get better, he said. By July, Jemima was practically bald. We kept her rugged in her horse blanket but the weather was closing in and she was cold and wretched. John and I knew what we had to do and I found a donkey-breeding neighbour willing to take in the still healthy Jamaica so she'd have company and not pine too much for her mate.

On a crisp autumn morning, John fetched the shotgun from the workshop. Through the rising mist, I followed him into the Big Paddock. We knew where to find the sick jenny—she'd be catching the first weak rays of sunlight as they appeared over Mumbulla Mountain. Sure enough, Jemima saw us coming and plodded over to meet us at the gate. In a typical equine greeting, I snorted a few blasts of air into her nostrils and she stood patiently as I released the straps on her horse rug, removing it for the very last time.

'Who's a good girl, then,' I said tearfully, kissing her muzzle and running my hand along the furry inside of her ears. As I held out a small tuft of hay, the unsuspecting animal reached forward trustingly to nibble the treat from my Judas hand.

'Come on. It's time,' John said huskily, roughly wiping a tear from his cheek. And flinging my arms around the donkey's neck, I buried my nose in a patch of thinning fur and inhaled her sweet musky scent. 'I'm sorry, Jemima,' I sobbed before stepping out of the way.

'Good donkey. Hold still now,' John said as he raised the gun and placed the end of the barrel on Jemima's forelock.

I stuck my fingers in my ears and shut my eyes. At such close range, the gunshot was a deafening, bone-jarring shock, followed by a soft thud as Jemima the donkey slumped dead to the ground; the acrid whiff of gunpowder caught in my nose and throat.

XXX

Although it was part and parcel of life on the land, John disliked killing fatally injured wildlife, terminally ill pets or old and unproductive farm animals. But at the end of one particularly long, hot summer, it was obvious that our batch of elderly hens had gone permanently off the lay so my pragmatic husband decided it was no longer economically viable to continue their upkeep.

'It's time to make way for some young and sexy egg-laying chicks,' he declared.

One by one, John grabbed the scrawny senior citizens from their pen and carried them flapping and squalling to the chopping block at the wood heap. With a tight-lipped grimace and a sharp-edged axe, he adeptly lopped off their heads. Employing a tried and true strategy perfected as a child whenever my parents fought, I remained indoors, plugging my ears with my fingers and singing *Mary had a Little Lamb* at the top of my voice, while walking briskly in circles round the room.

A few minutes later, gauging that the coast was clear, I ventured outside only to be handed a blood-soaked hessian sack stuffed with the freshly assassinated chooks. It was my job to bury the dead; the sinewy old fowls being past eating, even as chicken soup. I slung the bag over my shoulder and lugged it down the ridge to the orchard where the carcasses would be put to good use. Buried around the fringes of the fruit trees, they'd make excellent blood-and-bone fertiliser. But that year the drought was in full swing; the ground turned hard as concrete. Even with the aid of the heavy-duty crowbar I struggled to dig a hole deep enough to hold the grisly remains; after fifteen minutes, I'd hollowed out barely ten centimetres of dirt. Fed up, I reached into the sack, pulled out a still-warm cadaver and threw it unceremoniously into the shallow crater; the headless body sitting proud of the cavity—a white, blood-stained wing poking towards the heavens as if saluting me farewell from the grave. It was then, frustrated and momentarily taking leave of my senses, that I had a brainwave. If I stomped on the corpse I could squash it into the hole.

'*Bwaaaaaaaaaark!*' went the dead chook in what was a fine tribute to the great but not yet late Freddie Mercury as I brought my foot down, simultaneously leaping into the air like a startled springbok.

'*It's alive*! It's alive. It's still alive!' I screeched as, with arms flapping, I flew up the hill to John.

John followed me down to the orchard and pulled the flattened wad of gore and feathers from the ground.

'Look,' he said disparagingly, dangling it under my nose. 'It's dead, you idiot! You must have jumped on its voice box.'

ꭗ ꭗ ꭗ

Admittedly, John had a little assistance when it came to dealing with the emotional trauma associated with killing an animal. Rolling himself a stout, carefully crafted three paper joint, he'd sit and smoke it on the veranda before tackling the heinous task. But John wasn't the only one in the area partial to the wacky baccy. Every new settler in Brogo was cultivating cannabis and, for the men in the community, there was rarely an occasion in which marijuana didn't play a part.

'How's it going, man?' a male hippy would say when coming into contact with one of his own, already crumbling a dry bud into a pair of stuck-together cigarette papers.

'Time for a scube?' a bloke would ask, while helping his neighbour pour a concrete slab or raise a roof on a shed.

'I'll just roll a joint,' others would say before sharpening a chainsaw or heading to the wood heap to chop firewood.

Winter or summer, in sickness and in health, when he was happy or sad, at rest or at play, night or day, in good times or bad, it was always appropriate to smoke some weed.

'Would you all just *fuck off* and go home!' I yelled one afternoon at the small circle of stoned men sitting on an assortment of tool boxes, eskies and bricks stacks on our building site.

'Can't you see we're trying to *work*?'

Blinking at me impassively, the shambolic group of spaced-out males mustered themselves and reluctantly got up to leave. Mumbling their goodbyes to an apologetic John, they shuffled off—back to their respective shanties, harried wives and whinging,

68

ragamuffin children. They'd nicknamed me Attila the Hun, but I didn't care. Maybe *they* didn't want to achieve anything in their dope-addled lives, but *I* had an agenda. This fierce warrior princess was in desperate need of running hot water and a proper flush toilet.

Dope became a bone of contention in my marriage. John smoked so much of it that, if I needed to discuss an issue possibly leading to conflict, I'd wait until he'd lit a joint before broaching the matter. Over the years, I'd come to know that he was more amenable to reasonable discussion whilst semi-anaesthetised with marijuana. Ironically, the amount of dope John smoked also made him paranoid. Petrified of getting busted, he lived with a constant ear out for the *thwop-thwop* of police helicopter blades. When a mate told him you could see a matchbox on the ground from a hovering chopper he began to grow his plants deep in the bush under a dense canopy of foliage where, starved of sunlight, they never amounted to much.

XXX

Of course, living in the hippy heartland was not my first encounter with illicit substances. I was eighteen and about to complete my first year at art school when my mother's father died and left me $3000 in his will. With twelve weeks off before the next academic year, I purchased the cheapest airfare available and flew to London, missing Gough Whitlam's dismissal altogether. From London, I caught the train north to Manchester to stay with my grandmother, my father's mother, in Oldham. As I boarded the flight in Melbourne, I noticed a tall, good-looking young man, a boyish version of Butch Cassidy with a mop of sun-bleached hair, stowing his luggage in the overhead locker. He noticed me, too. When the plane levelled out, the vision in a body-hugging Rip Curl singlet, thongs and very short shorts that left nothing to the imagination, rose from his seat and swaggered up the aisle to introduce himself.

'Hi, I'm Craig,' said the blue-eyed surfer with a diamond stud in his right earlobe. 'Mind if I take a seat?' And without waiting for permission, the fitter and turner from New Zealand eased his tanned, muscular physique into the vacant space beside me, proceeding for the next nine hours, to chat me up.

On arriving in Bangkok, I was told my connecting flight to London was delayed for three days.

'Come with me,' said Craig. 'I know a great hotel.'

Not keen on being in a foreign city by myself and figuring that bunking with the tradie from Auckland was a safer bet, I climbed into the taxi with my new escort. However, on our first two nights in the hotel the handsome Kiwi left me alone, only to stagger back in the wee hours of the morning to pass out like a light on his bed. I was both curious and alarmed. The next night when my roommate went out, I decided to take a look through his stuff; unzipping his backpack, I removed T-shirts, jeans and sandshoes. And there they were at the bottom of the bag: twelve rectangular clear plastic pouches filled with snow white powder. I knew it wasn't icing sugar; it was the seventies after all and, with my proclivity for collecting experiences, I'd dabbled with just about every type of drug available at the time: marijuana, LSD, speed, magic mushrooms and even 'smack'.

When Craig finally returned that night I was sitting cross-legged on the bed.

'What's this?' I demanded, waving a packet of heroin in the air as he walked through the door.

'Oh, yeah,' he replied sheepishly. 'I was going to tell you about that. Listen, babe,' he continued, turning on the charm. 'Why don't you take some in your suitcase and when we get through customs we can hit the town? I'm getting ten thousand pounds for this lot!' he declared, flashing his brilliant white teeth.

It was one of those watershed moments where the course of your life can go one way or another. I was young and excitable and the idea of hanging out in London with the cashed up and spunky New Zealander was appealing. But I wasn't totally insane; I told Craig there was no way I was going to smuggle heroin out of Thailand. On that last night in Bangkok, sleep an impossible dream, I lay sweating on the bed with my eyes glued to the front door; praying that the Thai police wouldn't come crashing in and drag me off to prison.

Twenty-four hours later, safely installed in my grandmother's house in the north of England, the phone rang.

'It's for you,' my grandma said as she passed me the handpiece. It was Craig. He'd made it through customs.

'Hi, babe. I made it!' he announced triumphantly. 'How about you jump on a train and come down to London?'

For the second time that week, I said no to the drug smuggler from the Land of the Long White Cloud.

✗✗✗

Unlike some men in Brogo, being perpetually stoned didn't seem to affect John's motivation or his ability to work, which was fortunate because although we were, for the most part, living off the land, we still required money. John found part-time work as a tussock digger, or, when it was required, a human sheepdog. Tussock digging was a lonely job. His boss, a tight-fisted, pot-bellied farmer, would send John out to the far reaches of his property to root out the bothersome weeds with a mattock. Out there alone on the bare, wind-blown hills John would go at it like a man possessed for a couple of hours, then take a well-deserved break; sipping his tea, smoking a joint and admiring the arc of scenic splendour from the desolate hilltop. Sat on his corpulent behind astride one of those bulky quad bikes, John's boss would often ask his fit, young employee to help him bring in the sheep for shearing or drenching. John worked in tandem with Rosie, a professional border collie sheep dog. The pair would run non-stop, up-hill and down dale rounding up hundreds of flighty and exceedingly stupid ewes until by day's end, man and dog were exhausted, Rosie's tongue hanging from her mouth like a floppy slice of luncheon ham.

Making my contribution to the coffers, I found work as a cleaner for the wealthy squattocracy down the road. Mrs Macintyre, a stout and buxom middle-aged busybody, and a local councillor, employed me at well below the minimum wage to scrub, wipe, polish, vacuum and sweep her capacious house. On cleaning day, Mrs Mac would head into town to attend to council business. As the LandCruiser drove up the track and disappeared over the hill, I'd race to the bathroom, run a hot bath and immerse myself in the heavenly hot water for half an hour before beginning a day of hard labour.

Sometimes, like many other new settlers in the community, we worked *gratis* or in exchange for labour or produce. Neighbours Alan and Vera Jeffreys were traditional dairy farmers who'd lived on Warrigal Range Road for decades. Putting aside their natural suspicion of these scruffily dressed and hairy blow-ins, they'd come to accept the hippy families sprouting up like clusters of field mushrooms around them. One day, they let slip it'd been years since they'd had a holiday, so John and I offered to give them a break. The Jeffreys were thrilled, immediately booking a trip to the Gold Coast. Alan and Vera had a week to teach their inexperienced young neighbours how to milk their seventy-odd cows and run a dairy. Every morning, John and I rose at 3 a.m. and made our bleary-eyed way to work. It'd still be dark when we arrived; the milking shed lit up like Woolworths. On automatic, the slow-plodding milkers would have already moseyed into the yard.

From a distance, out in the paddock, a cow looks a benign and gentle creature but at close quarters, you realise they are a massive and formidable beast. Our first task was to usher the bovine giants into their stalls. Locked in place, we'd give them a handful of hay to keep them occupied while we washed their swollen udders with a disinfectant-soaked cloth.

'Hygiene is paramount in a dairy,' Alan told us. 'If the yield is contaminated with organic matter it's rejected,' he earnestly explained.

The cows seemed to enjoy having their pink bits cleaned with a warm, soapy rag but when it came to positioning the suction cups on their teats, there were always one or two (you know who you are) that, with an uncanny skill at hitting their target, would kick out with their hind legs or swipe you with their shit-encrusted tail.

The milk was drawn through pipes into a refrigerated stainless steel vat. Soon afterwards, a man in a milk truck came to test it for contamination before siphoning it into his tanker. Our initial two batches failed to pass the test and had to be ditched—John and I watching in shame and awe as the snow-white tsunami flooded the emerald grass. We soon got the hang of it, though, milking twice a day as if we'd done it all our lives. There was something deeply satisfying, almost transcendent, about being in a dairy at that time of day—the cows contentedly chewing their cud, the tart but not unpleasant smell of fresh manure in the air, the rhythmic suction sounds of the milking machine; the eastern sky seamlessly shifting from dark inks to pale pastels. Apart from the odd explosive fart from a Friesian, the atmosphere was serene. As the sun rose behind Mumbulla Mountain, the cattle slowly ambling back out to pasture, John and I would head home to cook a hot and hearty breakfast.

Tanned, rejuvenated and grateful, Alan and Vera returned to their herd and their unremitting milking routine—their two weeks in Surfers Paradise a life-restoring tonic. John and I hung up our dairy aprons, hosed the dung off our gumboots and reset the alarm clock to a more civilised hour. But being up before the birds turned out to be good practice. Feeling nauseous, I suspected it well before taking the pregnancy test; the human addition to our little animal family was due in eight months' time—New Year's Day, 1983.

'We'll need a trip to the bookshop, now,' I said to John with a grin.

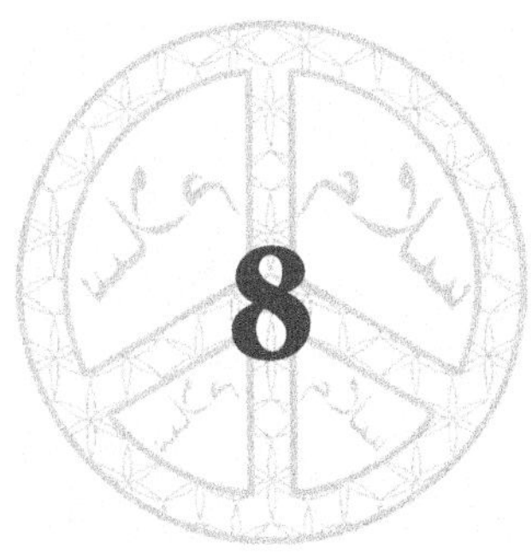

8

Eva

It must have been bang on midnight when my waters broke. I could hear the muffled cheers above the distant and repetitive thud of the New Year's Eve celebrations as they filtered up from the valley below. There was a distinct pop and I felt the warm splash on my bare feet. Over the dome of my naked belly, I could see the clear liquid seeping into the cow dung and sawdust mortar I'd tamped into the crevices between the hand cut, redgum wood rounds three summers ago.

'Will you be alright?' my neighbour Julie had asked, when an hour earlier she'd driven me home from the party.

'Yeah, I'm okay,' I replied. 'Just tired. I think I'll go to bed.'

I stood on the veranda of our wattle and daub hut watching as the headlights of Julie's Land Rover made their way up our track, winding through the towering stringy barks in a halo of illuminated dust.

Now I was alone in the black bush and as the terrible vice began to grip my body I realised my predicament. Ushering in 1983, the entire community including John, was at the festivities being held in a paddock a kilometre away as the crow flies. I had no one to call.

75

From the outset, the contractions were barely a minute apart. This is happening way too fast for a first delivery, I thought. I spotted my dog-eared copy of *The Spiritual Midwifery Handbook* buried under the pile of birthing and baby books on the bedside table, but it was too late now to do the research. Between white-knuckling the furniture in excruciating pain, I had precisely one minute to figure out how I was going to get to the hospital. What am I going to do? I can't give birth by myself. I'm going to die, I thought, with mounting panic. And then I remembered. Somewhere in the desk, scribbled on a piece of paper, was the number of the fellow who'd bought the property next door. I'd never met Harry Shields and John had only spoken to him once on the phone. But it was the Christmas holidays and although I knew Harry hadn't moved to the area permanently, I hoped he'd come to spend the weekend in the ugly clip-lock shed he'd erected on our boundary last Easter. Harry wasn't known by the locals and was rumoured to be pretty 'straight'. So, if he was here, I reasoned, he probably hadn't been invited to the shindig in the valley. Frantically, I rifled through the bureau, stopped in my tracks at regular intervals by breath-taking pain. Finding the precious scrap of paper at last, I waited for a powerful contraction to ebb, then dialled the number.

A whole eon passed.

'Is that Harry?' I blurted the second the man answered the phone. 'You don't know me but I'm your next-door neighbour. I'm in labour. I need you to go and get my husband. Right *now*!'

There was a brief silence but I sensed the well-seasoned cow cocky, with his years of experience delivering slippery, icky wet calves, was unfazed by the prospect of an imminent birth.

'Don't you worry, love. I'll go and get him straightaway,' was Harry's brisk response to my stammered directions to the party. Then the line went dead.

As I waited for John, I crawled across the rough timber floor on my hands and knees, moaning and cursing. For a change of scenery, I dragged myself outside to writhe about on the scrubby patches of tussocks, bellowing at the night sky in agony. The sky didn't care, no doubt bored with my overwrought paroxysms of torment, having seen it all before. In the ever-diminishing gap between contractions, panting on my back in the eerie silence of the bush, I looked up at the billions of stars and felt like some small primal creature, part of something vast and unknowable. Then all too quickly the pain returned, the mystic moment shattered and I was clutching at the earth—crying out into the dark and infinite void. One of the Jeffreys' cows mooed back in consolation.

I was inside when John burst into the hut, his face littered with faint, bleeding scratches, twigs and gum leaves sticking out like antennae on his head and the thin plait draped over his shoulder. Inexplicably, his jeans were drenched and dripping all over the floor.

'I'm so out of it,' he gasped as he leaned against the doorjamb trying to catch his breath, a puddle pooling at his feet. From my perspective at ground level, I had a worm's eye view of the water as it trickled into the crevices between the rounds of wood.

Our neighbour had found the expectant father smoking hashish from a home-made hookah in the back of a Ford Falcon panel van. But John, refusing Harry's offer of a lift on his motorbike, chose instead to run home, calculating that sprinting cross country over ditches, rabbit holes and jutting rocks, scaling barbed-wire fences, navigating thick bush and traversing a running creek in total darkness, was a more direct route and the quicker option. Fortu-nately, coming to the end of a horrendous contraction, I had just enough time before the next one began to pull myself up off the floor, stagger across the room, grab John by the lapels of his denim jacket and shake the bejesus out of him.

'*Get it together!*' I shrieked. 'I'm having the baby. We have to go to the hospital *now!*'

Instantly sober, John sprang into action. In a whirlwind of activity, he bundled me and all my paraphernalia into the car and sped down the deserted highway to the hospital. In the delivery room, the father-to-be rubbed my back and massaged my shoulders, ran to and fro emptying my bed pans or sat stoically by my side as I cut off the blood supply to his hand or dug my nails into his arm. Bearing up under a wall of harrowing sound, John's breathing technique deserved an Oscar and he didn't take offence when I called him an idiot for forgetting the hand mirror I'd planned on using to watch the baby's head crown. In those final moments, the 'mirror' I'd use would be John's face as he witnessed his daughter come into the world; her punctual, no-nonsense entrance the first clue I had of my child's fastidious and determined nature.

The midwife brought John and me a cup of tea, turned down the lights and left the three of us alone. It was the 1st of January and I could hear the magpies greeting the sultry new year with their familiar warbling song. Our freshly washed and naked baby lay peacefully on my deflated stomach. With a fixed gaze, she examined her father and me, a concentrated expression on her scrunched up tadpole face, obviously assessing the situation and coming to the conclusion that these two jokers were nowhere near up to the task ahead.

The next day I woke to find John standing over the clear plastic crib intently scrutinising his sleeping offspring, a picture of fatherly concern.

'You can pick her up and hold her,' I said. 'She won't bite.' Awkwardly, tenderly and ever so carefully, John gathered his daughter in his arms and held his breath.

It was then I noticed that he was covered in black soot, his hair plastered to his scalp, large panda eye circles streaked by rivulets of sweat. He smelled like a campfire and I could see the trail of charcoal Blundstone prints he'd made on the lino while tiptoeing around the maternity ward waiting for me to wake up.

'What an earth have you been doing?' I asked him.

'There was a lightning strike in the Top Paddock and it started a fire. But don't worry,' John said quickly as I rose from the mattress in concern. 'I put it out.' He flashed me a big grin and I saw that even his teeth were covered with an inky film of grime. A fleck of ash, momentarily suspended in the air, settled on the tip our newborn's nose.

Over the next few days, whenever John came to visit, we'd pull our chairs up to either side of the crib and with eyes glued to its soundly sleeping occupant, like watching a movie on the silver screen, sit riveted as our tiny starlet blew milk bubbles, yawned, made sucking movements with her lips, hiccupped or passed wind.

'Phew, that was a good one,' John would whisper proudly after a particularly loud, protracted and flatulent performance.

I spent seven glorious days in the Bega District Hospital, the longest stay permitted before they threw new mothers back out into the world. Compared to our mud hut in Brogo, it was like holidaying at a Four Seasons Hotel. There was electricity, running hot water, air-conditioning, telly and cooked meals served three times a day. Piles of soft towelling nappies, perfumed lotions, talcum powder and wet wipes appeared like magic. Clearly, the nurses were angels in disguise. During visiting hour, I'd prop myself up in bed with a couple of plump pillows, take my sweet-smelling baby in my arms and, like a Hollywood celebrity, receive my visitors—my mother, sister and much to the chagrin of matron, two or three of my bra-less, breastfeeding, kaftan-clad neighbours.

I didn't want to leave but at the end of the week, with my daughter having already instituted her own well-structured and consistent feeding and sleeping regime, I reluctantly packed my bags and, with some trepidation, prepared myself for the return to the bush. As I stood at the hospital entrance waiting for John to pull up in the ute, I looked down at the swathed and serene bundle of human existence we'd labelled Eva and felt, in equal measure, the weight of unconditional love and responsibility flood the very core of my being.

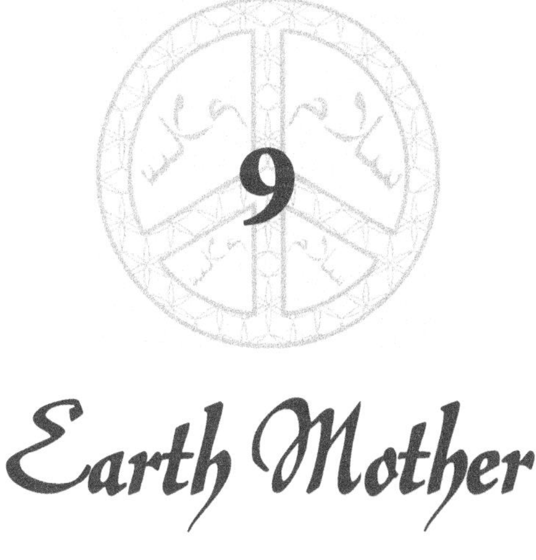

9

Earth Mother

Following my father's death, my mother stayed on in Bairnsdale but after two years, as soon as Lisa and I left home, me to art school in Melbourne and my sister to live with her boyfriend, Mum, escaping the town gossip and the stigma that came with her husband's suicide, packed her bags and 'got the hell out of Dodge'. Determined to bury the past, hoping to meet a decent man and eager to start anew, she relocated to Sydney. However, three years on, her Vaucluse knight in shining armour having never made an appearance, she followed John and me to the Far South Coast of New South Wales, settling into a flat overlooking the harbour in Bermagui and resigning herself to a celibate life.

Compared to our wattle and daub hut, my mother's place was a high-tech, carpeted palace of plumbed luxury and automation which I'd try to visit as often as possible. Leaving John to his own devices on the land, I'd pack the car with Eva and her mountain of miscellaneous baby gear and head to Bermagui for the weekend. There, I'd take a long, hot shower and do a few loads of washing.

With Eva fed and settled, Mum and me would have a cup of tea and a Tim Tam or two and watch *Days of Our Lives* on the telly.

Motherhood was a shock to my hitherto self-serving system; my freedom had been hijacked, my needs totally eclipsed by this wailing jot of energy, star-dust and will. I'd raised all manner of creatures—asinine, hircine, canine, feline, ovine and a few other 'ines' I can't recall now, but nothing had prepared me for raising a human being—for the unbearable responsibility, the crushing exhaustion, the meld of jaw-dropping love and gnawing concern. Not only that but the division of labour between John and I, which up until this point had been relatively equal, was completely thrown asunder. Overnight, the dynamics of our egalitarian relationship changed. Having lived through the Women's Liberation Movement, I considered myself a feminist yet suddenly, here I was, thrown back in time: a 1950s' housewife—child-rearing, cooking, cleaning and washing; John the Bloke, in the great outdoors—constructing fences, puddling mudbricks or chopping a load of firewood.

With no electricity or running hot water, nappies became the bane of my life. Determined to stay true to my sustainable principles, I refused to use disposable diapers; no bona fide hippy would dream of polluting the earth with those putrid wads of plastic and poo. We purchased a vintage mangle and an antique copper boiler from a bric-a-brac shop in Bega. At the far end of the carport, next to the concrete laundry sink with its mangle newly installed, John built a granite fireplace and placed the boiler on top. Every day, I'd fill the copper with cold water and light a fire beneath. After hosing off the worst of my baby's poos under a fruit tree, feeling the smug sense of satisfaction a hippy feels when they've recycled their own human waste, I'd throw the nappies into the boiling water, twenty minutes later heaving them out with a stick and threading them through the mangle. During this labour-intensive procedure, my eyes stinging and streaming with tears from the smoke, somehow, I'd always manage to scald myself on the scorching, hot cloth.

It wasn't long before I went on strike. Following one particularly brutal washing day, I marched down to the orchard where John was tamping in fence posts.

'I want a generator and a washing machine,' I cried in desperation.

Seeing my swollen, red hands and the fresh burns on my forearms, John realised it was the beginning of the end. His wife's bourgeois roots had bubbled to the surface; her ecological principles thrown out with the bathwater. By the end of the week, I had a second-hand washing machine and a loud, diesel-fuming generator to power it.

But next washing day, I got more than I bargained for. On becoming a mother, I'd made a deal with the snakes on our property.

'As long as you stay in the bush we won't have a problem' was the telepathic message I sent out across the land. 'But if you come anywhere near my daughter, it's hasta la vista, baby,' I added.

One red-belly black snake must have taken a sickie that day and not got the memo. I'd just put Eva down in her wicker bassinette next to Stephen the Chainsaw in the workshop and was on my way to the clothesline when I saw it, bold as brass, coiled up only metres from the front door. John had gone to work so I knew I'd have to deal with the situation myself. Abandoning the washing basket, I went to grab a shovel from the carport, hoping the snake would've slithered off by the time I got back. But on my return, it was still there, black and glossy; basking in the warm sunshine on a freshly mowed patch of kikuyu. Banging the shovel on the ground and stamping my foot, I tried to scare the snake away, but it didn't move. Tentatively, I poked at it with the implement until suddenly the rudely awakened reptile sprang into life, hissing and rising up to face me full-on.

My motherly instincts ignited. I took a swipe at the angry serpent—not killing it outright as intended, just lacerating its flesh with a nasty wound. Still very much alive but badly injured, the snake tried but failed to lunge in my direction. I felt ill. I've started this, now I have to finish it, I thought.

I struck at the writhing snake again, missing it by a mile. By now, I was desperate to put the poor creature out of its misery, bashing it over and over with the back of the shovel until I was sure it was dead. Alarmed and horrified by the intensity of my own violence, I dropped my weapon to the ground, ran to the workshop for a hessian sack and rushed to throw it over the snake's pulverised body; blindly stumbling inside to cry into a pillow in shame. I'd just killed an innocent being, a magnificent creation minding its own business on what began as a perfect day for doing the washing.

What was that about, I wondered afterwards? What had happened to the hippy idyll, to living in harmony with nature? Had I become desensitised by the harsh realities of life in the bush?

But I wasn't the only woman in Brogo battling the forces of nature. It was the women living an alternative lifestyle in hippy communities who bore the brunt of their primitive living conditions. My softly spoken, mousy-haired, and perpetually pregnant neighbour, Julie McNeil, did it tougher than most. Toting an Indian tepee and two boys under three, she and her ginger-bearded husband Brett, a bricklayer from Melbourne, arrived in the Bega Valley twelve months after John and me. Immediately hitting it off, John and Brett cleared a site and erected the tepee—by late afternoon the magnificent ivory structure glowed like an otherworldly craft in the saffron-tinted light. The following day, the men lay a floor of river stone and a fire ring of granite inside and the McNeil's moved into their cramped but cosy new home; an inquisitive wedge-tailed eagle circling in the sky above.

'It's a sign,' said John as he rolled a huge and beautifully made five-paper joint to commemorate the occasion; the stoned, new best mates *Doin' the Eagle Rock* round the tepee within minutes of finishing the reefer.

Dinner at the McNeil's was a nerve-wracking experience. Sitting crossed-legged on our flaps of sheepskin, plates of hunza pie and tabouli balanced on our laps, John and I would spend the evening poised to save a tottering toddler from falling headlong into the fire as it negotiated its way across the uneven floor. Although the tepee was joy to behold, when the canvas became impregnated with mould and the dark treacle residue of wood smoke, it was a dungeon in there. Julie's kitchen and bathroom, bark-walled structures open to the elements, were stationed outside. Under the blinking light of the Tilley lamp, sometimes in wind-driven rain, the worn-weary mother would stand at her wood-burning stove and cook her family their dinner. The kids were constantly battling colds and Julie's back ached from stooping to and fro through the tepee's low-slung entrance.

Brett and John began a bricklaying business. Setting off for work at seven in the morning, they'd drop by a mate's place for a beer and a joint on the way home and not get back till dark. I was stuck without a car, day in day out, in the pokey wattle and daub hut. When Eva was teething, they were long and fraught days indeed. I was torn between wanting to tear out my hair or bang my head against a mudbrick wall. Desperate for adult company, I'd bundle my fretful daughter into her stroller, pushing her with great difficulty up our rocky dirt track and along Warrigal Range Road to visit another mother. Or taking comfort in sharing a cup of lemon-grass tea and a slice of banana cake with someone in worse circumstances than myself, I'd strap Eva into a harness on my back and hike down the hill to see Julie. It wasn't long, though, before I'd had enough of my life in captivity.

'I need the car one day a week,' I demanded one night when John got home from work. He could see his wife, cheeks flushed and eyes feverish, like a number of other young mothers in Brogo, was in imminent danger of coming down with a severe case of cabin fever, or even worse, the dreaded 'rural malaise'. From then on, one day a week, John made sure I had the car at my disposal—to take a trip into town, visit my mother in Bermagui or simply get out of the house and go for a drive.

As if we didn't have enough to contend with, we were also living with the threat of getting burnt to a crisp in a bushfire. Much to the horror of the old guard, the hippy majority of the Brogo volunteer fire brigade elected John captain, assigning him the fire truck that went with the position. Fire brigade meetings were usually a bit of a lark. After gathering at the Brogo Community Hall to discuss strategy, new settlers and traditional farmers alike would set off in convoy to do a spot of fire hazard reduction in the forest. Out there in the bush, they'd back burn, chop down trees and create fire breaks. At midday, the hippy bloc would park themselves on one side of the campfire, smoking joints, drinking tea and joking around as if they were part of some bohemian *Biggles Boys Own Adventure*; sitting opposite, the farmer faction would eat their luncheon meat sandwiches and lamingtons in stony, disapproving silence.

One scorching hot and gusty day, John got a call from neighbour Brett when he'd heard that a fire was burning out of control some 20 kilometres away. Assuming he'd be asked to go fight it, John implemented the necessary precautions: plugging our downpipe with a tennis ball, filling the gutters with water, nailing sheets of corrugated iron to window frames and raking the ground clear of sticks and leaves; a pile of musty, wet hessian sacks at the ready. He'd just finished topping up every available bucket, bowl and receptacle when he got the call.

'It should be alright,' John assured me as he and Brett climbed into the fire truck. 'They reckon it's not headed this way.'

Standing on the veranda, jiggling my baby on my hip, I watched as the vehicle disappeared over the ridge before turning to take in my surroundings. Encircled by a forest of tall, wildly oscillating eucalypts, it occurred to me that Eva and I were sitting ducks. Despite the intense heat, an icy dread rose in my veins. Had I known about the fatal fire that had swept through the Brogo district thirty years earlier, I'm sure my dread would have turned to terror. Prior to that catastrophic event, fires had been burning in the rugged and isolated Brogo wilderness for weeks. On 25th January, 1952, a north-westerly gale swept the fires out of the bush and onto grassland. *'The whole countryside exploded in a horrible pattern of racing, terrifying fire'* the Bega District News reported. Five people died in the inferno, including fourteen-year-old twin sisters who were incinerated as they tried to outrun the blaze on horseback.

As they drove up the track, John and Brett began to have misgivings about leaving their wives and children alone and defenceless in the bush. What would happen if there was a change of wind and the fire started heading in their direction was the gist of the conversation in the Land Rover. By the time the two men reached the front gate, they'd worked themselves into a frenzy.

'Fuck this, mate,' John said as he turned the vehicle around and headed for home. At the next fire brigade meeting John was deposed as Fire Captain and his fire truck unceremoniously confiscated.

Although we were spared that day, John became obsessed with fire and its potential to kill and destroy. With his newly purchased state-of-the-art flamethrower, he'd set off on a fiery mission the minute the burning-off season commenced; everyone in the district aware that their apprehensive neighbour was up and about as the smoke rose in great, grey plumes above our property. As my fearful husband cleared more and more bush, I felt as if I was living in a manicured English park. But still John didn't feel safe.

One day, he decided to set alight a steep and previously unburnt tract on the far side of our land—mostly undergrowth and wattles; next morning he insisted I come to see the result. Standing side-by-side on the ridgetop, I was confronted with a shocking and eerie sight—devoid of birdsong or any other sign of life, a sparse forest of slender, charred posts jutted from an ocean of ghostly white ash; the all-too-familiar odour of burnt bushland stinging the inside of my nostrils. I could see why John was so paranoid about bushfires and why he'd so often shot down my objections to, what I'd considered to be, his unnecessary burning off operations. For those living in the bush, fire was not only a benign and useful servant but also a terrifying and destructive tyrant.

✕✕✕

Eva was eighteen months old with full command of the English language when, keen to resume working with John on the land, I convinced my mother to come and live with us. She was fifty-five. Evicting Honey the goat, we converted her living quarters into a dwelling fit for a *homo sapien*.

'Good one, mate,' all the Brogo blokes said to John. 'You've put the old goat in the Goat Shed!' But I was the envy of all the mothers on Warrigal Range Road.

Our extended family experiment was a great success; nearly everyone was happy with the new arrangements. Eva could visit her grandma and look for fairies in her garden. My mother could spend time with her granddaughter and watch her grow up. Not only did I have my beloved mum to talk to, I got a break from parenting whenever I needed it. Least pleased was John. My mother's arrival meant he had to cut extra firewood and pump more water from the dam. Outnumbered by women three to one, I think he felt besieged. Very soon though, he realised that the advantages of having my mother around far outweighed the disadvantages when I was able to help him on the property more often.

In addition, John figured he'd earned the right to use Mum's newly installed gas hot water system—the canvas pull-up shower in our mud hut left dangling, dried out and abandoned. At the end of the day, he'd head for my mother's timber-clad, single-roomed cottage. While Mum cooked her dinner, John, always in the mood for a chat, would talk as he showered. Bemoaning the evils of the market-driven economy or railing against the Right faction's dominance of the ALP, he'd poke his head out from behind the shower curtain and wag a soap-sudded finger to emphasise a point. Stood an arm's length away at her kitchen bench, Mum would be forced to listen to her son-in-law's rants and ramblings, handing him a fried fish finger if she wanted to shut him up.

✗✗✗

After years of being fussed over and doted upon, our fruit trees had grown into lumbering giants, dripping with tonnes of ripe fruit and demanding my constant attention. Watering, fertilising, pruning, weeding and keeping pests and disease at bay kept me on my toes, but at harvest time I was run off my feet. Mum became another pair of hands. Together, we'd spend the day in the wattle and daub hut bottling apricots, peaches and plums.

'Look at that!' Isn't that the most beautiful thing you've ever seen?' I exclaimed at the end of one summer as we stood back to admire the bottles of fruit on the kitchen shelves—on one shelf, orange apricots in brandy, purple plums in claret and yellow peaches in sugar syrup; below, red peppers in olive oil, green asparagus spears in brine and white pears seeped in honey. It was an art installation, a glittering shrine to the Goddess of Fertility and I was reluctant to remove even one of the carefully arranged components and ruin the display.

My mother took over the care of our chooks. Under her doting guardianship, the plump, sleek-feathered Rhode Island Reds began pumping out 'bum nuts' like there was no tomorrow; wire baskets filled with the bloody things proliferating in the pantry, the fridge and on the kitchen bench.

'Why don't you make something to sell at the market?' John suggested, as if I didn't have enough to do.

However, I did spend a pleasant afternoon flicking through my collection of cookbooks and decided on almond biscotti, a delicious crisp bread requiring large quantities of egg whites. My mother used the leftover egg yolks and lemons from our lemon tree to make her renowned lemon butter.

'We'll make a killing,' she said with a glint in her eye.

The following Sunday, Mum and I rose before dawn, packed the car with our freshly made produce and set off for the Candelo market, arriving just as the customers rolled in. It wasn't long before we had a queue in front of our display. But it soon became clear which product the punters preferred. While my mother's jars of lemon butter flew off the table, my Italian delicacies sat languishing and ignored in a pile.

✕✕✕

The garden became Mum's refuge. With her inquisitive grandchild in tow, she'd potter around for hours—weeding gazanias, fertilising pot plants, pruning jasmine and watering her pink scented geraniums.

'Granna, I saw one! Hurry up!' Eva would cry, her fluffy head of blonde ringlets framed in sunlight as she looked for fairies in the lavender bushes.

'Hang on, Evie. I'm coming,' my mother would respond. And hand-in-hand the odd couple would wander off—in search of pixies and elves.

One day, I dropped by the goat shed for a chat. Bent over her patch of gazanias, Mum was pulling out the wily strands of kikuyu that were threatening to strangle her precious flower bed. I noticed two pronounced welts on her left wrist. They looked like puncture marks to me.

'What's that on your wrist?' I asked her.

'Oh, that,' she replied, brushing me off. 'It's a snake bite. But it's okay. I think it was only a baby.'

'This is ridiculous,' Mum protested as I broke the speed limit on the way to the hospital. 'I could've had that patch weeded by now.'

Determined to keep the grass down and snakes at a distance, Mum became obsessed with mowing. In the zone, heedless of the fact that she'd be pushing up daisies if she didn't stop soon, she'd get behind the mower and go at it as if the Russians were coming.

One day, I came home to find her steering the Victa in ever-widening circles around her humble abode.

'Mum, *stop*!' I implored when I saw her face—her cheeks as red as one of her poinsettias. But my tunnel-vision-impaired mother just ignored me. Putting her troubled past behind her, she merely adjusted her throttle and pushed on to longer and greener pastures.

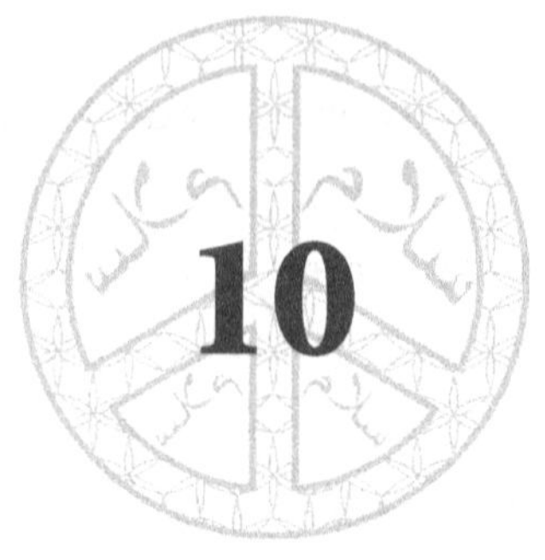

10

Reefer Madness

Eva may have been three years old and long out of nappies but I was still up to my armpits in shit. Our toilet was a tin dunny can in a small, bark-clad building at the back of the wattle and daub hut and when it was full, someone had to empty it. This entailed digging a hole in the recalcitrant drought-hardened ground and, to avoid shriek-inducing splashes on bare feet and legs, pouring the contents of the heavy, unwieldy pail of disgusting slush into the freshly dug hole. It was the most dreaded chore of all. For obvious reasons, there was often a standoff as, with grim resolve, John and I waited each other out to see who'd cave first and undertake the odious deed. Sometimes, sexual favours were promised in exchange for a dunny-can emptying reprieve. Ultimately, one of us would crack when the pile of excrement rose in a sloppy brown pyramid above the toilet seat and taking a dump was out of the question.

My daughter's aversion for our outhouse was understandable. Born under the Sign of the Goat and true to her astrological traits, Eva was growing up to be a pedantic and pernickety child and would not entertain the thought of entering the dingy booth until I'd carried out a comprehensive sweep for spiders with a straw broom. If it was raining, we'd don gumboots and raincoats and with a torch, umbrella and broom in hand, trudge outside into the dark, dripping wet night. Poking her head inside the cubicle, Eva would inspect my handiwork, refusing to cross the threshold if I'd missed so much as one gossamer thread of web.

'*No, mummy!*' she'd say as I'd encourage her to take a pew.

'*Look!*' she'd demand, pointing her stubby index finger insistently at the farthermost reaches of the gloomy stall.

'There's still some up there.'

Shivering under the umbrella, I'd shine the torch on my constipated child as she squatted on her haunches on the damp timber seat—the tribal posture her ingenious adaptation to her natural environment.

For some women in the hippy community, though, the lack of a flush toilet was the least of their worries as their dreams of creating a utopian life in the bush was shattered by family violence. Domestic violence became a topic of conversation at mother's group. A woman abused by her partner in the Bega Valley had nowhere to turn—her family or any support she may have had, left far behind in the city. Appalled with the lack of services for women—merely a handful of doctors and a local family planning clinic—we decided to take action. With babies at our breasts and children on our laps, the Southern Women's Group, as we'd called ourselves, met in each other's homes over cups of tea and biscuits to discuss strategy. Having grown into a large collection of women from a diverse range of backgrounds, we petitioned the government to fund a Women's Refuge. Signed by new settlers and locals alike, our petitions were successful and we were given a red-brick, two-storey, Federation-period building, a former bank in the centre of Bega, at a peppercorn rent.

On taking possession, laughter from our excited kids bouncing off the walls, we clambered up the wooden staircase to hang a banner from the balcony. 'SOUTHERN WOMEN'S GROUP', the banner proclaimed, each letter emblazoned on a pegged towelling nappy flapping victoriously in the wind.

Buoyed by our success, we secured funding for a women's housing scheme so that women who'd taken shelter in the refuge didn't have to return to their violent spouses. Instead, they could be housed for a nominal rent; supported for up to twelve months in one of nine, fully-furnished and equipped houses bankrolled by the state government. Initially, I was employed as a 'Stock Acquisition Consultant', sourcing and purchasing housing stock for the scheme. With a million dollars of the Department of Housing's money to spend, as word got around, I was courted by every avaricious real estate agent in town.

Once established, Southern Women's Housing needed employees to support their tenants. Those were the days of affirmative action, especially around women's issues and, with no experience whatsoever, I landed a job as a support worker. Riding the wave of feminism and endeavouring to raise the social value of what was traditionally considered to be unpaid women's work, from local councils to federal bureaucracies, the new policy was to place women, preferably with no or limited academic qualifications, into support roles; the idea being that we wouldn't alienate our clients with theoretical jargon but rather draw on our own life's experiences and relate to them with compassion and understanding.

I didn't know what I was doing, but it soon became apparent that neither did anyone else in the workplace. At first, I simply listened to my clients, sensing I should acknowledge and validate their feelings. Strangely enough, my hastily cobbled-together approach was effective. If I got out of my depth, which was often, I'd refer our tenants to a relevant community service. Along with the dairy industry, with its new settler population booming, the Bega Valley Shire had come to enjoy a thriving welfare sector.

Three days a week I'd set off for work leaving Eva at home with John. She was happy to hang out with her daddy and fit in with whatever task he was doing that day. At 4 o'clock, I'd come home to find her sound asleep on her sheepskin rug in the workshop, sprinkled with sawdust, her dainty ears protected with a pair of industrial earmuffs from the whining of the circular saw or the blaring of Bruce Springsteen on the cassette player.

'Come on Evie,' I'd say, gently nudging her awake and brushing the wood particles from her hair. 'It's time for your bath, and there's eggs and toast soldiers for dinner.' Taking her grubby little hand, I'd lead her to the wattle-and-daub hut up the hill.

The Department of Housing, realising they needed to address the lack of counselling skills among their newly appointed employees began to provide us with training. On all-expenses-paid junkets we'd fly up the coast to Sydney to attend workshops on *The Cycles of Abuse, Effective Parenting* and *How to Recognise Co-dependent Behaviour*, squeezing in shopping excursions to Myer or DJs to buy shoes, bed linen or a decent bra.

But more than anything else, we could have done with some training in drug counselling. Cannabis was wreaking havoc in the new settler community; the counter-culture ideal of love and peace all but destroyed by the side effects of chronic marijuana abuse.

'How much dope does he smoke?' was the first question I'd ask my hippy clients as they described their partner's textbook dope-smoking behaviour—the mood swings, paranoia, lack of motivation and sometimes, psychosis.

'How do you know he smokes dope?' the twitchy and hollow-eyed women would ask.

Little did they know that I had only to look in my own backyard to see the devastating impact marijuana addiction had on families and relationships. Living with his long-suffering wife and three children in a double-decker bus at the end of Warrigal Range Road, the shaggy-haired, be-whiskered Tom walked around in a permanent cloud of dope smoke. When he began to think of himself as the Messiah (admittedly there was a resemblance to the implausibly fair-skinned, blue-eyed JC we've all come to know) rumours began to circulate that he was breaking into his neighbour's chicken pens and sacrificing their chooks.

John was in the workshop one afternoon sharpening the chainsaw when Tom dropped by to share a joint; Eva on the other side of the room keeping herself occupied with her eclectic assortment of toys.

'Gotta get back to work, mate,' John said, sucking the guts out of the last of the reefer before stubbing it out, hoping that Tom would take the hint and leave. But Tom was off with the fairies. Noticing John's rabbit-skinning knife on the workbench, he picked it up and began to twirl it almost lovingly, in the palm of his hand, running his thumb down the recently sharpened stainless-steel blade and glancing sideways at Eva.

'What would you do if I killed your daughter with this?' Tom inquired in the voice of an angel.

Like a Japanese ninja, in one swift leap, John grabbed the knife from Tom's hand, propelled our lord and saviour out of the shed and sent him on his way.

A few weeks later Tom really lost the plot, bailing up a neighbour on her property and threatening to rape and kill her. Taking refuge in the rafters of her unroofed house, the terrified woman clung to a beam in horror as Tom delivered his sermon of fire and brimstone below. Fortunately, once he'd preached himself hoarse, the drug-crazed and mentally disturbed man took off, only to be picked up by the police and bundled into a divvy van later that afternoon.

Although John and Brett's bricklaying work was sporadic and I was employed at Southern Women's Housing for only three days a week, we were determined not to end up, like Creedence Clear Water Revival's, 'working for the man every night and day'. When we stumbled on an idea for a home-based business, we hoped it would keep our dream of an autonomous life alive.

The concept originated when John felled an enormous yellow box, a tree so big that three men with arms outstretched could have encircled its girth. According to my cautious husband, it was growing too close to the workshop and had to go. As the fallen goliath lay dead on the ground, I noticed the thin outer rim of wood and the rotting black pulp filling its gaping belly. John was right. The ancient specimen had been on its last legs, set to blow over in the next storm, I reassured myself, feeling guilty about its demise. There wasn't much timber to salvage so John amputated a tree knot (the scar tissue that forms when a branch breaks off) to keep as a memento.

'I'll make a mirror out of this,' he declared as he removed the bark from the knobbly ring of wood before placing it like a yoke round his neck.

Next time it rained, with nothing else to do, John sanded the cut surface flat, inserted a piece of mirror into a chiselled rebate and covered it with ply. Afterwards, I smeared the frame with a paste of beeswax and eucalyptus oil, rubbing it with a soft cloth until it developed a waxy satin glow. Hung in pride of place, the hand-crafted mirror was greatly admired by all who entered our rustic abode.

Before long, John and I had set up a production line making 'Mumbulla Mirrors'; an outlet in The Rocks on Sydney Harbour that sold furniture made from Australian timber, agreeing to take them on consignment. In the beginning, we scoured our property looking for knots. When there were no more to be found, we went further afield. John would load the ute with the chainsaw, a ladder, some iron wedges and an axe; I'd feed and dress Eva, pack lunch and fill the thermos with tea. And off we'd go, in search of our woody prey; our daughter delighted to be strapped into her car seat between her mummy and daddy.

It was a treat to be off the property, to drive around the country-side down the long gravel roads and winding dirt tracks; the colours of the landscape shifting in subtle increments from morning to afternoon like a living, breathing Arthur Streeton painting.

While John drove, I'd keep an eye out for the distinctive rings of wood.

'*There! Stop!* I see one,' I'd exclaim excitedly like a kid on a treasure hunt. John would pull over and unload his equipment while I set Eva up on a rug on the ground; surrounding her with stuffed animals, wood blocks, Lego, a drink bottle and some slices of banana and segments of peeled apple and orange. As John climbed the ladder, I'd grip the side rails, trying to keep it from wobbling on the uneven terrain whilst dodging an asphyxiating shower of sawdust as he made his cut with the chainsaw.

'*Timber!*' my husband would cry as the heavy hunk of wood fell to the ground, me ducking out of the way just in the nick of time. Having sealed the wounded tree with fungicide, we'd be back on the road, on the hunt for another elusive knot.

The mirrors sold well, but within twelve months similar items began to saturate the market, so with John and Brett's bricklay-ing business gaining momentum, we decided it was time to shut up shop.

While Tom the Messiah had done little else but grow dope, smoke dope, spread the word and bump off chooks, John and I weren't afraid of hard work, in fact we had a reputation in Brogo for being overachieving workaholics: John's inclination no doubt instilled by his hard-working father, mine borne out of a fear of ending up like my aimlessly drifting and dispossessed parents. Occasionally, however, we'd treat ourselves to some time off and head for the local tip. Old Gus lived in a dilapidated wooden caravan onsite and would turn a blind eye as John and I spent a few hours clambering over piles of hard rubbish looking for building materials or anything else we could put to good use. One day, doing her own foraging on the fringes, Eva unearthed a prize—a bedraggled, tabby kitten with a marmalade patch round its eye. The obstinate child refused to let the mewling critter go, so after a mighty struggle, in which we tried but failed to pry the kitten from her clutches, we took Tipsy (named in honour of her humble origins) home.

A clearance sale was a legitimate excuse to down tools; a big day out for the whole community. When a geriatric dairy farmer kicked the bucket, the family, having picked the eyes out of his stuff, would have an auction to rid themselves of the remaining household belongings, machinery and farm equipment. A lifetime collection of cherished possessions spread out over the House Paddock for all the world to see would be disposed of in an afternoon—everyone chafing at the bit to pick up a bargain or have a leisurely poke around in someone else's personal effects.

Although it went against the grain, we did take some time off at Easter. In a clearing owned by the members of the local commune *Mumbullazoo*, the Brogo hippies would gather for a highly anticipated annual event—The Brogo Olympics. Preparations for the festivities occupied the entire community for the week leading up to the big day. A pyramid of straw sat waiting to be seeded with mini chocolate Easter eggs; trestle tables were set up and a tarpaulin lean-to erected in case it rained on the day. A goat was slaughtered for the occasion and everyone ramped up their production of homebrew. Trifles, pavlovas, zucchini fritters along with beetroot dip and hummus lined refrigerator shelves; toffee apples sat upturned and dripping on bench tops and window sills. Someone wrapped handmade trinkets in butcher's paper to fill the lucky dip and one of the fathers pegged out a marathon course.

Arriving around 10 o'clock, we'd converge on the clearing and release our impatient offspring from our vehicles; the squealing youngsters darting off in all directions, startling timid wallabies and scattering cranky currawongs in their path. In the nippy autumn air, the sun not yet high enough to breach the tree line, a damp-earth-fragrant mist still lingering in dark pockets in the bush, the women arranged their plates of food on the trestle tables while the men lit a campfire and set up the rotisserie.

The day began with a series of races—sack, three-legged, foot, obstacle and the obligatory egg-and-spoon; depending on the outcome of the race the sound of laughter, cheers and sometimes dismay reverberating throughout the valley. At midday, we'd break for lunch, plundering the laden trestle table and digging into barbecued sausages, lentil patties, salads and homemade bread, washed down with beer for the grown-ups and fruit juice for the children and followed by an adults-only dessert—a hash-laced double choc-chip cookie.

By now, the kids would be desperate, begging to be let loose on the mound of straw and pillage its hidden treasure; parents watching on with amusement as their little ones dived head first into the heap; spindly legs sticking out like brightly coloured pins in an over-sized grassy pompom. The afternoon schedule included gumboot and horseshoe-throwing competitions, an apple bobbing contest, a tug-of-war and a wood chopping event; whilst a disorderly cluster of men and adolescents set off on the cross-country run.

By eight o'clock the younger children would be tucked into bed on the back seat of their parent's cars and the Brogo Olympics closing ceremony would commence. Encircled by the deathly silence of the bush, scrappy beige clouds racing across the luminous crescent above, our ruddy-cheeked faces lit by flickering firelight, we'd sit around the campfire amidst the fragrant drifts of wood smoke, recapping the day's events as we ate our charred goat meat off the bone, drank our yeasty homebrew and smoked the unlimited supply of dope. The raw night enveloped us in its pitch-black shroud until there was nobody but our small, like-minded community on the planet—a clan, like all clans since the beginning of time, feasting, drinking and getting high under the waxing moon and arc of glittering stars.

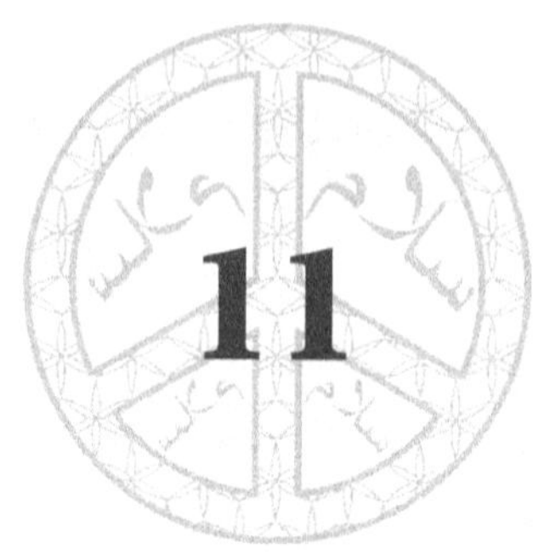

11

Aragunnu

Rudolf Steiner, a nineteenth-century Austrian philosopher, artist and social commentator developed a holistic education philosophy that emphasised the role of the imagination and encouraged artistic expression in the formative years of a child's life; formal reading and writing skills being taught much later than in a conventional school. Like many others in the new settler community, Brett and Julie McNeil were opposed to traditional approaches to child rearing and schooling. They became the driving force behind the establishment of a Steiner School in the district. On top of his regular chores and bricklaying gigs with John, Brett volunteered his skills and labour to construct the school buildings.

When it was time to send Eva to school, John and I had an important decision to make. Should we send her to the Steiner school or to the public school in Bega? If Brett and Julie's parenting of their demanding progeny, now four and counting, represented the Steiner method we weren't convinced that it was the education approach we wanted for our daughter. According to the Meister, you should never say 'no' to a child lest you thwart its sensitive nature. Instead, you should distract the little darling, gently encouraging him or her to stop what it's doing. Sometimes, it would take a good hour to coax a badly-behaved McNeil into compliance; it was a gruelling process.

'*Mummy*! Tegan stole my doll!' one of them would wail as its sibling ran off with a handmade humanoid-shaped toy, deliberately left faceless in order to stimulate the imagination.

'Tegan, wouldn't it be fun to share with Noah?' Julie would reason with the toy thief. 'How about we all play a game?'

'*No*!' Tegan would yowl, clutching the scruffy doll to her chest.

'It's *mine*. I want it.'

'Oh, look at that!' Julie would say, pointing to an eagle soaring high above the tepee.

If that didn't diffuse the situation, the eternally patient mother would suggest they all take a walk to the creek or have a glass of goat's milk and a home-made tahini ball.

When the boys came to our house to play with Eva, they must have been in shock.

'*Right!*' John would declare, lining the motley crew up on the veranda.

'There will be *no* running in the house. There will be *no* slamming of doors. You *do not*, under *any* circumstances touch my tools. *Is that understood*?'

'Yes, John,' the quivering group would reply.

One day, I overheard the eldest McNeil boy chastising his younger brother for slamming the back door.

'*Don't do that!*' he hissed. 'We'll get into trouble with John.'

Despite running a household which must have felt like a military camp to these children, most weekends, two or three of the McNeil tribe would traipse up the hill to play with Eva and I'd find them standing at the front door waiting to be let in, noses streaming with green candles of snot, hair matted in clumps and fingernails rimmed in dirt. On entering the house and not before I'd wiped their noses and washed their grubby hands and faces, the boys would make a beeline for the television, pestering Eva to turn it on.

'Mum, they won't come outside and play,' my daughter would complain bitterly when the boys sat glued to the set. And I'm sure they'd be sitting there today, eyes wide and jaws dropped in wonderment, if I hadn't switched it off and shooed them outdoors.

I could only imagine how tired Brett and Julie were, neither of them ever getting a full night's sleep or even having a bit of a lie-in. Every night one or two of their brood shared the parental bed or woke up for attention and comfort. Trudging around their dimly lit abode, a baby in their arms or a toddler slung over their shoulder, the exhausted couple would take turns singing lullabies, patting backs and shushing their fretful offspring.

In the end, after much debate, John and I agreed that forewarned is forearmed. Eva's education should equip her for a future in a ruthless and competitive world: we enrolled her in the public school in Bega.

Along with the McNeil's and the rest of the local hippy population, we'd spend at least part of the Christmas school holidays camping at Aragunnu, in those days a relatively unknown beach just south of Bermagui; everyone staking a claim to a campsite on the tea-tree-covered cliff top overlooking the South Pacific Ocean. It took us a day or two to stop thinking about what we could and should be doing at home but like everyone else, John and I soon settled into a leisurely routine of swimming, sleeping, reading, eating and going for walks on the beach.

Clad in black, body-hugging wetsuits and looking for all the world like a pod of sleek, shaggy headed seals, the men would go diving for abalone, tenderising the meat with a mallet and marinating it in a bowl of lemon juice and crushed garlic on their return. In the darkening amethyst light, the whiff of wood smoke, grilled mollusc and Reef Oil permeating the air, we'd stand around the campfire, sun-kissed and salty-skinned, in board shorts, bikinis or sarongs gorging ourselves on the sweet, rubbery delicacy as the swishing paperbarks creaked like a forest of rusty gates in the breeze. Down on the beach, we dug a large pit in the sand and covered it with a framework of driftwood and sheets of blue plastic. Between baby-sitting shifts, we'd douse fire-heated rocks with water and sit around the sandy crater sharing stories and telling jokes until the steam became too much to bear. Then, bursting into the night, we'd race laughing and squealing to the seashore to dive naked into the cold, inky sea, catching our breath in a frisson of fear as we plunged into the possibly shark-infested depths.

For me, New Year's Eve was a 'dry' event because the next day, as soon as the dappled sunlight filtered through the trees and onto our tent, my exuberant daughter would be bounding out of her sleeping bag demanding her birthday presents; I couldn't risk a hangover. One year, John and I were invited to a party at the campsite across the way. Around a blazing bonfire, dreadlocked Rasta devotees played bongo drums; hippies silhouetted by the flames stomped to the throbbing beat. Someone suggested I try some hash butter, so thinking the effects would be minimal, I popped a water cracker smeared with a nanoparticle of the bitter paste into my mouth. Two hours later, begging John to take me to hospital, I thought I was going to die. My experienced husband stayed with me all night, talking me through the griping pain and panic attacks. Wary of taking me to the emergency ward where he may have had to field questions about my condition, he thought it prudent to sit tight, unless I suddenly took a turn for the worse.

'You'll be right,' he repeated at regular intervals. 'It'll all be over soon.'

Crawling around the bush in a feverish sweat, my body eliminating the poison from every orifice, trying to moan as quietly as possible so as not to wake Eva asleep in the tent, I hoped to God that it wouldn't literally be all over soon and I'd be alive in the morning to ice and decorate my birthday girl's cake.

XXX

After approximately six years of concerted effort, we'd come to the conclusion that our dream of achieving a totally self-sufficient lifestyle was just that—a dream. There were just some goods and services that even we hippies couldn't do without. As landowners, we were obliged to pay rates. Bartering for petrol with a bunch of asparagus or a litre of milk was out of the question, and I refused to go without a decent haircut, a telephone or a doctor's appointment, if it was necessary. On her birthday and at Christmas, Eva, who didn't share her parent's distaste for conspicuous consumption, went, year to year, from being satisfied with plasticine and a colouring book to pining for a Cabbage Patch doll to demanding a pony with all the trappings. We realised we'd never escape the system and that money, and quite a bit of it, was an unavoidable necessity.

In addition, like the hacienda Gabriel Garcia Marquez described in *One Hundred Years of Solitude,* our wattle-and-daub hut was returning to the earth. I was fighting a constant battle to hold back the forces of nature. Tendrils of kikuyu grass would find their way inside to coil around a saucepan at the back of a kitchen cupboard. Spiders made webs in the nooks and crannies of the mud facades. Bracken fronds doggedly pushed their way up through the manure-and-sawdust crammed crevices in the floor. Lizards weren't shy about using the room as a thoroughfare to get from A to B; mould proliferated as the rising damp climbed the walls, and cute little antechinus were taking up residence in the hessian lining that served as our ceiling. Looking for something under the bed one morning, I spotted a solitary, pure white toadstool glowing in the dark in the corner. On top of its reclamation by the local fauna and flora, prolonged and driving rain waterlogged our walls—great hunks of mud slaking off and dropping to the ground in big squishy plops. It was only a matter of time before the whole structure disintegrated and disappeared without a trace. I wanted a proper house and I wanted it now!

Unfortunately, John had an allergy to banks. The idea of being drawn into a lifetime of crippling debt by the evil arm of capitalism, otherwise known as the financial system, was anathema for him. But the owner builder is in a dilemma. If you work, you don't have time to build. If you don't work, you don't have the money to purchase building materials or pay for tradesmen etcetera. With price rises always one step ahead, saving for materials was a daunting and frustrating task. Desperate for a real house, my dream house, I knew a housing loan was the only way I was going to get one. It was a battle and there were arguments and tears—mine as usual—but eventually I convinced my ideologically driven husband to take out a mortgage.

xxx

The Bega Valley had been in the throes of a severe drought when John and I arrived in 1979. Dusty tornadoes zigged and zagged from one paddock to the next, dams baked dry sat cracking under the merciless sun; a zillion desiccated rabbit droppings scattered on the barren ground like the star-strewn Milky Way. Desperate to stop their livestock from dying, farmers loaded their starving cattle onto trucks bound for Victoria where drovers would herd the emaciated creatures along the grassy stock routes in the hope of keeping them alive for another couple of weeks.

Sometimes, I could swear I smelt rain but in the end it was just wishful thinking or my powerful imagination at play. Dark clouds, full of potential, came and went, teasing the whole district with their empty promises. One day, out of sheer desperation, I decided to perform a rain dance; under the cloudless blue sky, stomping barefoot in a circle where grass once grew, I recited my chant.

'*Rainnnn. Rainnnn. Rainnnn,*' I beseeched Gaia, the Aboriginal ancestral beings, the Native American spirits, the Nordic gods or anyone else who might be listening.

Next day, a menacing bank of gun-metal black thunderclouds, much like those in El Greco's painting *Toledo*, gathered encouragingly on the horizon. Standing on the veranda, I watched as the storm approached. It was going to rain for sure. I was about to make a dash for it and grab the washing off the line when, directly above the mud hut, an ear-splitting crack sent me ducking for cover, my arms instinctively wrapping themselves around my head. Realising I wasn't hurt and certain that the tempest had passed, I got up to survey the damage. Just metres from the veranda, a bolt of lightning had struck a large gum tree, unzipping its bark and exposing, for all the world to see, its naked blond wood down its length. In a tree fork low down, small tongues of fire had sprung to life, licking at the frayed and fibrous tear. Any second now, a falling ember would ignite the tinder-dry forest floor and all hell would break loose. I ran to the water tank to fill a bucket with water and rushed to throw it on the flames. John, cutting fence posts in the Big Paddock, heard my calls of distress and arrived minutes later gasping for breath, by which time the fire was out. And did it rain, you ask? No, it bloody didn't.

However, it did start raining the minute we began building the house.

I was reminded of a much-loved early-twentieth-century Australian poem about the trials and tribulations of life on the land. 'We'll all be rooned', said pessimist farmer Hanrahan to his mates at the end of every stanza as they endured a never-ending cycle of droughts, floods and bush fires. The rain didn't let up, saturating the wattle-and-daub shed until we feared it would collapse. Cabbage and broccoli plants rotted where they stood in the ground, fruit turned to mush on the trees; our road repeatedly washed away by flood waters; JR and Sue-Ellen's dung-caked hindquarters flyblown in the humid conditions.

Our dream had been to build a mud-brick house, but when the rain didn't stop, John ordered clay-fired bricks from the local brickworks, laying them between downpours. It compromised our principles but by this stage we were past caring, already thinking about re-sale values. A conventional double-brick house would be a far easier proposition to sell than one made of mud, we reassured ourselves. I don't know precisely how or when it happened. Maybe we were worn down by the unrelenting toil and lack of creature comforts but slowly and surely, as we crept towards our forties, our idealism dissipating like an early morning mist after sunrise, we began to crave a more comfortable and convenient existence.

12

Salt Water

By her seventh summer, Eva had lost interest in the McNeil kids, becoming, like so many girls her age, besotted with horses instead. Granting her most fervent wish, John and I bought her a pony. A child-safe pony is worth its weight in gold and Winnie the Pooh was one such quadruped. He had no desire to rear up, buck or gallop; even a trot or a canter was too much effort. Winnie preferred to spend his days grazing in the sunshine, staring contentedly into the middle distance or, if it was absolutely necessary, flicking away an irritating fly with his tail. Anything else was just a nuisance, quite frankly. Standing at the kitchen sink window, I'd smile to myself as Eva, skinny legs flapping ineffectually on his big barrel of a belly, tried to kick him into action. Following what must have seemed an eternity to an eager and aspiring young rider, the horse would twitch an ear and with a sigh of resignation, half-heartedly take a step forward.

'Oh alright,' you could see him thinking. 'If I must.' And reluctantly the stocky, flea-bitten grey, my daughter on his broad back, would plod slowly up the driveway and disappear over the top of the ridge.

Eva's new best friend, the equally horse-mad Rebecca, lived on the *Mumbullazoo* commune with her hippy parents, the Kembles. On weekends and school holidays, Rebecca and her lanky chestnut Topaz would ride over to see Eva or vice versa; the girls mucking around with their horses from morning to night. If they weren't riding their ponies, they'd be brushing their coats, plaiting their manes, worming them, picking stones out of their hooves, dressing them in various horsey ensembles, oiling their bridles, collecting their manure from the paddock or feeding them equine snacks. On rainy days, confined to indoors, the girls, undeterred, would pretend to be horses. Resembling Monty Python's Knights of Ni, they'd trot around the living-room whinnying, neighing, shrieking with laughter and driving me crazy.

'Put your helmets on properly,' I'd instruct them before they set off for a ride. 'Are your girths done up tightly? Are the stirrups the right length?' I'd ask.

'Yes Mum,' Eva would groan impatiently. 'Can we *go* now?'

Little did I know that as soon as they were out of eyeshot, the girls would discard their saddles and helmets, stowing them by the side of the track before continuing bareback through the bush to the creek in the gully. There, Winnie and Topaz would be forced to stand whilst the girls took turns clambering up on the back of one horse before diving into the shallow water under the belly of the other; the long-suffering geldings remaining motionless, patiently waiting for the game to end. Next, the two friends would mix up a paste of wet silt and plaster their horses and themselves with muddy handprints, entwining kookaburra feathers and sun-bleached wallaby bones into their own blonde locks and the roughly braided tresses of their mounts. In the stippled afternoon light, you might have caught a glimpse of the naked warrior princesses flash past on their primitively decorated horses, the sound of their laughter trailing through the eucalypts.

Eventually, things got serious as they tend to do with girls and their horses, and Eva and Rebecca began lobbying their parents to take them to Pony Club. The Kembles owned a horse float, an old and rickety piece of junk that could be heard way in the distance as, attached to Martin Kemble's four-wheel drive, it clattered down our track early on a Sunday morning. After loading Winnie into the dilapidated death trap beside Topaz, John and I would follow Martin and the whole menagerie into Bega.

For the uninitiated, uninterested and un-aristocratic, Pony Club isn't exactly the ideal way to spend your precious day off work. Rolling up at the club grounds behind the ramshackle trailer, I couldn't help but notice the stares of disdain as we parked amongst the expensive, state-of-the-art, immaculately maintained horse floats. Oblivious to economic disparity, Eva and Rebecca would unload their ponies, saddle them up and trot off to join the group of well-groomed and impeccably kitted out Pony Club kids on the far side of the oval. Ensconced in the car, John and I would drink cups of tea and watch proceedings—the barrel races, obstacle courses and dressage lessons. But it wasn't long before I was reading a book and John had his head buried in *The Guardian*, surfacing occasionally to comment on the bovine-like appearance of the local female population as they lumbered past the car.

'Jesus, will you look at that heifer,' he'd rudely remark.

Taking a wander outside, my bored and fidgety husband would try to engage another dad in conversation or buy a sausage and tomato sauce sandwich at the sausage sizzle stall.

'Howz it goin' mate?' I could hear him jovially inquire. 'Nice day for it. Reckon it's going to rain? We could use some.'

Invariably, at least once in the course of the day, one of the girls would arrive back at the car in tears of pain, frustration or rage. Either she'd fallen off her mount or her riding gear had failed or her stupid horse was behaving badly and not doing what it was told; the same scenario was played out all around us as parents tried to soothe or scold their injured, sobbing or demanding offspring.

'Mum, I need another horse!' Eva would whine. 'Winnie can't jump over the jumps. He's too short and fat.'

I had to admit that Winnie was not exactly Pony Club material. He was adorable and he was doing the best he could but he didn't quite cut the mustard when it came to athletic performance.

'Mum, can I get another horse? *Please*!' Eva would beg. And to get some peace, I'd tell her I'd think about it, a response mothers must surely have repeated for millennia across the planet.

Finally, buckling under the relentless pressure from a determined daughter, I gave in. My eight-year-old already had her heart set on a replacement—a stunningly beautiful, wild and totally mad, dappled grey Arab filly called Meringue.

I found Winnie a good home where he'd be loved and cared for the rest of his life; his new family composed of five horse-crazy daughters aged from two to ten. But my heart contracted on the cold and drizzly day we dropped him off. As we drove away, I could see Winnie in the rear-view mirror being mobbed by the over-excited little girls; the sweet-natured horse, who just wanted a quiet life, would be in servitude for a long time to come.

'He'll be alright, Mum,' Eva said tearfully, reassuring herself as much as me.

In contrast to Winnie, Meringue was every mother's nightmare: one of those psychotic horses that sees phantoms at every turn. If you rustled a plastic bag anywhere near her or if she happened to tread on a stick, her ears would flatten, her nostrils would flare and she'd be rearing up on her hind legs like a charger in the *Lawrence of Arabia* movie. Then, tail arched and eyes rolling in their sockets, the maniac would take off, galloping off to God-only-knows where. The only option was to hang on until she calmed down and got it out of her system. My daughter was in heaven. The indefatigable Meringue would virtually fly. With our feisty fox terrier Billy running alongside, she and Eva would rendezvous with Rebecca and Topaz in the pale morning light, only to return famished and saddle-sore with the sinking sun at dusk.

One Easter, with Eva and Rebecca away on a Pony Club camp, I took a rare break from life on the land and set off on an adventure: a Shanka Prakshalana retreat. Shanka Prakshalana, a five-thousand-year-old Ayurvedic practice originating in India, involves consuming nothing but copious amounts of warm salt water over the course of three days. Purging the digestive system and drawing impurities from the internal organs the practice is supposed to open the practitioner to a deeper psychological/spiritual cleansing. Or so it is said. For months, I'd attended yoga classes at the Brogo Hall, a big tin shed used by the local community for aerobics, play group, fire brigade meetings, Christmas pageants and barn dances. Our yoga teacher, Bhav, an orange-robed Western swami with a shaved head and leather sandals had waxed lyrical about the merits of the ancient tradition.

'You'll feel renewed and invigorated,' the charismatic yogi promised.

Of course, back then, there was no internet to do the research. Had we been able to get online, we'd have probably thought twice about what we were about to do. Fifteen men and women enrolled in the retreat which was held in bushland on the coast in Bournda National Park. We all knew each other pretty well, having lived in the district for years, but at that stage, none of us knew how much more familiar with each other we'd become.

Arriving at base camp late on a Friday afternoon, we stowed our sleeping bags and rucksacks in the primitive open-ended A-framed huts, our living quarters for the duration of the practice, and made our way through the drooping, pine-needle scented sheoaks to the communal meeting ground where Bhav was setting things up. Instructing us to observe silence until the end of the retreat, Bhav asked us join him in the log pavilion for a session of meditation and a lesson on the methodology of Salt Water Cleansing. Afterwards, washed in mottled moonlight, above us a blinking and insubordinate tawny frogmouth disobeying our leader's order to remain silent, we stumbled mutely on the sandy track through the bush to bed—unpacking our few belongings by torch light before wriggling into our sleeping bags and settling down under the starry sky.

The following day, we rose at dawn. With mixed feelings of dread and excitement we gathered around the big vat of brine Bhav had prepared on the campfire while we were asleep. We knew exactly what was expected of us. Over the next three days, we were to drink nothing but the saline solution until our bowels eliminated pure water, uncontaminated by any hint of faeces. Standing silently in a circle, we held out our plastic cups; Bhav proceeding to fill them with a big metal ladle repeatedly dipped into the warm brew.

Together we raised our vessels to our lips. I took a small sip and was immediately racked by an overwhelming urge to gag. Some of the more macho men gulped their water in a single swig, promptly running into the bush to vomit. Eventually, I managed to quaff my first cupful but like everyone else, rushed to throw it up at the base of a nearby tree.

Our cups were filled again. Again, we drank, only to have the water erupt in violent projectiles from our mouths. Before long, everyone gave up looking for a private place to puke. Just like the under-age patrons outside the Tathra Pub on a Saturday night, we were spewing up at frequent intervals at each other's feet. That night, there were a few tears followed by some mutinies and our number decreased by a third. On the second day, the remaining 'true believers' managed to hold the water down. But there was worse to come. Once the solid matter had been expunged from our stomachs, loose stools began exploding like a geyser from below; every few minutes someone racing off to noisily evacuate the disgusting swill. By now we were in another world—physically, emotionally and possibly, as promised, even spiritually. The eruptions were coming fast and furiously. In the end, we lost all inhibition and squatted to relieve ourselves right out in the open; no one giving a shit who saw or heard the usually privately performed body function.

On the third day, keen to see if we'd achieved The Holy Grail, that chalice of crystal clear water, Bhav ordered us to bring him a sample of our emissions for inspection; weak and exhausted we formed a wonky line by the campfire. With trembling hands, we presented our offerings. One after the other, Bhav scrutinised our cups, each brimming with varying strengths of yellowish-brown liquid; a look of utter disdain on our guru's face when he realised that none in the congregation had attained the goal.

'You're the worst students I've ever had,' he said, goading us to drink more of the loathsome beverage.

But we'd had enough. In a simultaneous and unanimous act of defiance, we threw down our cups and walked off the job. Breaking our vows of silence, cursing and grumbling, we dragged our sorry arses off to bed. Trudging up the track with the others, I turned to look back at Bhav. I could just make him out between the gap in the trees, striding in a fury around his undrunk cauldron of salt water, pausing every so often to kick at the ground or stomp on a plastic cup.

On the final morning of the practice, sitting pale and listless at the timber picnic tables, we waited for our sullen swami to serve the *kitcheri*—a soupy porridge made from rice and mung beans, lightly flavoured with ginger and other spices. Traditionally eaten post fast, the meal allegedly creates a protective film on the intestinal tract and restores balance to the system. After three days of starvation, we stuffed our faces with the freshly made gruel. Never before had such bland food tasted so good. By now our group had bonded for life. Like war veterans, we'd endured so much and survived. We packed up our gear, gave one another a hearty hug and said our farewells. For years to come, bumping into each other at a party, down the street or at a committee meeting, like brothers and sisters-in-arms, we'd reminisce about that punishing ordeal.

Back home I produced my first bowel movement since completing the practice—a bizarrely odourless, snowy white turd, bobbing like a marshmallow in the toilet bowl. I waited for the sense of well-being and euphoria our teacher had promised, but instead, I began to feel terrible and by the end of the week I was almost bedridden. I made an appointment with the naturopath in town and told her about the Shanka Prakshalana retreat. She was horrified. I'd stripped my body of potassium and electrolytes, I'd altered my critical pH levels, I'd wiped out all my beneficial bowel bacteria and I'd tortured my kidneys. I was an idiot, the naturopath said. Shaking her head in disbelief, she sold me some bottles of expensive supplements before sending me on my way. Fortunately, within a few days, I was back to normal with nothing more than a salty taste in my mouth and a healthy scepticism for balmy swamis.

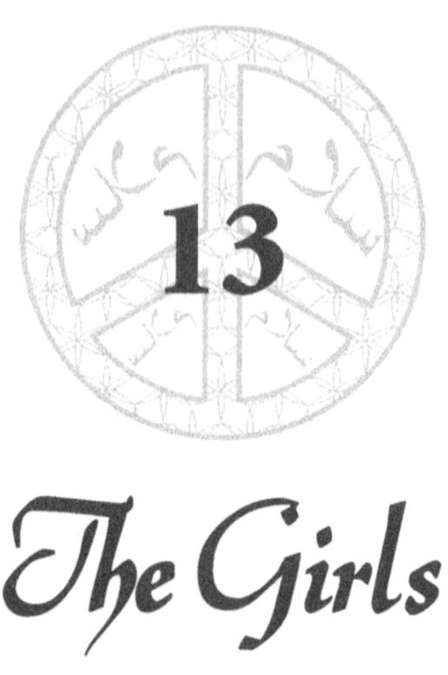

13

The Girls

There were times I'd daydream about the life I could have had: an easier life in a cushy job with regular hours, a steady income, annual leave, sickies, superannuation, nice possessions and a house with all the mod cons. If I hadn't dropped out of art school maybe I'd be an established and renowned Australian artist, winning grants and scholarships, undertaking artist's residencies and travelling the world to exotic locations, I'd think. By now, with a PhD in Political Science, John could have been a university lecturer, or even a politician with perks and the possibility of a parliamentary pension.

Like the vast majority of new settlers in the Bega Valley, John and I had sought an 'authentic' life: self-directed, creative, flexible and most of all, free. Endeavouring to dodge a lifetime of meaningless and repetitive work, we'd dreamt of creating a new world order outside the conventional monetary system. But to my knowledge no one in the Brogo hippy community ever entirely escaped the belly of the capitalist beast, and by the nineties, many of us were wage and salary earners, 'working for the man' in the very same jobs we'd struggled so hard to avoid. For some the dream had become a nightmare and, overwhelmed and defeated by physical and financial hardship, they abandoned their quest, fleeing back to a more comfortable existence in the city. As we edged towards the new millennium, the landscape of Warrigal Range Road changed dramatically; subdivision after subdivision brought a different type of property owner into the area. Small hobby farms began multiplying up and down the road; cars driven by people I didn't recognise hurtled by, going way too fast.

But for John and me, life on the land still had its precious moments. Like when we'd step back to admire a perfect stretch of fence that had taken months to construct, or when I'd finished weaving a magnificent Navajo design rug with my hand spun, hand dyed wool, or to see, at the end of an exhaustive and productive summer, the shelves in the pantry lined with a dazzling array of bottled pickles and preserves.

'Yum, Mum. This is the best batch ever!' Eva would declare whenever we stood at the kitchen bench laughing and stuffing our faces with freshly baked bread smothered in butter and lashing of homemade jam.

The crowning glory, though, was the day we moved into our newly built house. Side-by-side John, Eva, my mother and I stood admiring the magnificent structure. The three-bedroom, one-bathroom, brown-brick building rose from the ground like the sacred and rock-solid Pantheon—my favourite building on earth since I saw, at the age of fourteen, a tiny black and white photograph of it in one of my high school text books. At last, I had the house of my dreams. Our home. My home. Home.

'It kinda looks like the castle in *Sleeping Beauty*,' Eva said. Then we laughed and I cried and we hugged and slapped each other on the back; John threw Eva over his shoulder and tickled her till she got cross.

Initially, our eight-year-old wasn't all that impressed, the crumbling mud shack being the only home she knew; we had to coax her with promises of pyjama parties and room for more books and toys into the modern and unfamiliar mansion. It wasn't long, however, before Eva realised the advantages of having a bedroom she didn't have to share with a chainsaw or a stinky sack of wool; a place where she could spread her stuff on the carpet and invite friends for sleepovers.

In the beginning, I'd flounce from room to room just because I could. In an unprecedented display of vegetative behaviour John would take a whole day off to lie on the couch and watch cricket. At night, snuggled in bed under the doona, we'd listen to the sound of rain on the roof, for the first time since arriving in the valley feeling safe and secure in our fortress. There was mains electricity and months passed before the novelty of flicking a light switch wore off. We could have dinner parties for more than two people. We had running hot water, a laundry with a front-loading washing machine, a bathroom with a beautiful claw-foot bath, a white tiled shower and a fancy flush toilet. I couldn't wipe the smile off my face.

Seventeen years had flown by since my student days at the Royal Melbourne Institute of Technology. In all that time, occupied with building and making things, landscaping, cultivating fruit and vege-tables, preserving food, raising animals and taking care of Eva, I'd had little desire to paint or draw. Now, with the house built, the gardens established and Eva growing up, I had an urge to set up a studio and paint.

It had been a long time since I'd held a fine sable brush in my hand, though, or come face-to-face with an intimidating blank canvas. So I decided to start small. Inspired by my surroundings, I focused on microcosms of the natural world—forest floors, fungi, riverbeds, lichen, native flora and the sea shore. Like a child, I was seeing the landscape as if for the very first time and, awakened to its splendour, I was consumed by my creativity reborn. When my paintings were picked up by a local gallery, I was delighted. When they began to sell, I was ecstatic. At last, I was an artist. The future was full of the promise of good things to come.

Motivated by my new-found direction and a desire to use his brain and perhaps do something meaningful, John went back to university, undertaking a Bachelor in Work Studies at the University of South Australia by long distance education. In 1995, he put his hand up as the Labor Party candidate for the blue-ribbon state Liberal seat of Bega. Embraced by the Hard Left of the Socialist Left, John was tagged by some in his own party as 'that tree hugging communist from the bush'; in his typical larrikin response, he began to refer to everyone, whatever their politics, as 'comrade'. In an effort to tone down the vote-losing pinko perception, I bought him a hand-stitched Hugo Boss suit at the op shop (a bargain at eight dollars) ensuring he'd look presentable on the campaign trail and whenever the party bigwigs were in the electorate.

In a bizarre offshoot, posters of my husband's head began to pop up on gum trees, electricity poles and fence posts all over the district.

'Check it out, Mum! There's Dad again,' twelve-year-old Eva would proudly exclaim whenever we drove into Bega.

Sitting at home, I'd listen with bated breath as John extolled the virtues of the Labor Party on the local ABC radio station. At first he was stilted and obviously nervous, so I was a nail-biting wreck, but within three or four interviews he found his voice; like Eva, I was proud of my husband and his stance against the red-necks and silver-spoon conservatives.

'Good on ya, mate. Stick it to 'em,' the hippies in the shire would say, whilst the die-hard Liberals and National Party yokels were appalled by this articulate, brazen, weed-smoking 'red' living under their beds.

The electorate was huge—a three-hour drive from one end to the other. With John gone doorknocking for most of the day, I'd be left at home fielding questions from irate constituents.

'What's the Labor candidate doing about the new tip site at Jellat?' an elderly punter would ask. 'When are we going to get the Bega bypass?' another would demand. Like I would know. But worst of all, was the dreaded fundraiser. Having avoided lipstick and panty-hose my whole life, I was peeved I had to wear them. My mouth ached from smiling and my feet hurt from tottering around in high heels; but for the sake of my husband's new career, I played the dutiful wife and endured the tedious event.

After a gruelling campaign lasting six months, John and his party were conclusively trounced by the safely entrenched Liberal candidate; the only booth to win (50 votes to Labor, two to the Libs) was at Wallaga Lake—John and his politics appealing to the mostly Koori community.

John went back to bricklaying and me to making and selling art but on a long weekend in October 1997 our daily lives were turned upside down when two schoolgirls Bega High—fourteen-year-old Lauren and sixteen-year-old Nicole—were abducted and murdered. Although she was not in their class at school, Eva knew the girls, having been horse-riding with them on a couple of occasions.

That fateful weekend, Nicole's father set up a campsite for the girls and a group of their friends in bushland not far from their home near Tathra. From time to time during the course of the weekend, Lauren and Nicole would go back to the house to shower, change clothes and grab something to eat; and once or twice a day, Nicole's dad dropped by the campsite to make sure everything was okay. One night, unbeknown to their parents, the girls decided to check out a party nearby. They set off on foot down the road but hadn't got far before a car pulled up beside them. Leslie Camilleri and Lindsay Beckett, a pair of previously convicted criminals from Yass had spent the day cruising around the coast, drinking beer and injecting themselves with amphetamines. When they offered the girls a lift, Lauren and Nicole—country kids prone to trusting others—got into the car. For the next twelve hours, the men held the girls captive, driving from place to place where they repeatedly raped and assaulted their victims in and out of the vehicle. Just across the Victorian border, Lauren and Nicole were dragged from the car, marched gagged and bound through the remote and rugged terrain to be brutally murdered.

When the schoolgirls were reported missing a massive manhunt was launched; police and volunteers combing the area but failing to find any trace of them. Then came the tip-offs—members of the public from all over Australia claimed to have seen the girls in a shopping mall in Adelaide or a cinema complex on the Gold Coast. Every night we'd watch the news on TV, hoping and praying that the friends had simply run away; and that they'd be found alive and well.

Six tense weeks passed before the bodies were discovered, and it was months before police investigations led to the arrest of the men. Finally, everyone knew, in graphic detail, exactly what happened the night Lauren and Nicole were abducted. The entire community, new settlers and locals alike, was in shock; our illusion that the Bega Valley was a safe place to live was shattered. A heavy pall of grief fell over the district, some needing to talk incessantly about what happened, others unable to mention it at all.

With talk all over the school ground, I couldn't prevent Eva from learning the facts. At thirteen, she was just becoming interested in boys; I was afraid her opinions of the opposite sex and sex in general would be irrevocably tarnished before she'd even had a chance to form any.

Over the next few weeks, Eva became picky about what she ate, cutting back on carbs, dairy and anything with fat or sugar. She began to lose weight but if I hassled her to eat she'd become angry. I tried to reason with her but she wouldn't listen. I backed off but that didn't work. I encouraged her to talk but she didn't want to. I suggested she see a counsellor. She refused to go. When she stopped menstruating, I took her to the doctor.

'This isn't an isolated problem. Other girls have lost their periods since the murders,' the doctor told us. Then, drawing her chair beside her under-nourished patient she began to describe the damage Eva was doing to her young and developing body.

Worried sick, the questions whirled in my mind: was my daughter, albeit unconsciously, delaying her physical development so she wouldn't be seen as a sexual object and therefore a potential rape victim? Confronted with unspeakable evil, her world spiralling out of control, was she trying to reclaim a sense of control by over-regulating what went into her mouth? I'd seen documentaries about anorexic teenage girls and the complex psychological issues involved and I knew how difficult it was to treat the illness. That night, John and I talked and talked. Fearful for our precious and only child, we decided to contact an eating-disorder clinic as soon as possible.

Next day, as I drove Eva home from school, I glanced across at my little girl's emaciated frame slouched in the car seat beside me; her face pinched and bloodless, the delicate skin under her eyes pearlescent and purple like the inside of a freshwater mussel. How brittle and fragile she looked. My heart ached—not just for my daughter but for Lauren and Nicole, for their families, for the terrible physical and emotional abuse perpetrated on women and girls in a world that seemed overly populated with predatory and violent men.

Back home, I parked the car and sensing that Eva had something she wanted to say, I sat in silence, waiting.

'I'm so tired,' she said presently, a fat tear rolling down her hollowed cheek. 'I don't want to be hungry anymore.' Reaching across I took her baby-bird hand in mine, inwardly dropping to my knees and kissing the ground in thanks.

The following morning, I came into the kitchen to find Eva sitting at the table ploughing through a big bowl of muesli, yoghurt and sliced banana.

'Morning, Mum,' she chirped, smiling from ear to ear through a mouthful of wheat germ and oats. And although I couldn't be a hundred percent sure she was entirely back on track and I knew I'd have to keep an eye on her, I had a feeling my sensible and resolute daughter had decided she wanted to live.

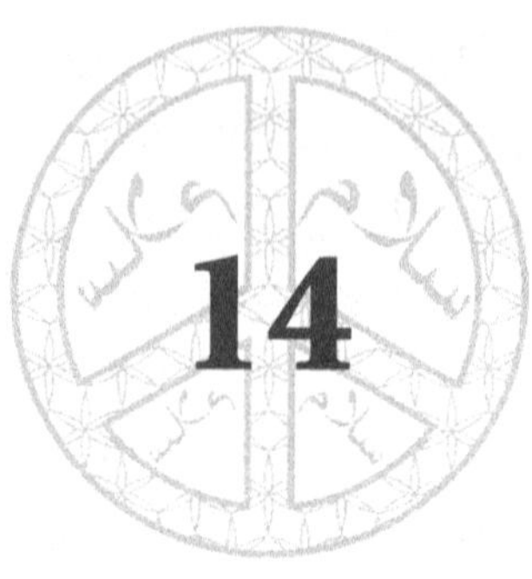

14

On Fire

My life-long association with fire began with my father. It was he who snatched me up into his arms when, as a toddler, I stumbled on our slate hearth and almost toppled into the flames. And it was he who had my grandfather set me alight with a blowtorch when I was three. Attempting to make his name as a young freelance photographer in England, Dad was contracted to photograph the non-inflammable qualities of a popular brand of children's nightgowns.

Dressed in one of the long-sleeved, full-length, buttoned-to-the-neck nighties, I was placed next to my kneeling grandfather and told to keep still as he directed the flame of the blowtorch at the hem of the rabbit-and-daisy patterned garment.

'*Smile!*' Dad must have said just before clicking the shutter; but one look at the photograph and you can see the terror in my eyes.

XXX

On a stinking hot day in Melbourne, fresh off the boat from England, I was recruited for another photo shoot. Insisting I wear

126

a scratchy, unlined red woollen dressing grown (thrown together on the Singer by my mother in an afternoon) my father stationed me in front our 'crazy paving' fireplace.

'Pretend you're an angel,' he said encouragingly.

As I stood squirming below the mantelpiece trimmed with tinsel, felt stockings and yuletide baubles, sweat streaming down my tubby little trunk and my ponytail wilting in the heat, I struck a decidedly un-angelic pose. Setting the scene, Dad sloshed a capful of petrol on the roaring log fire, sending the temperature in the room skyrocketing whilst Mum hurried across to dab my beaded brow with a hanky.

'Not much longer love. There's a good girl,' she said trying, without success, to placate me.

Dad positioned his tripod, covered his head and shoulders with a square of black cloth and adjusted the lens on his box brownie camera. At long last, he was ready to take his Christmas card photographs.

When we started school, Lisa and I had the fear of God put into us when it came to bushfires. In 1965, East Gippsland was ablaze. For seventeen days and nights, an out-of-control fire ravaged the region. Our teacher had given us instructions on what to do if the fire came: fill a pillow case with important items and stow it under the bed. When the flames were upon us, we should hold the pillow in front of our bodies and jump through the window pane to safety, Miss Balfour said. It sounded like a brilliant plan to me. That day, when I got home from school, I filled my pillow case with my teddy and other stuffed-toy essentials, ready for any contingency.

Dad had gone off to help fight the fires but on his first day had arrived home from the fire front in disgrace. Knowing nothing about the occupational health and safety aspects of firefighting, he'd unwittingly sat on a tin of kerosene used by the volunteers for back burning. The Kero container leaked and the fuel soaked my father's trousers, burning the skin on his pale, Pommy bum. He couldn't sit down for a week. Tucked into bed at night, I'd listen to the muted conversations between my mother and the other women in the street as they stood with their garden hoses saturating their weatherboard homes. Trying hard not to fall asleep, the tang of burning bushland in my nose, I'd imagine jumping like a jumbuck through the window while I waited for the fire to come.

✗✗✗

It was fire that reduced my marriage to ashes just weeks before 9/11. I didn't know it then but the beginning of the end was on the news that night—three national park rangers burnt to death in a routine burn-off operation in the foothills north of Adelaide; another in hospital in a critical condition. An image of the injured ranger flashed on the screen. It was our neighbour, Michael.

Michael and his partner Jessica owned a block of land down our road and were about to leave Adelaide to come and live permanently in the Bega Valley. John and I had become good friends with the pair, inviting them for dinner whenever they came to check on their property. Ten years our junior, they made a stunning couple: Michael reminiscent of a sultry James Dean, Jessica a softly-spoken Eurasian beauty, a curtain of black satin hair hanging to her waist.

On that unspeakable day, Michael sustained fourth-degree burns to eighty percent of his body. Rarely does anyone survive that degree of physical trauma, the doctors explained and Michael's family prepared themselves for the worst. The burns had penetrated deep into muscles, bones and internal organs. Michael's ears had been burnt away and he'd lost his fingers extinguishing the flaming clothes of a colleague as they tried to escape the fire. The doctors kept their patient in an induced coma and, over multiple operations, took skin from his feet (spared by his heavy-duty work boots) to cultivate into sheets of membrane for grafting onto his fleshless frame. Constantly battling infections and still on the critical list, Michael was airlifted to the Burns Unit at The Royal North Shore Hospital in Sydney, a distraught and traumatised Jessica at his side.

By coincidence, John had a lucrative three month building contract in Lane Cove. Each afternoon after finishing work, he'd go back to his rented digs, take a shower, dress in clean clothes and steel himself for a visit to the Burns Ward. I was holding the fort back on the Far South Coast. Eva, just sixteen and already master of her own destiny, had left home, refusing to complete her Higher School Certificate at the under-resourced Bega High School. Off her own bat, my indomitable daughter had enrolled at Narrabundah College in Canberra, finding board and lodgings with a nice family nearby.

Over the next few weeks, John and Jessica sat on either side of the bed as Michael, fighting for his life, lay unconscious between them.

In time, I came to understand how the pair fell in love. But when, on a visit to Sydney to see John, I woke in the middle of the night to find him at the kitchen table texting Jessica on his mobile phone, I was mortified to discover the affair.

'Who are you texting?' I demanded before he had a chance to hide his treachery.

'No one,' he blurted out, a look of horror on his face.

'It's two in the morning. *Who* are you texting?' I demanded again, my heart beginning to pound in my chest, my stomach churning with hot poison. John looked away, refusing to answer.

'Jesus,' I said softly with the dawning realisation, 'you're having an affair. Who with?' I asked, feeling strangely numb inside.

Still, John didn't reply.

'Who *is* it?' I yelled, my fear and anger rising in a slow and deadly wave. Then it hit me.

'*Oh, my God!*' I gasped. 'It's Jessica?'

John put his head in his hands, his shoulders convulsing as, making barely a sound he began to weep.

'I'm sorry,' he stammered, looking at me at last, eyes brimming with tears, anguish and shame.

I left Sydney that night, returning to Brogo alone. In shock. Sickened. Appalled and disgusted. How could the man I knew and trusted, the man who'd been by my side since I was a girl, who'd shared a lifetime of struggle, achievement, hardship and joy have done this to me? Not only that, how could he do such a despicable thing to his suffering friend?

Within days of arriving home, I packed my car and drove down the Princes Highway as it follows the south-eastern coast to Melbourne, weeping and wailing through an indifferent and primeval landscape. Eight hours later, I arrived on my sister's doorstep with nothing but my clothes, paints, brushes and a box of photographs. It was the spring of 2002; I'd turned forty-five in June.

I'd left my husband, my friends, my house, my land, my worldly possessions and my little fox terrier, Billie. Worst of all, I'd abandoned my mum, who by then was living in a retirement village in Bega. Our break-up sent shock waves throughout the Brogo community, some criticising me for leaving 'poor John'. I wasn't able to explain or justify my dramatic departure fearing that Michael, having finally regained consciousness, would learn about the hideous betrayal—miraculously the fire hadn't killed him, but that devastating disclosure just might.

'Will you be okay?' Lisa asked anxiously as she helped me unpack my few bits and pieces, clearly disturbed by her big sister's ravaged appearance.

'*No!*' I cried shaking with fear and fury in equal measure. 'I'll never be okay again!' And, as I fell to my knees, Lisa knelt too, putting her arms around my heaving shoulders.

In the following days came the howling into a pillow, the retching over the toilet bowl, the hyperventilating and frantic pacing around the living room. I pounded at mattresses, tore at my hair, ripping up photographs as I drank red wine and smoked one cigarette after another. There were also the hysterical, acrimonious and often pathetic voicemail and text messages to my duplicitous husband who refused to take my calls or reply to my messages.

Bless Coco the cat, Lisa's Burmese moggy, who allowed me to kiss and cuddle her, saturating her sleek, seal-like coat with tears and snot, only scrambling to escape if I squeezed her too tight.

'What am I going to do? How am I going to *be*?' I would bawl under the shower when Lisa went to work. I was finding it hard to breathe.

I'd spent years surviving financial hardship, floods, fire and drought, struggling to achieve my dream—our dream—only to have everything I'd worked for, all I'd accomplished, the promise of a secure and comfortable future and growing old with my partner, snatched away overnight.

I had absolutely no idea how to be alone.

Unfortunately, my mentor Juliette de Bairacli Levy, never got around to writing *The Complete Herbal Handbook for The Jilted and Deceived*, so I had nowhere to turn. I rang my mother instead.

'Have you told Eva?' she asked. I'll call her, I promised. As soon as I got myself together.

When I rang her a week after arriving in Melbourne, my heart ached for my all-grown-up little girl. I pictured her face on the other end of the line when I revealed the truth about her father—the disgust, the disappointment, the anger—no doubt a mirror of mine when I became aware of my own father's shortcomings. I was incensed. Not only had I been cruelly betrayed but it had fallen to me to inflict this pain on my daughter; John too cowardly to do it himself.

Although Eva, with my encouragement, eventually forgave her dad, for a long time she was her predictably intractable and resolute self. 'I never want to speak to him again,' she said that day.

'He's your dad,' I was able to say twelve months down the track when I'd recovered from the shock and healed a little; John's relationship with Jessica having come to a bitter end. 'He stuffed up, but what if something happened to me? You'll need him.'

To John, when we were on speaking terms again, I was less conciliatory.

'She's your only child. Your blood.' I said. 'You're an adult. Act like one and fix this.'

Over the next few weeks, I lost a lot of weight—living on wine, coffee and cigarettes: unable to sleep, constantly ruminating over the treacherous liaison that had destroyed my life. I set about painting Lisa's flat—wall after wall of purifying white paint obliterating the grubby surface. I lay new lino in the bathroom, rendered the brick fireplace with a concrete slurry, replaced the benchtop in the kitchen with a slab of laminated pine and built bench seats on either side of the balcony. Lisa let me get on with it.

Why hadn't I seen it coming? How could I have been so stupid? The questions roiled around in my mind as furiously I rolled on the Dulux. But by the end of my manic makeover, I knew what to do. I would paint about fire. What better way than to harness fire itself to make the work.

I purchased a gas bottle, an assortment of blowtorch fittings, some wood-burning tools and sheets of plywood and set up a studio in the garage at the back of Lisa's flat. Day after day, I'd don my overalls, march downstairs and wreak havoc; one minute, scorching and branding a timber panel with flames, the next, chiselling it with deep and purposeful wounds. I swapped traditional art materials for the non-traditional media with which I'd become so familiar in the bush—experimenting with wood stains, bitumen, varnish and liming solution. It was only subsequently that I learned about my great-grandfather and his father before him—both artists—head wood-engravers at the London Illustrated News whose job it was to churn out illustrations for the celebrated newspaper before the advent of photography. Obviously, my predilection for gouging wood had been passed down through the generations.

After six intense and therapeutic months, I'd produced a dynamic and evocative body of work about fire and the Australian landscape and was invited to exhibit the paintings in Artefact Gallery in St Kilda. Entitled *On Fire*, the exhibition was a sell-out; my career as bone fide artist ignited. *I* was on fire!

As my professional life gained momentum, I began to look after myself—eat better, sleep more, go for walks by Port Phillip Bay. But in the city, my sense of connection to the land was fading. The St Kilda Botanical Gardens became my sanctuary; lying in the mottled light under a leafy oak or elm, I'd put my nose to the ground, inhale the loamy scent and remember.

My hippy days had come to an end. I didn't have so much as a pot plant to fertilise or a goldfish to feed. I stopped scanning the sky for clouds or wondering if it was good weather for drying fruit. I missed the smell of the bush, the magpies yodelling and kookaburras cackling at dawn; ripping an ear of corn from the stalk and nibbling it moments later, piping hot and dripping with melted butter. I missed bumping into people I knew down the street, the warm ache in my limbs after a strenuous day of weeding and digging. I longed for Billie the fox terrier falling over backwards to greet me when I got home. There'd be no more sun-ripened apricots plucked from the tree or sweet, eucalypt-tainted rain water drunk from the old tin mug at the tank. Never again would I need to be on the look out for kangaroos dashing in front of the car as I drove down Warrigal Range Road or have to pick up a bale of hay and a bag of chook pellets from the stockfeed depot in Bega. Instead, my world became populated with grim-faced strangers, the sound of sirens in the night, trams dinging and rattling throughout the day; flowery apples, tasteless tomatoes; garrulous neighbours living above and below. But then again, I could shop for trendy clothes, see the latest movie release and visit a gallery whenever I chose. I began to feel the possibility of loving again, of living my new life to the full. But some part of my hippy heart would always be in the veggie garden—standing at dusk with a hose in my hand, listening to the stringy barks rustle in the breeze and watching as the purple shadows deepened over Mumbulla Mountain.

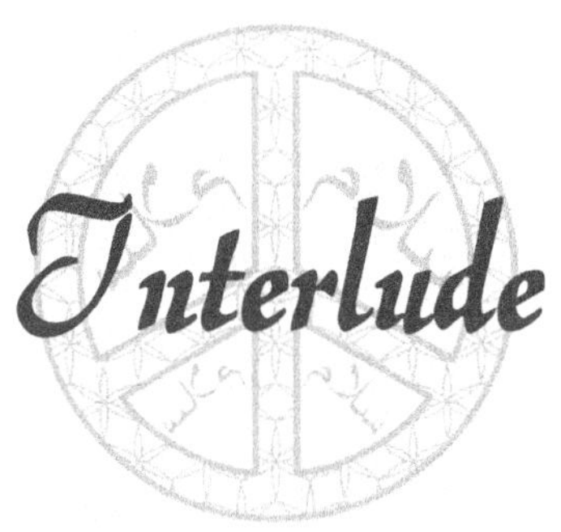

Interlude

'Why don't you get a job you hate like everyone else?' my hard-nosed daughter would say if I hadn't sold a painting in a while and my coffers were running dry. Despite her anti-materialistic upbringing, or maybe because of it, Eva had grown up to become a career-driven, goal-orientated, insured-to-the-hilt, Gen Y member of the upwardly mobile; she and her economist partner were Chardonnay socialists who rarely drank. Thinking back to her birth and the worried expression on her newborn face, I shouldn't have been surprised. Having spent her formative years with a pair of hard-core hippies from the sticks, there was no way on God's earth Eva was going to emulate her parents and drop out of university to live off the land. Instead, she chose to become an exercise physiologist, a champion mountain bike rider and health and fitness fanatic, at one stage awarded a scholarship to undertake a PhD at the Australian Institute of Sport.

But Eva's sensible advice notwithstanding, I was determined to be an artist, however rocky the path. 'Difficult pleasure' is how celebrated Australian painter, Brett Whiteley, described the creative process before dying of a heroin overdose in 1992. Making art can be exasperating, stimulating, challenging, joyful, confronting, exhilarating, soul destroying, nerve-wracking and utterly engrossing, all in the same day. Some mornings before breakfast, I'd pop into the studio with the intention of taking a quick look at the painting I'd been working on the previous day, only to find myself at four o'clock standing, paint brush in hand, unwashed, unfed and wearing only my undies—belly bare and breasts streaked with paint.

XXX

On the opening night of my *On Fire* exhibition, as I sipped champagne and mingled with the collectors, red dots proliferating like measles on the walls, I was introduced to the clever, charismatic, cocaine-sniffing, Croatian architect Vicko. Wow, who's this, I thought, after five minutes of witty and animated banter, the charming man's twinkling and mischievous blue eyes trained on mine, making me feel as if I was the only woman in the room. Owning two penthouse apartments in a building around the corner, one his architectural practice, the other his residence, the well-heeled Vicko, wearing a three-day growth, a chunky stainless steel earing and an Armani suit teamed with lime-green Converse sneakers—had just purchased the most expensive painting in the show; the ultimate turn-on for any artist and the beginning of our fiery and ill-fated relationship.

We'd been together only a few months when Vicko, after thirty years as a professional architect, decided to take a sabbatical to develop his own long-envisaged building project. Letting go of his staff, he vacated his apartments and installed tenants. Signing a lease on a 400-square-metre basement carpark in Mirka Lane in St Kilda—former stomping ground of one of Australia's best-loved artists, the eccentric and bohemian, seventy-five-year old, Mirka Mora—we moved in. As they walked through the garage doors, past Vicko's pair of vintage E-type Jags into the vast open-plan cavern, friends and acquaintances concurred that *Debasement*, the name we'd given our new home, was the funkiest studio-cum-living space in Melbourne.

While I painted, my *bon vivant* kept me plied with Mount Mary pinot; and, using every utensil and receptacle in the cupboard, make the most god-awful mess I've ever seen in a kitchen as he tended his osso bucco between mixing techno/trance vinyl on his state-of-the-art turntables. Our parties were debauched, drug-fuelled and legendary, as were our arguments. It was a far cry from my life in the bush but, for the next two years I made up for lost time, revelling in my bacchanalian existence.

In the spring of 2005, Vicko and I locked up *Debasement* and went to live in Italy, taking out a six-month lease on a rustic, fifteenth-century farmhouse in Umbria, thirty minutes' drive from the region's capital, Perugia. I set up my studio in a large stone-walled workshop attached to the house and, experimenting with European timbers such as elm, oak, ash, cherry wood and walnut, began creating a body of work inspired by the Italian landscape. Amid concentrated bouts of cooking, Vicko would join me: quaffing vino rosso and playing records, he'd sit at his makeshift architect's desk drawing up plans or fabricating balsa-wood models of the house he dreamt of building. Every two or three weeks, we'd make forays to an Italian city or another province, returning after a few days away to rest and work.

As the time to return to Australia approached, however, Vicko became increasingly tense and agitated. Our Italian adventure had cost a lot of money. He was starting to wonder, not only about the wisdom of closing his business but also about how, when he'd been out of the industry for so long, he was going to make an income and maintain his decadent lifestyle.

My lover had never married or had kids and his experience of living under the same roof with someone was limited. Before I came along, his girlfriends were inclined to be much younger and in awe of the great man. He'd become accustomed to being listened to and agreed with, not challenged. As Vicko's anxiety intensified, so did his drinking, our arguments escalating in frequency and ferocity.

On the pretext of buying cigarettes one night, I took the car and drove to the local village ten minutes down the road. Vicko had been drinking since lunchtime and we'd been arguing for hours. I needed some time out. When I returned, however, the front door was locked and for some reason my key wouldn't open it. I knocked insistently and waited. Vicko didn't come. I knocked again, steam pouring from my mouth as I called his name into the freezing night air. No answer. I went to stand beneath the upstairs bedroom window, begging Vicko to let me in. After a long and bitterly frigid minute, I realised to my horror that he wasn't going to open the door. I rushed to the car, quickly jumped inside and switched on the heater. But at minus five degrees, the heater was as good as useless and in tears of panic, I abandoned the vehicle.

By now my teeth were chattering, my fingers and toes, ice. I ran to the studio to see if there was something I could use to keep warm; nothing—only a handful of turpentine soaked rags strewn on the flagstone floor. I returned to the front door—kicking and pounding it, howling and wailing, pleading with Vicko to open up. It was then I spotted a small wooden hatch to my left which I'd never noticed before. Juddering with cold, I tried my keys in the lock and to my relief, the fourth key swivelled in the keyhole. I opened the flap, squeezed through the tiny aperture into the kitchen and made my way to the living room.

Entering the room, I stopped in my tracks. Stacked against the front door was our entire collection of furniture—the solid wood dining table, the writing cabinet, the chest of drawers, the couch and four dining chairs. In my absence Vicko had barricaded me out of the house. A dark venom rose in my veins. I found Vicko upstairs in the bedroom, spreadeagled on his stomach on the bed, snoring like a trooper and reeking of alcohol. Flinging back the doona without a thought as to the consequences, I began, in a frenzy, to pummel his back with my fists.

'*You bastard!*' I screamed. 'I could have died out there!'

Instantly awake, Vicko sprang from the bed, threw me onto my back and straddled my torso, pinning me down on the mattress.

I can't remember how many times his fist slammed into my face, my brain jarring in my skull with each powerful blow; the pain raw and searing. I could feel my eye turning to mush in its socket, smell the sickly stench of sour wine on his breath, see the madness in his eyes. I struggled to get free but to no avail. Half his size, I was no match for the enraged and hulking big man. There was nothing I could do but wait for the torment to stop. When Vicko finally exhausted himself, capsizing sideways and unconscious onto the bed, I fled, clambering down the spiral staircase to the living room.

I don't know how long I squatted on the cold, terracotta tile floor, crying, trembling, rocking and hugging my knees. Eventually, I dragged myself to my feet, dismantled the fortifications in front of the door and stoked the wood heater. Still dressed in my puffer jacket, jeans and fleece-lined boots from the drive to the village, I covered myself with a rug and some bath towels before curling up on the couch to shiver and weep until dawn.

In the harsh and pitiless light of day I staggered to the bathroom to be confronted by a grotesque and unrecognisable face in the mirror. I looked like a car accident victim or an extra in a zombie movie: my eye gummed shut, engorged with blood and ringed in dark purple;

my cheek and jawline blue-black and swollen like the time I had my wisdom teeth removed.

'Look at you. Look at what he did to you,' I whimpered to my mutilated reflection, torn between wanting to rip Vicko limb from limb and wanting my mum.

It was late in the morning when Vicko made his shame-faced appearance. He could barely bring himself to look at me. When he did, for a split second, before he had a chance to rearrange his face, I saw the mortified expression in his eyes. He was drunk, he said. He didn't know what he was doing. It would never happen again, he vowed. But I'd heard it all before from the domestic violence survivors I'd counselled during my time at Southern Women's Housing; their partners having made the same lame excuses and hollow promises. When Vicko went into town to pick up some supplies, I photographed my battered face with my mobile phone. That night, the phone, which I'd kept with me at all times, even sleeping with it under my pillow in case Eva was in trouble and needed to contact me or something happened to my mother and Lisa called, went missing. Considering I hadn't left the house, it was strange that I was unable to find it.

Why didn't I go the police? That's what I would have done back home. But in a foreign country with no family or friends to come to my rescue, emotionally traumatised and physically debilitated, I couldn't face the prospect. Unwilling to involve the Italian authorities, I stayed put. With the language barrier, who knows how they'd have dealt with the situation.

For the next few days, Vicko took care of me—cooked my favourite meals, kept the wood heater going, plumped my pillows, bought me treats and did all the housework, washing and shopping. I slept a lot or, if I wasn't asleep, I'd lie on the couch staring at the wall, trying to reconcile how someone who claimed to love me one day could beat me half to death the next. At the end of the week, in an effort to jolly me up and restore my feelings for him, Vicko suggested we take a trip to Rome; a city I'd been desperate to see for as long as I could remember.

'We shouldn't dwell on what happened,' he said. 'We need to move on.'

Rome was a blur. Fragile and still shaken, my condition exacerbated by a niggling urinary tract infection, I traipsed in a stupor from a cathedral, to a museum, to a gallery, to an ancient monument; silently crying myself to sleep in bed each night. I just wanted to go home.

Back in Australia, I tried to put the events of that horrific night behind me. But with my trust in Vicko lying dead and buried in the black Umbrian soil, it was a lost cause and I ended the relationship. A few years later, I came across a photograph taken in the City of Lovers. Standing before the Trevi Fountain, I'm smiling weakly into the lens of Vicko's camera; sunlight dancing on the cascading water and bouncing off the magnificent marble statues—a romantic holiday snap. But as I looked at the picture, I saw something else, something no one but me could have possibly seen—a shattered heart and a fading bruise hidden behind a pair of dark glasses.

✕✕✕

The next three years were all about my art. I was single when I flew to France to undertake a two-month studio residency in a medieval village in the Dordogne; a long-held dream come true. After a lengthy stint of city life, it was a joy to be in the countryside again; to glean materials from the surrounding environment and incorporate them into my work. I experimented with 300-year-old oak beams I found at a recycled timber yard, unrefined beeswax I bought from a local honey farm and beige-coloured clay which I dug from a river bed on the edge of the village. I discovered *bru de noi*—a stain distilled from walnuts that can be used like ink and *la chaux*—a powdered limestone which I added to paint to make *impasto* medium.

As a self-confessed Francophile, I'd been learning French on and off for years and when I wasn't at work in my gloomy but extremely atmospheric, slime encrusted, stone-walled studio—a dungeon in the twelfth-century I was told, I'd wander through the cobble-stone streets in the village; dropping into *la boulangerie, la charcuterie* or *la fromagerie,* not only to sample or purchase the produce but also to practise my French. One weekend, I came across a local flea market called *un vide grenier*, meaning 'empty attic'. Haggling with the wily stall-holders, I managed to get a good deal on a blowtorch, a cast-iron saucepan, an electric hotplate and some second-hand carpentry tools. I'd been inspired to make sculpture; to create a body of work I'd entitle *Beyond the Black Stump*—that iconic Aussie expression that spoke to how far I was from home.

I spent the following days sawing and chopping my oak beams into smaller, roughly-hewn blocks before charring them with the blowtorch; scraping back the residual charcoal with a chisel to fashion the shape I desired. Next, I cooked up a batch of encaustic medium—a concoction consisting of beeswax and dammar resin crystals melted together in a saucepan on the hotplate. In thrall of the eerie gothic setting, I applied the warm, golden syrup to the blackened cubes of oak, breathing in the heavenly perfume of burnt wood and molten wax; the base notes so redolent of the Australian bush and a medieval church.

By the end of the residency I'd produced a considerable body of work—sculpture, paintings, ceramics and photography. I invited the locals to an exhibition in my studio and was delighted to witness the pleasure they took in seeing their village interpreted through an outsider's eyes.

It was that same year that I first set foot in America. I was fifty-two. I'd been awarded a scholarship—a studio residency at the Art Students' League of New York's residential campus situated on the outskirts of Sparkhill, Rockland County, a small and tidy town on the Hudson River, forty-five minutes' drive from Manhattan. It was February so the imposing 1820s, three-storey weatherboard mansion with its profusion of steep, slate-gabled rooves, dormers, bay windows and a tower, sat in fifteen acres of woodland (home to white-tailed deer, squirrels, wild turkey, raccoons, chipmunks and coyote) was encircled by a knee-deep layer of snow.

I settled into my quarters on the second storey—a large sun-lit room graced with original timber floorboards, a faux Persian rug and period furniture—basking, as did my frequent visitor Elvis the tabby cat, in the heat emanating from the magnificent nineteenth-century cast-iron radiator. Sitting at my desk, I'd gaze out over the dazzling, white carpeted forest, captivated by the novelty and beauty of the scene. At night, with the moonlight filtering through the sheer lace curtains, I'd lie buried under my duck-down quilt listening to the long, plaintive wail of a freight train in the distance. How long ago and far away John and my life in the bush seemed then. How grateful I was that, in spite of the pain and heartache, I was there in that time and place, tingling with a sense of adventure.

Allocated a studio on the ground floor, I spent much of my five-week residency exploring and photographing the area, or looking for natural materials and found objects with which to make art. The property adjoined a massive cemetery where revolutionary soldiers from the American Civil War were interred; and rugging up, I'd often go tramping in the snow through the skeletal elms and lichen-encrusted headstones. It was getting late, when one after-noon a cluster of ominous-looking clouds began to gather over the graveyard. In the fading light, I turned towards home. Passing through a small clearing in the trees, I came across a breathtaking sight—a scattering of flawless, dove-grey feathers, each individually nestled in a shallow concave in the crystalline snow. I scanned my surroundings for signs of life, but a pall of electrifying stillness hung in the air, the colour sucked out of the landscape. I was totally alone. There were no tracks or any hint of a skirmish so something dire and violent must have occurred, seconds before my arrival, in the sky above. Floating to the ground, the feathers, still warm from the heat of battle, had melted the snow to form the tiny, frozen tombs.

Inspired by my surroundings and a long-standing interest in Buddhist philosophy, I set about creating a body of work entitled *The Art of Living and Dying in Rockland County*, planning to hold an exhibition in the campus gallery at the end of my residency. Two or three days a week, I'd walk into Sparkhill, past the neat, mono-chromatic, timber-clad homes all flying the American flag in some form or another (from a flagpole, a letter box or a lawn adorned with a fluttering riot of red, white and blue) and catch the coach into Manhattan.

An Aussie's notion of America is shaped through American film, television, music and literature. I was in a familiar land and as I stood on the deck of the tour boat, staring wistfully across the bay at the Statue of Liberty, I was overcome with a strange and misplaced nostalgia. What struck me the most about America, however, was how *American* it was. People actually say 'have a nice day' and 'you're welcome'—*all* the time. The characters and scenes I'd seen on TV were just like those I was experiencing in real life—the *Happy Days* diners, the burly cops in Brooklyn, the Andy Warhol types in Chelsea with their turtle neck sweaters, skinny jeans and thick-framed glasses, the gesticulating taxi drivers, the pinafore-wearing waitresses, the pizza joints, Jewish guys with their cork-screw side locks, the homeless loitering outside the Port Authority Bus Depot, the African

American men in their full length camel-hair overcoats, draped cashmere scarves, trilby hats and chunky gold bling, the lycra-clad joggers in Hyde Park, the steel bridges, the diminutive Colombian nannies pushing their prams up Madison Avenue, the purposefully striding, briefcase-swinging, bespoke-suited businessmen and the plum-in-their-mouth women behind the counters in Tiffany's uptown. New York City felt like the twenty-first century equivalent of Ancient Rome where all roads led and if I'd had one regret, it was that I hadn't lived for at least a decade in that fascinating place.

All day long I'd ride the subway, criss-crossing the city, surfacing to visit galleries, museums and iconic landmarks. Come nine o'clock, satiated and exhausted, I'd catch the last coach back to Sparkhill. It'd be dark and the streets deserted when the bus pulled up at the stop outside the local Mexican restaurant. Yanking on my mittens and wrapping my scarf around my neck, I'd start the chilly trek back to campus. One night, as I trudged past the power substation on the fringes of town, I paused to admire the giant metal structure, its icy framework glowing like the skeleton of a church in the moonlight, a perfect image to include in my exhibition. I unzipped the camera bag and took out my Nikon. I'd been shooting for a couple minutes when out of the corner of my eye I noticed the silhouette of someone standing at the second-storey window in the house across the road. I waved but the shadowy figure didn't wave back and, dismissing them from my mind, I continued clicking. Suddenly, three black-and-white police cars, charging in from three different directions, sirens wailing and lights flashing, came screeching to a halt at my side. I was surrounded. What on earth have I done? Intending to beg forgiveness or prostrate on the ground if necessary, I took a step towards the nearest car.

'*Step away from the vehicle!*' a male voice boomed from a megaphone the second I lifted my foot from the turf as, simultaneously

I jumped back and snapped to attention like a Fort Knox military cadet. A car door swung open and out climbed a blonde, snugly attired female police officer about Eva's age, handguns dripping on either side of her sturdy hips.

I explained who I was, where I was from, where I was staying and what I was doing. Fortunately, I had my passport in my bag.

'This is America ma'am,' the young woman in uniform gravely declared. 'We don't take photographs of power stations here,' she said, watching over my shoulder as I deleted the possibly terrorist intel from my camera before motioning the other squad cars to move on.

After a few more formalities, we got chatting, the lady cop and her partner even offering to drive me home. With lights strobing, we pulled up outside the campus and I could see my fellow resident artists' jostling for position in the windows above. As a suspected terrorist no less, I'd unwittingly become an overnight legend.

'Female exiting the vehicle,' crackled a Robert De Niro voice on the two-way radio as I scrambled out of the car.

PART TWO

Arabian Nights

Out beyond ideas of wrongdoing
and rightdoing there is a field.
I'll meet you there.

— Rumi

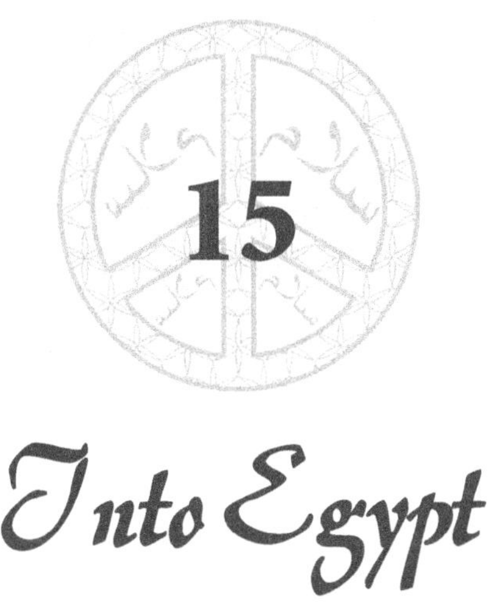

15

Into Egypt

It was late in 2010, just two months before the Egyptian Revolution, when I flew into Cairo for the first time. I'd never had a burning desire to visit Egypt nor been particularly interested in Ancient Egypt or the Pyramids. I knew next to nothing about Egypt's political situation, culture or the Islamic faith. Now, in my capacity as an established Australian artist, I was invited by the Egyptian Ministry of Culture to participate in an all-expenses-paid International Artists' Symposium in Luxor, over six hundred kilometres south of Cairo set on that legendary, almost mythical, river of ancient lives and religions—the Nile.

From the air, Cairo appeared bleak—a sepia realm of brick cubicles and satellite dishes swallowed up in a brown haze of pollutants. The vast metropolis looked as if it had been dusted with taupe icing sugar, resembling one of my childhood finger paintings in which the colours turned to mud if I fiddled with it too much; the mosques, with their slender minarets and plump, tiled domes the only structures standing out in the mire. To my Eurocentric eyes with their preference for flying in over patchworks of green, lushly vegetated valleys, densely forested mountain ranges and picturesque medieval ruins, Egypt appeared inhospitable, almost uninhabitable. I tried to imagine what it would be like living in one of those apartment blocks, driving on those roads or walking in the streets. It seemed as if one apocalyptic sandstorm could bury the whole place alive. Perhaps in a hundred years' time, there'll be nothing left but a sea of satellite dishes poking through the desert sand like huge metallic seashells. Squinting to see the pyramids, I was unable to make them out in the gritty atmosphere.

Down there, somewhere in that sprawling mass of humankind and masonry was Gamal. I wouldn't meet him until I arrived in Luxor in a few days' time, and I had no inkling of the epic journey we were about to undertake. As the plane banked, I took a last look outside before stowing my tray table and fastening my seatbelt. And there it was: the mighty Nile, glinting and snaking its way through the Egyptian capital. My heart raced as we hit the runway and taxied into Cairo International Airport.

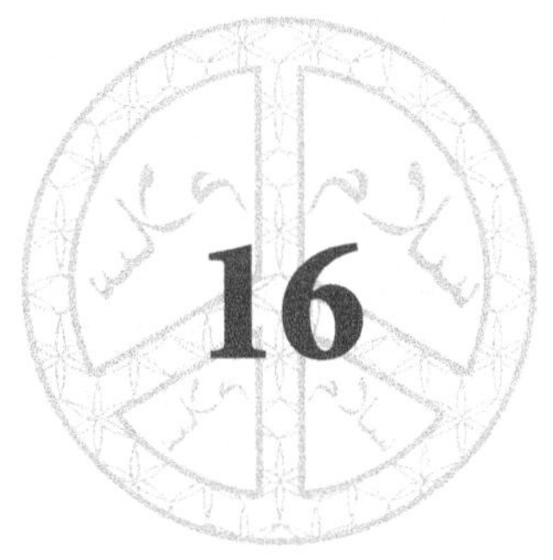

16

The Derelict Palace

The first thing to strike me when I got off the plane and entered the terminal was *The Veil*. Of course, I'd seen Muslim women wearing the hijab and niqab in Australia but having never visited the Middle East, I was taken aback by the sheer number of women swathed in head-to-toe black robes—some sporting designer sunglasses, Prada handbags and patent leather Jimmy Choo pumps; gold rings gleaming on ebony gloved fingers; dark eyes glancing this way and that. With my loose, mussed up hair and travel-soiled clothes creased from the flight, I felt positively exposed and bedraggled. I grabbed my suitcase from the carousel, purchased my tourist visa and passed through customs, joining the host of elegant apparitions as they glided majestically through the plate glass exits into the hazy and sweltering afternoon light.

Outside, hundreds of families struggling with trolleys piled high with luggage navigated their way through a gridlocked sea of cars; hot-tempered taxi drivers yelling at each other from the open windows of their battered vehicles; horns tooting and blaring. Egyptian pop music, overlayed with doleful incantations of the Qur'an drifted from the idling cabs to fuse in the diesel-saturated air. Boys with fuzzy upper lips and gaunt men in long robes and turbans begged for piasters in exchange for carrying bags or minding cars. Lined, worn-weary women in dusty veils and sandals, babies bound to their backs, roamed the car park selling boxes of tissues or packets of biscuits, their pitiful pleas lost in the din.

Dazed and exhausted from the twenty-five-hour flight from Melbourne, I perched myself on my suitcase on the pavement, engrossed in the scene as I waited for my lift to arrive. But I didn't have long to wait. The polite young man from the Egyptian Cultural Development Foundation had no trouble finding his unveiled Western passenger and, after bundling my luggage into the boot of his car, we set off, merging into the lava flow of traffic to my hotel in Tahir Square. I'd wanted to spend some time in Cairo before flying down to the Luxor at the end of the week.

For the next few days, I did the things tourists do—the pyramids, the museums, the mosques and souqs. Strolling past the row of open-air mechanic workshops in Champollion Street one day, trying to catch a glimpse of the immaculately maintained early model Rolls Royces garaged behind, I came across an imposing nineteenth-century palace, spectacularly run-down like Havisham Hall in *Great Expectations*. Arriving back at the hotel, I asked Wahid, on reception, about the building.

'It belonged to Prince Said Halim. And after that it was a school, but now it is empty,' he explained. 'I heard it was sold to a rich guy from Alexandria who will turn it into a hotel.'

I asked if, as an artist on invitation by the Egyptian government, I could possibly get permission to take photographs of the interior of the palace.

'Of course,' Wahid said. 'It will not be a problem. Leave it with me. I will arrange everything.'

That night, I googled the palace on my laptop and found an intriguing reference:

Halim was obsessed with Rome—the city in which, ironically, he would eventually be assassinated by Arshavir Shiragian, an American agent, in December 1921. It was only natural that he should commission Antonio Lasciac, the Italian who designed, among other regal downtown buildings, the palace of Princess Neamat Kamaleddin and the headquarters of Bank Misr, to build his Cairo residence in 1896. In line with the extravagant tastes of the house of Mohamed Ali, materials were imported all the way from Italy. And despite his wife's preference for the Bosporus, where she eventually died, Halim spent much time in this, the envy of his blue-blooded cousins. The palace was confiscated by the British in the wake of World War I, in which Halim had sided with the Ottomans, and later transformed into Al-Nassiriyah Secondary School for Boys—many a deputy and cabinet minister would receive their education there—before the latter's gardens, once the site of marble fountains and unique species of tree, were cordoned off and occupied by apartment buildings. It was then, too, that the street was named after Champollion and the rumour spread that the Egyptologist was living there while he deciphered the Rosetta Stone, unlocking a limitless cache of ancient mystery. Early in 2000, the palace was finally included in the register of the Institut Français d'Archaeologie Orientale, which seeks to document all monuments.

Next morning at breakfast, Wahid told me to be ready to leave at 2 o'clock as I'd been authorised to access the palace. He would take me there himself, he said. That afternoon as we approached the building, I inquired about the official permission I assumed he'd obtained.

'*I* am giving you the permission,' declared the proud, self-appointed ambassador to his country.

'But Wahid, what if we get caught?' I asked apprehensively. 'Won't we get into trouble?'

'Do not worry,' the confident young man replied. 'Come. This way, Miz Kasrin,' he said, veering sharply into a dark and deserted alleyway.

Before I had a chance to object or voice my concerns, we were there, standing at an inconspicuous side entrance to the derelict building. Pitching his bony shoulder against the rusty metal gate, Wahid pushed hard until with a pronounced creak, it opened—just enough to let us pass through. As I followed my fearless guide into the grounds, I could see the caretaker in the distance engaged in a heated argument with his wife. Like a couple of Bond characters, we made a stealthy dash to the ornate portico and slipped unnoticed through the front door.

Catching my breath, I took in my surroundings. In Australia, we rarely get the opportunity to experience crumbling grandeur, the Heritage Council pouncing on old structures and restoring them the minute they start to deteriorate. But to me, like many artists fascinated by the fleeting nature of existence and by fading beauty and decay, the dilapidated palace was enchanting.

The interior was wonderfully ramshackle; a layer of pale, grey powder carpeting the disintegrating parquet floor, not a footprint marring the surface. At the far end of the once-grand entrance hall, a magnificent, branching wrought-iron staircase sat before a vast panel of murky lead-light windows. Soaking up the hushed atmosphere, I tiptoed from room to room, taking photographs and visualising what must have taken place during the *belle epoch* of the building;

the perceptive Wahid, obviously aware of my need for solitude, made himself scarce. I scaled the increasingly narrowing staircase, emerging onto a flat expanse of rooftop overlooking a parapet to the bustling streets below. Returning to the ground floor, I found a crumbling stone staircase leading to a labyrinth of dim passages and dungeon-like rooms beneath the palace, where I assumed servants had once lived and worked.

Oblivious to the passing of time, I was startled from my reverie by the sound of a small cough from behind.

'Excuse me, Miz Kasrin,' Wahid said quietly. 'We must leave now. It is dark soon.'

Unbelievably, over three hours had passed since we entered what, for me, was an Aladdin's den. Wahid poked his head outside the front door and turned to give me a thumbs-up. Following right on the tail of my fellow trespasser, we stepped onto the portico and took off. We were halfway across the forecourt when the caretaker spotted us. Striding furiously in our direction, his billowing *gallabiyah* emphasising his considerable bulk, he was clearly incensed that we'd entered the building without his permission. I glanced across at Wahid's diminutive frame but surprisingly my featherweight companion appeared unfazed by the rapid approach of the irate man. On the other side of the grounds, I could see his wife locking the gates, blocking our only avenue of escape. At that point I needed the bathroom.

Without further ado, the battle commenced. As I stood anxiously out of the way, legs squeezed together and heart pounding, Wahid and the caretaker launched into a clamorous and wildly animated argument in Arabic.

'Do you have money?' Wahid asked me after a while.

I opened my wallet and he fished out ten Egyptian pounds which he promptly passed to the caretaker. However, rather than having a mollifying effect, the man threw his hands in the air and bellowed his indignation. You would have thought that Wahid had insulted Allah Himself. Both men resumed their argument with even greater intensity, yet it was dawning on me that their quarrel was unlike any real-life drama I'd ever seen. On the contrary, I had a front row seat to an over-acted pantomime at Her Majesty's Theatre; a ritual preformed in this part of the world since well before the reign of the Pharaohs.

'I need another ten pounds,' Wahid said following a few more minutes of theatrics. The moment he clasped his hand on the money, the big man's fury evaporated. Wahid had obviously met his foe's expectations. The former adversaries shook hands, clapped each other heartily on the back and beamed at one another like the best of friends. Next, the caretaker turned his attention to me. Suddenly metamorphosing into the most congenial tour guide in Egypt, he gave me a winning, practically toothless smile and with a flourish of his dinner-plate-sized hand and a charming bow, the trium-phant fellow beckoned me back inside to continue my tour, politely pointing out the things that he considered might be of interest.

'Welcome to Egypt,' Wahid said smiling wryly. '*Baksheesh*. That is how it is done.'

At the end of my stay at the Cairo Downtown Hotel, I thanked Wahid for his assistance, trying to press upon him a modest tip. But despite my insistence, he repeatedly refused to accept the money.

'No worries, mate,' he replied with a perfect Australian accent and a winning grin, warmly shaking my hand before turning his atten-tion to the Japanese tourists at reception.

'*Konnichi wa*,' I heard him say as I wheeled my suitcase out the door.

17

Hotel Pyramisa

Twenty-five artists from around the world arrived crumpled and bleary-eyed on a red-eye flight from Cairo in the ancient city of Luxor. Plonking ourselves on the brocade sofas under the gilded chandeliers and fake palm trees in the foyer of the Hotel Pyramisa, we waited for the symposium organisers to check us in. It was a lengthy process and I was dozing when a party of besuited men with five o'clock shadows, entered the building. When an artist from Romania nudged me awake, I grudgingly rose to meet the assembly. One by one, we were presented to the Egyptian government officials, but I'd already noticed the stunningly attractive man long before I was introduced to Mr Gamal Bahar, our translator and it was obvious, when I saw his eyes repeatedly return to meet mine, that he'd noticed me.

He was paler than his companions, tall—at least six foot, broad shouldered with smoky brown eyes, full, curvaceous lips and a head of tight, dark curls that reminded me of the emperor statues I'd seen in Rome. Undone two buttons down, his powder-blue shirt revealed a glimpse of the wide expanse of his chest and a sprinkling of

157

hazelnut hair. There was an air of gravity about him, a reserve; not, I got the impression, from being arrogant or aloof but rather from being quietly self-possessed. I watched the women in our group fluster as with a cordial smile, a small bow and a warm handshake the beautiful young man greeted the artists.

At last, it was my turn. As we shook hands, I looked up and into his eyes. For an instant, it seemed as if he'd been struck; his composure dissipating in an instant. I felt it too and, shocked by the flash flood of our immediate attraction, with a racing pulse, I quickly disengaged before anyone had a chance to notice what was happening between us.

My God, Katherine. What are you thinking? I thought as I scurried to the ladies' loo to catch my breath and take a look at my sleep-deprived face in the mirror. He's way too young and you're far too old; I was unaware then that he'd only just turned twenty-six so that would turn out to be the understatement of the century.

Reminiscing later about the meeting in the foyer, Gamal described his version of events.

'I saw you first,' he recollected. 'On the sofa.'

Oh shit, I thought, mentally scrambling to picture my dishevelled self on the couch. I must have looked a wreck.

'It felt as if I already knew you,' he continued, oblivious of my dismay. 'The moment I saw you, you entered my soul and I knew you were my destiny.'

'Be still, my beating heart', was the famous quote that sprang to mind, as both smitten and amused by his highly romantic and poetic words, I concealed my smile and pleasure.

✕✕✕

My hotel room at the Pyramisa, which would also serve as my studio during the two-week symposium, although not five-star, was clean, bright and airy and to my delight overlooked the majestic Valley of the Kings; the Nile virtually lapping at my doorstep. Abandoning any notion of unpacking, I threw my suitcase on the bed, slid open the sliding glass door and stepped outside onto the terracotta tiled, bougainvillea draped porch. In the pale pink-blue light, the sun not yet up, six hot air balloons, like giant upside down teardrop gems, hung motionless in the tepid sky above the sandstone mountains in the distance. I could hear a rooster crowing and a goat bleating across the other side of the wide and glassy breadth of water; see the flat-roofed mud buildings set amongst the slender palms and lush, lime-green undergrowth; the faint smell of engine oil wafting in from the watercraft already up and about on the river. I didn't have long to savour my new surroundings, however. Following a quick shower and a short rest, we were summoned to assemble in the hotel foyer before being whisked off to visit the Luxor Museum. Walking through room after room of tastefully lit antiquities, I rounded the corner of a pharaonic burial casket and bumped into Gamal. Our eyes met and I knew there and then I was, as we say in Australia, 'a goner'.

The following night, the whole menagerie of artists and organisers loaded onto an assortment of open-air wooden boats to take a short cruise up the Nile to a Nubian restaurant where we were assured there'd be delicious food, alcohol and belly dancing. By the time we arrived, the outdoor eatery, festooned with colourful traditional rugs and Egyptian pinprick lanterns, was packed with groups of merry, sloshed and badly sunburned English tourists. Half male, half female, our group, an eclectic assortment of professional artists from Turkey, America, Italy, France, Australia, Romania, Korea, Tunisia, Austria, Pakistan, Saudi Arabia as well as Egypt and ranging in age from thirty to eighty, joined them; tucking into the smorgasbord of Middle Eastern dips, lentil soup, lamb tagine, roast pigeon, flat bread and rice. Gamal sat by my side as we ate and watched the succession of fervent performances by Nubian drummers, whirling dervishes and belly dancers.

There wasn't much opportunity to talk but I was conscious of the heat from his thigh next to mine. When everyone kicked off their shoes and got up to try their hand at belly dancing, us Westerners laughing at our complete lack of expertise, he joined me on the dance floor; his arms bent at chest height, his palms facing his body; his gestures so distinctly Egyptian; so unlike the often ungainly and ill at ease dance moves of many Australian men. Under my partner's attentive gaze, I could have, like Eliza Doolittle in *My Fair Lady*, 'danced all night and still have begged for more'.

It was after midnight when we stumbled back on board. Beckoning me with his Omar Sharif eyes (what girl ever recovered from watching *Dr Zhivago*!), Gamal crossed the deck, and without a second thought—if you can't take a risk in your fifties, when can you?— I followed him up a narrow wooden ladder, emerging onto the flat, paint-peeled roof of the vessel as if stepping onto a film set. Is this really happening, I asked myself over and over again? Nevertheless, here I was on a boat on the Nile with this gorgeous young man who obviously wanted me as much as I wanted him. I was thrillingly alive; euphoric; undeniably in lust if not yet in love. I was in Egypt! *Egypt*, for heaven's sake. And at that moment, nothing or nowhere else existed.

A mild breeze refreshed the humid night; the scent of jasmine drifted across the black water from the dark and lushly vegetated river bank to our left. We had the rooftop to ourselves and when Gamal dropped to the timber platform and lay on his back, I did the same. Lying side by side, the soft throb of the engine pulsating through our bodies, we gazed up at the star-littered sky above as the boat made its leisurely half-hour journey back to the hotel. We didn't touch but I was acutely aware of the electric current zapping across the five-millimetre gap between our fingertips.

On shore, our rowdy and largely intoxicated group bid each other farewell, everybody dispersing and staggering off in different directions through the dimly-lit grounds to their rooms. Gamal, who'd drunk nothing but orange juice all evening, showed me to mine. As I struggled with the key in the lock, I found myself being spun by the shoulders from behind. Pushing me up against the door, he stole his first kiss—hard and persistent. I didn't resist. How on earth could I? This was not something that happened every day, not to me anyway. With a lifelong predilection for collecting experiences, I wasn't about to forego this one. But though I'd yearned for this moment since we'd met in the hotel foyer two days earlier—had thought of little else, in fact—I'd determined it was up to Gamal to make the first move.

Certain his advances would be welcomed, he'd seized the day, spurred on no doubt by Egyptian common knowledge that Western women have loose moral standards. Had he done this before, I wondered vaguely before dismissing the thought from my mind. With my head light from the wine, my limbs pliant in the blood-warm air, my whole body flushed with desire, free and unaccountable so far from home, I yielded to the exotic night.

'I must go now,' Gamal said, when our lips finally parted, smiling a smile that would have surely beguiled the gods. 'We shall see each other in the dining room at breakfast, *Insha'Allah*.'

And with that he was gone. Trembling and breathless, I let myself into my room and closed the door, sliding like jelly to the ground. Less than ten days ago, I was minding my own business in Melbourne. I hadn't asked for, looked for or expected this. It was surreal; life imitating art; a Salvador Dali hand-painted dream—molten clocks in the desert. Where was this going, I wondered as I lay wide awake tossing in bed that night; sensing even then that this was more than just some romantic holiday fling.

xxx

Forty-eight hours later. Room 212, the Hotel Pyramisa. *Please Do Not Disturb.*

It was an exquisite night of firsts. The first time Gamal had seen a naked woman—touched her pulsing skin, inhaled her primal scent, made her come. The first time inside. His eyes never closed.

'Oh dear,' he repeated softly as he looked at the female form lying before him, taking in every detail, lapping it up, drinking it in. I was Courbet's *L'Origine du Monde*, unveiled for the very first time.

It was also the first time Gamal had been touched by a woman. Tracing my fingertips across his skin, his body jolted with the newness of it all.

He smelled of Egypt. Not Egypt on the city streets, but Egypt in Khan El Khalili souq in Old Islamic Cairo, where dried jasmine petals, cumin seed and lotus flower oil layer the cloistered air. He tasted like a sun-ripened fig plucked from the tree—lips full, firm yet soft and sweet with nectar. Taking his hand, creamy and smooth like a boy's, I showed him how a man, slowly and surely, pleases a woman. By then he was hungry. Ravenous. Devouring everything at once.

'Whoa,' I laughed, pulling him up. 'Now try it slowly,' I suggested gently, setting the pace, our glistening bodies melding into one writhing creature—timelessly, languidly, slipping and sliding like silk on silk.

I felt him tremble, heard him cry out, saw the rapture on his face. I was the first to see. And as I stole it all away, that which we call innocence, I knew he'd found something, not lost it, and my heart filled with a warm and expansive joy.

As for me, his beauty, *The Statue of David's* beauty, was *my* undoing. I was in awe of it; consumed by it; was completely under its spell.

When I was young, I didn't take enough notice of the things that truly warranted it. But now, a lifetime from those careless days,

I know better. In that room, that moment in time and space, every fibre of my being finely tuned to every nuance of the senses, I said to myself—I am here. Remember this. Always remember this.

And Gamal got up to pray.

I didn't know that that was what he was doing. I thought he'd just gone to the bathroom, although I did wonder why he'd put on his T-shirt and tracksuit pants first. When I didn't hear flushing or taps running, I slipped out of bed and peeked around the alcove wall to see what he was up to. There he was, back to me, bent over on his knees with his forehead on the carpet. I was taken aback, feeling like an intruder witnessing some intimate moment I wasn't meant to see. I scuttled back to bed and pulled the sheets up to my chin. Wow, he must be really religious, I thought. Apart from the nuns in the catholic convent in Spain, I'd never knowingly met anyone *that* religious. Not someone who got to their knees and prayed five times a day, that is. What was he doing with *me*, I wondered, realising at the same time that I was somewhat aroused by the fact that he was so devout, remembering how titillated I'd been at the age of twenty when I'd read Colleen McCullough's best-selling novel *Thorn Birds* about a priest torn between his calling and his carnal lust.

We made love again, and then again and, as daylight seeped around the edges of the heavy block-out drapes, the air thick with the musky scent of sex, bedsheets in dishevelled disarray; a breakfast trolley rattling in the corridor outside, my spent and exhausted lover collapsed on top of me, burying me beneath the warm mountain of his body. Of course, there'd been no one to explain the do's and don'ts of après-sex etiquette and this time, his first time, I wasn't going to be the one to do it. When I could no longer breathe, I carefully inched my way out from under my lover's slumbering form and dressed; bending to kiss his cheek

and smell his tousled hair before making my way back to my hotel
room to catch a couple of hours' sleep before breakfast.

✕✕✕

For the next two weeks, the pace during the day was frenetic, and the
nights were no less so. As participating artists, we were required to
produce a body of work for inclusion in an exhibition to be opened by
the Governor of Luxor, at the end of the symposium. Every evening, we
were expected to attend discussion sessions where we'd describe our art
practice to one another and the symposium organisers with a Power-
Point presentation; Gamal was frequently required to attend these, too,
in his role as translator. Most afternoons there'd be organised trips to
visit the ancient sites, galleries and museums; my secret lover and I
staying at a close but discreet distance whenever we were in company.

Once I'd set up the studio, I decided, as I'd done in France, to
respond to the environment by making art from local materials and
natural resources derived from my surroundings. I was assigned a
studio assistant, Mido—well-mannered, fluent in English and eager
to please—a streak of a young man with angular features and slick,
black, short back and sides. Mido was a student at the nearby Luxor
Art Institute; it was his job to acquire my art materials and assist me
in any way possible. The first task I set my eager helper was to find
me a palm tree trunk.

The following morning, I was woken by the sound of my name
being called from somewhere outside. I jumped out of bed and ran
to open the sliding glass door. The voice seemed to be coming from
the direction of the Nile, so after scrambling into jeans and a T-shirt,
I raced to the riverbank, met by a sight to behold. There, in a wooden
skiff graced with an elegant calico sail was Mido, standing astride
a big hunk of palm tree as if he'd just hunted and shot an African
wildebeest.

164

'Could you possibly cut it into sections?' I asked tentatively when he'd dragged the hefty length of timber ashore, not yet comfortable with soliciting someone else to do my dirty work.

'Of course, Miz Kasrin. Your wish is my command.' Yes, he actually said that! before scurrying off to find an implement to do the job.

Two hours later, brandishing a bread knife and a blunt, second-hand saw, the triumphant Mido returned. That afternoon, under the shade of a leafy bay laurel, Russian tourists calling out encouragement from the passing tour boats, my sweat-drenched but uncomplaining assistant, proceeded to hack through the fibrous trunk with the flimsy utensils, supervised by his unlikely overseer. By the end of the day, both of us sneezing from the wood powder in our nostrils, I had the beginnings of an artwork.

My next request was for some slabs of limestone, like those used to clad the pyramids in Ancient Egypt. Again, Mido came through with the goods, delivering three pearly, delightfully cool-to-the-touch and irregular squares of stone to my studio. Sitting cross-legged on a rush mat on the banks of the Nile, the faint put-put sound of the river-boats heading upstream in the background, I set about carving the limestone with some rusty tools on loan from the Art Institute. It was late in the day when I looked up from my work and across the wide expanse of river, catching the sun's last rays as they illuminated the Valley of the Kings in an incandescent blaze of light. My back ached from bending, my fingers were blistered from handling the tools, my eyes scratchy with grit. But as I breathed in the muddy scent of the papyrus reed-covered river flats, listening to the 'keek, keek' calls of the spindly-legged stilts as they foraged for food at the water's edge, half expecting a herd of yawning hippos to come floating by, I felt an overwhelming exhilaration course through my entire being. This was an existence I'd craved. Personally and artistically, it was an opportunity I could only dream of as I trudged through back-breaking days building a life in the mist and shadow of Mumbulla Mountain.

Some days, Mido turned up with classmates in tow. Standing around my worktable, chatting to each other in Arabic, the curious young students would ask questions about my art and Australia, my versatile assistant acting as translator. As visiting artists, we'd toured their Art Department and were shocked by the lack of facilities, especially considering how much the Luxor Governorate had spent on funding our symposium.

Having already produced six pieces for the exhibition, my final project was a 'mummy painting'. Accompanying me to the local souq, Mido facilitated with negotiations over a copper-coloured wheel of raw beeswax and some rolls of muslin bandage. Back in the studio, inspired by the 1st-century BC encaustic mummy portraits I'd seen in the Egyptian Museum in Cairo, I bound a timber panel with the loose weave fabric and coated it with my warm, liquid wax medium.

Opening night was a grand affair. The Governor gave his speech and the international artists mingled with the Luxor glitterati and the media. Having integrated local materials into my work—limestone, palm tree, papyrus, muslin and encaustic, the Egyptian guests were intrigued, sidling up to me at regular intervals throughout the evening to ask questions and express their admiration. I was elated. In two weeks, despite all the sight-seeing, extra-curricular activity in Room 212 and the subsequent lack of sleep, I'd achieved what I set out to do—produce an evocative and aesthetically pleasing body of work that responded to the surrounding environment. Apart from a few red dots on the walls, what else could an artist ask for?

As the evening wound up, I went to look for Mido. Thanking my immaculately groomed and resourceful apprentice, I tried, as a token of my eternal gratitude to slip some Egyptian pounds into his hand, knowing that I wouldn't have been able to achieve what I did without him. But the polite young man would not accept my gift. I knew that his family were poor, that he would've been paid a pittance, if at all, for his labour and that he'd probably bought some of my art materials with money out of his own pocket. Yet despite my insistence, Mido adamantly refused to take the cash.

'I am very happy you are pleased with me, Miz Kasrin. It has been an honour to serve you,' he said with a big smile and a deep bow.

I knew I would never see Mido again, and I wanted to give him a hug. But sensing it wasn't appropriate, I shook his hand, brushing the tears from my cheeks as we said a sad goodbye.

✕✕✕

When we weren't working, Gamal and I tried to spend as much time together as possible. Along with the other artists and organisers, we ate together in the dining room, swam in the hotel pool and remained close during organised visits to the museums and ancient sites, not to mention our nightly rendezvous in Room 212. But we had to be careful. My young lover would have lost his job had he been found seducing a resident artist so it wasn't until everyone had gone to bed that I'd sneak to his room. Back then, I was unaware of the other risks involved. It was only later that I learned about the Adultery Police whose role it was to monitor hotels and arrest Egyptians discovered fornicating without a marriage certificate.

Despite our intimacy in the bedroom, a religious and cultural gulf set us worlds apart. Eagerly seeking to bridge it, we began the first of many discussions—about Islam, Egyptian history, politics and culture, about art, family, language, the role of women, relationships, marriage, death, birth, literature, humour, food, health, education, traffic, bed linen, toilets, cats and lizards. This last topic gave rise to what became my nickname for Gamal—Lizard Boy—his hysterical aversion to reptiles developing in childhood after hearing about the scheming serpent in the Garden of Eden.

I asked him about the veil.

'Will you expect your wife to wear a headscarf?'

'No, I will not,' he adamantly replied. 'It would be her choice, of course. The idea is that a woman keeps herself for her husband. She wears the niqab or hijab to protect herself from the harassment of men who are naturally more predatory than women.'

Naturally, I arced up with the usual feminist arguments against the custom, chastising Gamal for his paternalistic view of my sex.

'The veil has become a way of strengthening national pride, too' was Gamal's solemn response. 'My mother did not wear a veil when she was young. She wore miniskirts and dyed her hair different colours. But since the death of President Nasser many women choose to wear the veil to promote their Islamic identity. It is also how a woman dedicates herself to Allah.'

Surely, it's possible to have an Islamic identity and dedicate yourself to Allah without covering your hair with a headscarf or swathing your body in black, I thought. But thinking it might create friction, I didn't pursue the issue.

'I do not see why you have a problem with it,' he continued. 'You have nuns wearing veils in the West. It is the same thing; Muslim women want to take the emphasis off their bodies and their sexuality.'

'As long as they can accessorise,' I said cheekily, thinking back to the highly accessorised, niqab-clad women I'd seen at the airport in Cairo.

'It is true,' Gamal said, lightening up a little. 'Some women like wearing the veil because they cannot be bothered washing their hair or going to the hairdresser. And did you know that thieves, men who disguise themselves in niqabs, have been caught robbing people in the streets?' he exclaimed, his voice rising to the singsong level of indignation I was coming to know so well. This is why I do not agree with the full-face veil,' he said emphatically. 'It is a question of security. It is necessary to see the face.'

If we became exasperated by each other's values or beliefs, opinions and attitudes in those first giddy and besotted days of love and lust, we'd diffuse the tension with humour.

'You're so fucking backward,' I'd say.

'You are so fucking barbaric,' Gamal would counter, laughing.

'So, will you go to hell for sleeping with an infidel?' I asked him one evening.

'Allah is All Merciful,' he earnestly replied. 'I will pray for His Forgiveness.'

Although I was itching to know how he could so easily accommodate what seemed to me such a questionable, but clearly convenient rationalisation, for the time being at least, I bit my tongue. Why disrupt a delightful evening of lovemaking and pillow-talk.

'Have you ever been in love?' I asked that night, threading my fingers through the soft fur on his chest.

'I thought I had. But now I realise I have not. It was nothing like this. This,' he said, tucking a stray lock of hair behind my ear, 'this sparkles.'

One morning at breakfast, I asked Gamal if he knew where I could buy some reading glasses and he offered to take me to an optometrist in Luxor later in the day. That afternoon, during a rare break in the hectic symposium schedule, I made my way to the hotel foyer. As the lift doors parted, I glimpsed him surrounded by a small circle of fawning female artists across the other side of the room. Catching his eye, I watched with amusement as the handsome young man bowed, stepped backwards and seamlessly extricated himself from his admirers.

We grabbed a taxi to the town centre. Once we were out on the bustling streets Gamal took my hand, placing himself on my left flank presumably to protect me from a rogue car that might possibly mow me down.

'You're very chivalrous,' I teased.

'I must do this,' he said earnestly. 'You are my woman.'

I loved his gallantry, a quaint quality long lost in my own country. Conveniently ignoring the subset of infantilising implications around a woman's vulnerability and her need for a male protector, unambiguously unpacked by my feminist sisters decades ago, this strong, independent and feisty, snake-killing, bushfire-fighting, mud-brick-making woman from the Australian bush, was enchanted.

With my glasses purchased we joined the confusion of cars, scooters, donkeys and carts, peddlers, goats, beggars, pedestrians, couriers and loiterers, outside.

'Come with me,' Gamal said, shepherding me along the road and down a side alley until we reached a mud-brick, open-fronted kiosk where a number of men in long, pastel-coloured gowns and leather sandals waited patiently in line. Behind the counter, lengthy stalks of pale green sugar cane were being fed into a steel contraption from which gushed forth the sweet, freshly squeezed juice: something I hadn't seen or tasted since my hippy days during a visit to the Bangalow market near Byron Bay. Gamal ordered two frothing glassfuls, the colour of newly unfurled bracken fronds and in the balmy, ochre light, our backs against the sun-warmed wall, we stood in silence, sipping the delicious nectar and watching the world go by in that ancient Egyptian city.

I felt transported back in time. The narrow, unpaved street, lined with three storey brick buildings, their crumbling plaster facades daubed with mud or painted a faded pink, blue or yellow, washing and rugs hanging from laundry lines strung across latticework and Art Deco balconies, thronged with life; mostly male life, it seemed— men in turbans on daintily trotting donkeys, a father and son driving a horse and cart, half a dozen boys kicking a scuffed soccer ball, a vociferous street vendor vying with his neighbour to sell his cackling hens from an antique metal cage. I did see one woman—appearing from a dark laneway holding a cloth wrapped bundle on her head, her robed silhouette receding down the street in a sunlit aura of dust particles. Everywhere flashes of colour—a fire engine red downpipe, a cobalt blue doorframe, trays of oranges, bananas and sliced watermelon. Before my eyes, a floppy-eared Nubian goat skittered across the road, cleverly avoiding a head-on collision with a frenetically tooting man on a moped. The sound of Arabic music—classical, religious and pop, drifted from open windows and shopfronts. There were lots of cats—mangy, shrunken looking creatures that back home, had they been curled up asleep on the ground, would have been mistaken for roadkill. The sour yet herbaceous odour rising from randomly deposited piles of fresh donkey manure, perfume to my country-girl nose.

'You like this,' Gamal said with a quiet smile, visibly proud to be showing me his fascinating country.

'I do,' I replied as I reached across and squeezed his hand. I felt so close to him at that moment; as if there was something precious growing between us; fragile tendrils of emerging love, seeking the light in each other.

We drained the last dregs of juice from our glasses and taking me by the hand again, Gamal led me through the traffic to the local souq; a clamorous and congested undercover market selling souvenirs, ethnic jewellery, leather bags, brassware, cotton clothing and household linen as well as fruit and vegetables. Pushing our way past wicker baskets overflowing with dried saffron and hibiscus flowers, piles of beige pumice stones, pyramids of fat, brown dates and hills of yellow spice and indigo pigment, the individual aromas merging into one sweet and spicy scent, I was pleased to be away from prying eyes and spend some time alone with Gamal. Then, emerging from the crowded and stifling souq, there on the banks of the Nile, with a backdrop of the Valley of the Kings, sat, as it had for millennia, the Luxor Temple in all its golden splendour; life and traffic going on all around, oblivious to the fact that they were circling one of the most spectacular structures on the planet. The evening call to prayer rang out simultaneously from the mosques nearby; a row of nodding horses shackled to glossy, black-enamelled carriages waited for customers in the square.

'Would you like to take one of those back to the hotel?' Gamal asked.

Could I die and go to heaven, too, I wondered; horse-drawn carriages have been my thing since I was eight years old and saw newly-weds, Curly and Laurey hightail off into the distance in the finale of the movie, *Oklahoma*.

As the horse clip-clopped its way along the Nile, Gamal and I chatted about, well, relationships, of course. I was curious to know about the status quo of relationships between men and women in Egypt. How does it work? Where do people meet? Are you allowed to have sex before marriage? What's the deal?

'According to Islam, we cannot have sex before marriage. It is a sin,' Gamal said gravely.

Great, I thought. We're both going to hell in a handbasket. But since I didn't believe in the existence of the *Pretend, Weird, Beardy Guy in the Sky* as Australian comic and self-confessed atheist, Paul McDermott called Him, with opportunistic logic, I figured it would be okay. For me, at least.

'Approximately ninety percent of marriages in Egypt are "salon" marriages,' he continued. 'Generally, people do not marry for love. Couples are introduced to each other through family connections and their marriage is arranged in the salon of the family home.'

'*What*?' I shrieked. 'Are you *serious*? So, what about you? Will your family arrange *your* marriage?'

For some reason, I'd always thought that Egypt, or Cairo at least, was relatively liberal in comparison to some other Muslim countries, like Saudi Arabia, that were notoriously conservative from a Western standpoint. Clearly my knowledge beyond the narrow confines of Australian norms and expectations was sadly lacking—maybe I'd spent too long a sheltered life in the valley under Mumbulla Mountain. Here I was, falling for a man young enough to be my son, whose cultural beliefs and values alone should spell the death knell to any relationship before it had even begun.

'My family know that this does not fit with me. I will find my own partner and marry for love,' he said, a small frown creasing his brow. 'I will tell you something,' he continued. And at this point, leaning back against the padded leather upholstery, I made myself comfortable, knowing him well enough by now to know I was in for the long haul.

'Nowadays, it is very difficult to get married in Egypt,' Gamal began. 'In the country, it is easier. Life is simple. People are poor and a man is not expected to provide an apartment or a dowry. But in the big cities, parents want to ensure that their daughter is entering into a secure environment. In order to propose, a man must have a good job, a car, provide a dowry and have a deposit on an apartment,' he explained, bringing his fingers to his thumb and waving his hand to and fro to emphasise his point, a charming and frequently used gesture that always made me want to jump onto his lap and smother him with passionate kisses.

'It must take him forever to get that sort of money together,' I responded, reminding myself that public displays of affection were taboo in this part of the world.

'It does,' he replied. 'Engaged couples live at home with their family until they get married. It can take many years for a guy to accumulate his savings. Unless he receives financial help from his family, that is. My family is well off. They bought me a car and an apartment. Plus, I have a good income by Egyptian standards. But there are guys who will never get married because of this situation. Sometimes their fiancée leaves them to find a better prospect. Women are under pressure too. They need to marry in a reasonable timeframe to have children. No man will want them if they become too old.'

'So, during the time they're saving to get married, they don't have sex?' I asked incredulously.

I knew that sex before marriage was forbidden in the Gulf countries where Sharia Law applied but I'd assumed that Egypt was a little more moderate in this regard. Yet again, I was reminded of my ignorance.

'Not if they are following Islam correctly,' Gamal answered. 'Look, here is the thing: during President Nasser's time, everything was nationalised. Rents were fixed and very cheap. You could not be evicted if you did not pay. It was not necessary for a husband to own an apartment. Couples could marry, find a place to rent and be secure. But when Sadat came to power, landlords and property investors agitated for new laws to be introduced and rents were raised to the current market value,' he said, just as his mobile phone rang.

I thought back to a conversation I'd had one day in the Cairo Downtown Hotel while taking a break from the relentless sightseeing. Sitting in reception, drinking cups of sugary mint tea, smoking Cleopatra cigarettes and chatting with Wahid and another young Egyptian man, the pair told me how unhappy the Egyptian people were and how angry they'd become with their situation.

'Are you married?' I asked. 'Do you have kids?'

'No,' they replied in weary unison.

'I work sixteen hours a day, seven days a week in this place but I do not make enough money to get married,' Wahid said, sighing. I noticed the dark circles under his eyes.

At the time, just weeks before the Egyptian Revolution, I didn't know anything about their cruel dilemma. I didn't ask Wahid or his friend to elaborate as I was reluctant to pry but afterwards I thought about the contrast with the experience of Australian couples, young and in love and setting up house quite often despite their financial circumstances—an aspiration that seemed far from the Egyptian reality.

✗✗✗

So, that explains why Egyptians Gamal's age are still virgins, I thought, as the carriage picked up pace on the last stretch of the palm-tree-lined boulevard. They can't have sex before they get married. But they can't get married until they can afford it. But they can't afford to get married so they can't have sex.

'Did you ever read *Catch 22* when you were studying English literature at uni?' I asked.

But the carriage had pulled up to the entrance of the hotel and our pony ride had drawn to a close.

175

18

Revolution

Either I was a good teacher or he was a fast learner because in a very short space of time Gamal had perfected the art of lovemaking. In terms of experience, I could've been compared to a fully-fledged masterpiece, he to a pristine blank canvas. There were obvious advantages for us both. Unlike many older men with their tired, pre-conceived and often weird ideas about how to satisfy a woman, Gamal actually listened. He was keen to learn, and aspired, more than anything else, to please. His feel for the different moods of love, however, was instinctive, poetic; our nightly trysts like the changeable Melbourne weather—hot and furious; warm and sensual; sunny and playful; teary-wet and tender.

'How come you don't have an Egyptian girlfriend?' I asked my gifted student, following a glorious evening of ten out of ten sex.

'The most important thing in life for an Egyptian woman is to find a husband,' he replied. 'They are very materialistic. They want only a big wedding and the status of being married. I do not like this mentality. After the marriage, many Egyptian wives become fat and nag their husbands. They do not want sex anymore. This does not suit me,' he said, idly kissing my neck.

'*No!*' I mocked as I thought about how often we'd made love in our few days together.

'And anyway, so far I did not find someone I liked. Until I met you,' he added, ignoring my jibe.

'Did you know that because of the arranged marriage situation, cheating has become a big problem in my country?' he said. 'It is like an epidemic now.'

'So why is this happening?' I asked, intrigued by his fascinating disclosure.

'Many couples do not marry for love so they become unhappy. They feel they have missed out on something. They want passion in their lives so they have affairs. It is terrible,' he said, sighing. 'It was not like this in my parents' day. Marriages were arranged but husbands and wives were faithful.'

It was only later that I learned about *musalsalat*—Arab soap operas which are produced *en masse* for viewing during Ramadan. Brimming with drama and intrigue, the over-the-top love stories provide not only a distraction from hunger and thirst but are perhaps fodder for the soul in a boring or loveless marriage.

'But according to Islam, isn't adultery an even greater sin than sex before marriage?' I asked.

'Yes, it is,' Gamal answered, a look of disgust on his earnest young face. 'Adulterers are punished in hell. But why we are speaking of this? We are wasting time. You are denying me my rights,' he said with a devilish grin. 'Come here,' he demanded, hard again and grabbing me by the wrist.

With only two days of the symposium to go and prompted by a desire to look my best for my young lover, I treated myself to a facial. After all my hard work, I figured I deserved it. Fitted out in glass, marble and chrome, and milling with loud and buxom Russian women with bronzed leather skin, magenta-painted nails and lashings of gold jewellery, the beauty parlour was on a par with those I'd experienced back home. Salma, the petite, young woman attending me spoke excellent English and like women all over the world, we spent the session talking about men and relationships.

'In Saudi Arabia, all marriages are arranged,' Salma said as she applied my turmeric and orange blossom mask. 'Couples do not meet each other until the wedding ceremony. The husband has sex with his wife in order to produce children, then leaves her alone.'

'Yes, this is true,' Gamal said when I relayed the conversation. 'Many Saudi men have affairs when they go away on business. Women are not permitted to drive so they rely on a driver when their husbands are not there. It is rumoured that Saudi wives are having affairs with their Indian drivers.'

How odd, I thought at the time. It seemed like the vast majority of Middle Eastern men and women had given up on the idea of a loving marriage altogether.

✗ ✗ ✗

By the end of our two weeks in Luxor, Gamal and I knew we wanted to see each other again and eventually be together. But the question was how? Neither of us had the funds to be flying backwards and forwards across the globe. Despite holding down two jobs—his nine-to-five position at the Ministry of Culture and an after-hours gig researching material for Egypt's most famous television news anchor-woman, by Western standards, Gamal's income, was relatively low. As an artist, my income was sporadic—one moment feast, the next famine. I'd managed to survive the global financial crisis that had decimated the art world by borrowing against the equity in the property I still owned with John. But having had it on the market for what felt like forever, I'd almost given up any hope of it selling. I needed a miracle and, until then, I wasn't going anywhere.

On the sorrowful eve of my departure, daylight seeping too quickly around the edge of the block-out curtains, the customary sound of crockery chinking in the corridor, we made love for the last time; a sad and lingering *pas de deux* of passion and tenderness; a bitter sweet farewell. For two fleeting weeks, we'd lived a dream. But now the dream was over. I was leaving this young man whom I'd come to know and love and I wasn't sure if I'd ever see him again.

'Please, may my property sell immediately,' I beseeched the mythical Arabian genie, my palms together in supplication, laughing through my tears.

Later that morning, I checked my emails and there, at the top of my inbox, was a message from my real estate agent in Sydney. He had a buyer.

When I told Gamal at breakfast, he didn't seem surprised.

'Destiny,' he said, grinning like a Cheshire cat who'd just devoured a saucer of creamy *mihallabiya*[2]. 'Allah is great!'

That afternoon, my glum-faced lover accompanied me to the airport. Squashed in my suitcase was a large, unwashed T-shirt impregnated with his spicy cologne and musky male scent.

'Do not cry, my love' he said, wiping my wet cheeks with his fingertips as the final boarding call was announced. 'We will see each other again very soon, Insha'Allah.'

And as I kissed him goodbye, reluctantly tearing myself away from his loving embrace, I felt my aching heart break into two; for the time being at least, one half would remain in Egypt with Gamal.

XXX

---

2   A milky Middle Eastern pudding.

Back in Australia, we began to talk about our future in our daily Skype sessions. Mountains would be climbed, rivers forged, deserts traversed. I felt like Lance Armstrong on steroids— except the medication I was popping was HRT for hot flushes!

Unsurprisingly, there were mixed reactions from my family and friends when I spoke about Gamal and our plans; my mother was the most concerned. Gamal was Muslim and possibly a terrorist.

'Oh, Kathy. Are you sure about this?' she said, her eyes wide pools of fear.

Eva was mortified. Who can blame the poor girl? Her mother's boyfriend was only one year younger than her.

'*Mum*!' she exclaimed in horror, 'this is *so* embarrassing.' And in her renowned brand of wit she began to refer to Gamal, if she deigned to refer to him at all, as 'The Foetus'.

My Buddhist and happily unattached sister, who'd spent most of her life rescuing feckless men like our father, was her usual unruffled and tolerant self, momentarily feigning interest but soon wandering off to contemplate more profound revelations. Unsurprisingly, there were a few patronising comments from male acquaintances.

'Fuck your brains out. Get it out of your system. I give it twelve months,' one or two said, with a disparaging chuckle. The aging Lotharios considered it perfectly acceptable for a balding, over-weight, soft-cocked, rotten-toothed man with yellow toenails and grey bristles sprouting from every orifice to bed a woman half their age, yet baulked when the roles were reversed. Caught up in the romance, my girlfriends thought I was lucky to have found such a young, handsome and passionate lover.

As the weeks went by, though, the doubts crept in. What was I thinking? What am I doing? Have I gone completely mad? I'd ask myself, eaten at by an insidious and insistent uncertainty. Yes, my policy had always been to 'feel the fear and do it anyway'.

I'd adamantly maintained that I'd rather regret doing something than regret doing nothing at all. But this was ridiculous.

'You've really lost it now, Katherine,' I said to my reflection in the bathroom mirror, noticing the brown sunspot on my cheek that had definitely not been there the day before.

Apart from the age gap, there were the cultural and religious differences to consider, not to mention the question of getting into another relationship, particularly a long-distance one. After my cheating husband and the turbulent liaison with Vicko, I'd convinced myself that relationships were too much trouble. Thinking back to my father, I'd come to the conclusion that generally speaking, men were a bit of a disappointment. Although I sometimes got lonely, I'd become accustomed to my uncomplicated single existence. Having loved and been loved, I was finally enjoying some of the advantages of being alone, of not having to compromise or accommodate somebody else's agenda. With its innumerable challenges and countless complexities, did I really want to enter into a relationship with an Egyptian Muslim man half my age whose beliefs and experiences were often diametrically opposite to mine?

But each time I signed into Skype and saw the lovesick look on Gamal's face, heard the sound of his all too familiar voice, my heart would leap; my reservations dissipating like photons in cyberspace.

Then, overnight, the world as Gamal knew it, changed dramatically. For the time being, at least, I pushed aside my creeping misgivings.

On 25 January, 2011, a million people gathered in Tahrir Square in the centre of Cairo, calling for the resignation of their President, the tyrannical Hosni Mubarak. Many Egyptians were inspired by events in Tunisia where, denied a permit to sell his wares and make a living to feed his family, a humble fruit seller had set himself alight and perished. Taking to the streets in protest, the Tunisian people had forced their government to stand down.

In Egypt, young, mainly secular university students and activists hijacked Police Day, an annual public holiday held on the 25th January (ironically a day honouring the despised and corrupt Egyptian police force) to demonstrate against the police for the torture and subsequent murder of the twenty-six-year-old activist, Khalid Said. Social media networks were harnessed to muster huge crowds. Not to be outdone by the Tunisians, the Egyptian people, day-by-eventful-day, became galvanised against the regime, convinced they had the power to force Mubarak out. The Arab Spring was on.

On the 28th January, coined 'The Friday of Wrath', the situation became violent and, after Friday prayers, two hundred people were killed, allegedly by the police, in Tahrir Square. Frightened for their lives, the police withdrew from the streets and an indefinite curfew was imposed. When I found Gamal online, he was grey with shock and sleep deprivation, his fraught face a totally different vision from the happy, loved-up one I'd known in Luxor. Like the rest of the world, he was shocked by the unfolding events and alarmed by the chaos spreading like wildfire across the country.

'I do not know what is happening,' he said wretchedly. Despite the weak and distorted video connection, I could see he was on the brink of tears.

Reports were circulating that protesters had stormed the jails, releasing scores of prisoners onto the streets. Hardened criminals were breaking into private property, stealing whatever they could. With no police presence, the city was on the verge of anarchy.

Concerned for his safety, I asked Gamal about the criminals. His response, however, did little to dispel my fears.

'Do not worry,' he declared, his fighting spirit restored. 'I am in the streets with my knife and a sword. I will do whatever it takes to protect my family. And do not forget—I am three times National

Karate Champion,' he added, giving me what I'm sure he thought was complete reassurance.

I'd witnessed an impressive demonstration of Gamal's martial arts skills one night in Room 212 in Luxor, but picturing Harrison Ford in that gun-versus-sword scene from the *The Temple of Doom*, the one where Indy casually pulls out his pistol and shoots dead the swashbuckling Arab assailant brandishing his flashy steel sabre, I have to admit I wasn't all that reassured.

That day, the regime cut all communication between Egypt and the outside world. For the next three days, I had no contact with Gamal whatsoever. In the meantime, while I was either painting, pacing the floor glued to Al Jazeera TV or on the phone to my mother, contracts were exchanged in a blessedly quick property settlement. Theoretically, I could now afford an airfare to Cairo. The Australian government, however, had issued a 'Do Not Travel' warning for Egypt and I knew going back any time soon was out of the question.

When the communication blackout was lifted and Gamal could Skype again, he appeared to be in relatively good spirits for someone going through the upheaval of a revolution.

'It has been like living in the Middle Ages,' he said, his face taut with tension but strangely electric. We have not been able to use our mobile phones or the internet. We cannot go to work because of the curfew. Most shops and businesses are closed. There are no police on the streets or anyone directing traffic. It is chaos.'

'So, what have you been doing?' I asked, having imagined him toppling a bronze statue of President Mubarak on horseback in Tahrir Square or getting teargassed while throwing chunks of concrete at riot police on the Sixth of October Bridge.

'It is very boring,' he sighed. 'I am going crazy. I sleep during the day and watch TV. In the evening, I go outside with the other guys to make sure no one comes into our street to steal or make trouble.

We light a fire and smoke *sheesha*. It has become like a coffee shop atmosphere. The women make hot drinks and sandwiches and bring them to us.'

On a number of occasions, I'd tried to ascertain on which side of the political fence Gamal sat. But he was cagey.

'I am a journalist,' he would say. 'I must remain neutral.'

As a left-wing hippy from way back, it goes without saying that I'd rather drink from a poisoned chalice than sleep with the enemy—a conservative party voter. Yet here I was, clearly blinded by love, hooking up with someone whose political inclinations could be, for all I knew, to the far right of Genghis Khan. Employed in a high-ranking position in a government department, Gamal's father had close ties to the ruling elite; his son's career, should he choose to go down the same path, a fait accompli. The current situation did not bode well for Gamal; his well-laid, nepotistic plans for his illustrious future were rapidly slipping through his fingers.

'Aren't you pleased with this revolution?' I asked. 'What about Mubarak and the corruption and torture? What about the state of your country—the poverty and illiteracy?'

'Yes, yes, I know,' Gamal replied gloomily. 'You are right. Things could not continue as they were. I am proud that the Egyptian people have done this. But there will be a price to pay. It will be many years before things are back to normal. But tell me something,' he said in a small voice so far away, his face a pale and distorted ghost on my computer screen. 'Do you love me?'

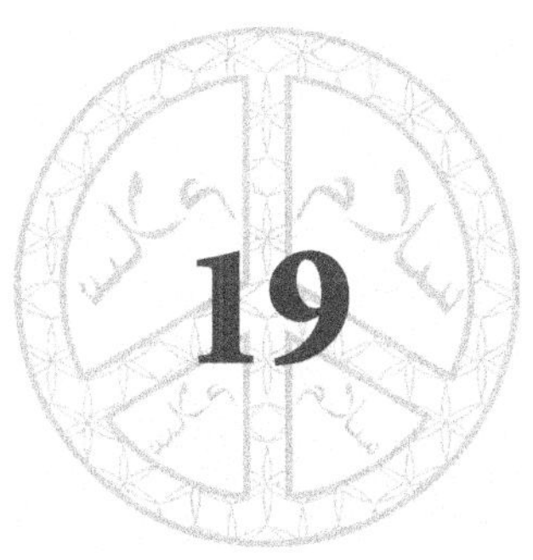

19

Biscuit

Ten weeks later I was back in Cairo, about to spend a whole two months with Gamal. Everything had gone according to plan. In a whirlwind of activity, I'd managed to complete the work for a solo exhibition in Melbourne. My representing galleries in Australia were stocked with a selection of paintings in case the global financial crisis abated and art began selling again. Back in Egypt, President Mubarak had left the stage, the military forming an interim government. The Australian Department of Foreign Affairs had downgraded its travel warning for the region to a more user-friendly 'travel with caution'. The volcano in Iceland that had grounded thousands of flights had petered out. I was good to go.

Gamal had warned me that, apart from a bit of handholding, we wouldn't be able to display physical affection to one another when we met at the airport or in fact anywhere else in public. We risked arrest, he said. So, after a curt and courteous greeting, we loaded my suitcases onto a luggage trolley and quickly exited the terminal.

Outside the airport, a very different scene from my last visit to

Cairo awaited. Grim-faced soldiers in full battle gear atop army tanks with water cannons seemingly aimed at the passing cars, lined the highway as we sped back to Gamal's father's apartment in New Cairo City. When I took out my Nikon, Gamal almost ran off the road.

'Oh, my God! Are you *crazy*?' he exclaimed. 'You cannot take photographs. It is the *army*! They will arrest you. They are here for a show of military strength.'

Got it, I thought, quickly pushing the camera under the car seat. Note to self: to avoid arrest and possible torture and/or execution do not kiss in public or take photographs of tanks. That wimp Brigitte Jones thought she had it tough!

Exiting the freeway, we merged into the maze of streets, the traffic a mess. With only a handful of traffic lights and millions of vehicles, Cairo was pandemonium at the best of times. But since the revolution, fearful of reprisals from the people, the generally despised Egyptian police were unwilling to return to their duties, leaving no one to direct the staggering number of cars, trucks, pedestrians, motorbikes, donkeys and carts and sometimes, herds of goats, on the roads. At one intersection, young men in jeans and T-shirts had bravely and conscientiously taken it upon themselves to direct the four or five lanes of honking and careening automobiles bearing down on them from all directions.

Eventually, we made it to New Cairo City and Gamal parked the car outside his father's apartment block, pointing out his own flat across the other side of the street. We grabbed my luggage from the boot and bundled it and ourselves into the stuffy shoe-box of a lift in the foyer; hips and lips locked in a passionate embrace as we rose to the top floor of the building. The lift doors parted and rearranging my clothing, I stepped out onto the landing, bracing myself to meet the Bahar family as, opening the front door, Gamal ushered me into the apartment.

I found myself standing in a bright and spacious room filled with reproduction baroque sofas and formal armchairs; an elegant chaise lounge upholstered in bands of cream and burgundy satin and adorned with a staggered row of tasselled cushions took pride of place. Faux rococo vases and chintz porcelain ornaments jostled for position on a carved mahogany sideboard and a collection of bow-legged occasional tables. On one wall, a heavy floor-to-ceiling reproduction colonial TV unit was adorned with an assortment of faded stuffed toys, on another, a gilt-framed 'chocolate box' land-scape hung above a plush, red velour couch. It was late afternoon. Slanted sunbeams together with imperceptible drifts of air filtered through the gauze curtains causing a cut-glass chandelier to deli-cately tinkle and shards of rainbow light to waltz across the Persian carpets that graced the grey and white marble tiled floor.

The artist in me would have liked more time to take in my surroundings but I needed to focus my jet-lagged attention. I was being presented to Gamal's siblings—kid brother, Tarik, and sisters, Safiya and Halima. Unveiled behind closed doors, black, unruly tresses cascading over their shoulders, the young women welcomed me with air kisses and greetings in English. Safiya was a beauty— tall and slender with startling grey eyes, a long, fawn-like neck and cheekbones to rival a Nubian limestone bust. Halima was tiny like me. Set in the face of a child, her dark eyes shone shyly above dimples that appeared on either side of her mouth when she smiled. Shaking my hand, the lanky Tarik, a Middle Eastern equivalent of Bronte's brooding Heathcliff, excused himself with a bow, gesturing that his English wasn't up to conversation level.

When Safiya asked if I'd like to see the rest of the apartment, I followed her and Halima down the hallway to the bedrooms, noticing with interest that the girls shared one room and Tarik and Gamal shared the other. Having divorced the mother of his children, not once but twice, Gamal's father Abdul had the master bedroom to himself while his ex-wife lived in an apartment down the street. Gamal's uncle Ibrahim lived in a flat across the landing, an aunt lived downstairs and cousins Ahmed and Mohammed lived around the corner.

Leaving Gamal and I alone on the couch, the sisters disappeared into the kitchen to make tea and I grabbed the opportunity to question Gamal about his living arrangements. Obviously, he didn't reside in his flat over the road. He lived here with his family. I knew he'd installed a new bathroom and kitchen in his apartment so I'd be comfortable during my visit and I'd assumed he'd be staying with me there. Keeping me updated on Skype during our ten-week separation, he hadn't, in all our communications, suggested otherwise.

'I have to tell you something,' Gamal whispered anxiously. 'We will not be able to stay together in my apartment.'

'*What!*' I said far too loudly. 'Are you *serious*?'

It would be an understatement that I'd been longing, especially after the cloak-and-dagger antics in Luxor, to sleep with Gamal at night, to wake up with him in the morning, have lazy and luxurious morning sex, go out for breakfast on the weekends, read the paper— do the things that couples do in Australia.

'We will be able to spend most of the evening with each other in my flat and you know … do stuff,' Gamal said, trying desperately to calm me down. 'But I must return to my father's apartment to sleep or else it would be a scandal for my family. The neighbours will gossip. We are not married.'

'Why didn't you tell me about this?' I hissed.

But I already knew the answer. Gamal was afraid I might not have returned to Egypt had I known the situation. Amazed at how quickly I found myself making excuses based on his youth and inexperience, I immediately adjusted my notion of how things were going to be during my time in Cairo. The extent of the differences in our cultures was beginning to hit home.

'What does your family think I'm *doing* here?' I asked, trying to keep my voice down.

'They know only that you are my guest and that I am hosting you while you are in Egypt,' he replied.

Our conversation was cut short when the sisters came back with the refreshments, following which I was led to Uncle Ibrahim's apartment across the hall to meet him and Gamal's mother, Naheema. As Gamal made the introductions, I watched Naheema's eyes glance anxiously from me to her son as she tried to gauge the nature of the relationship between him and the middle-aged, divorced, foreign woman, an infidel what's more, who had suddenly materialised into her life. Up until that point I hadn't been particularly nervous. I'd had no time. But now, wanting to make a good impression and start off on the right foot, my stomach fluttered like a moth trapped in a jar. It was Gamal's mother, after all. Clad in a caramel-coloured, polyester, buttoned-to-the-neck blazer and matching full-length skirt, Nahemma was dressed in a floral print hijab; a scuffed pair of Nikes on her feet. Her face, greyish and etched with lines, made her seem beyond middle age but I knew she wasn't a lot older than me. A few of Naheema's teeth were missing, the remainder in bad shape. Raising four children while teaching full-time had obviously taken its toll, not to mention the consequences to one's health living in a developing nation.

'I worry about my mother,' Gamal told me when we were alone. 'She lives on cups of tea, boiled potatoes and white cheese; recently she began to sleep on the floor because her doctor said it would cure her osteoporosis. She is still angry about the way she was treated by my father and his family before the divorce. I think that is why she has eczema.'

I warmed to Uncle Ibrahim immediately. Although he wasn't fluent in English and was forced to communicate mostly through his nephew, I got the sense the feeling was mutual. Ibrahim sported a sparse comb-over, his bright eyes twinkling through a pair of geeky steel-rimmed glasses. As a university professor, he'd devoted his life to teaching and had never married; according to Gamal, he hadn't had a girlfriend or even so much as kissed a woman either.

'Is he gay?' I asked Gamal.

'No,' he replied, laughing at the audacity of my question. Extreme homophobia being the status quo in Egypt, it was unthinkable that his uncle, or anyone else for that matter, could be homosexual.

'Ibrahim cared for his mother all her life,' he explained. 'Out of respect for her, he did not want to bring another woman into the house in case there was conflict. When she died he was too shy and stuck in his ways to go out and find a wife.'

By the time we made it across the street to Gamal's apartment and my home for the next two months, I was shattered from the long-distance flight and some rather intensive socialising. Nevertheless, reunited and alone at last, my young lover and I had one more thing to attend to before I could pass out. Desperate for each other after weeks apart, we dumped my luggage inside the front door and headed straight to the bedroom.

XXX

The insistent wail of the call to prayer was determined to wake me at dawn, but I'd merely opened one bleary eyelid and slipped back into heavenly unconsciousness, semi-accustomed from my last visit, as I was, to its insistence. When eventually I woke, alone, as stipulated by Islam, I got up to investigate the apartment. In a positive light, you could have described it as Minimalist but if you were a spoilt, affluent Western woman, you might have called it Spartan or even bleak, although the bathroom and kitchen were brand new and for that I was grateful. Bless his Egyptian cotton socks, I thought lovingly. As the ex-wife of a builder, I knew how expensive renovating could be and I calculated that Gamal had spent a lot on fixtures and tradesmen. Supervising the work whilst holding down two jobs must have been stressful in such a short timeframe. But true to character, Gamal had been too polite to mention the cost and had never complained about the work involved.

The bedroom housed an old double bed with a carved wooden bedhead, a rusty, metal army issue wardrobe, its doors seized permanently open, and a plastic outdoor table with a couple of matching chairs. An ancient and minuscule television sat on the white-tiled floor; while from the ceiling, a naked spiral light globe dangled on a frayed cord. The second bedroom was empty apart from some building materials stacked against the walls. A large reception room housed its only occupant, a lumbering, elderly fridge, coughing away asthmatically in the corner, too obese to be accommodated in the tiny kitchen that consisted of a single-bowl sink and a two-ring cooktop hooked up to a dodgy-looking gas bottle.

Eagerly, I flung open a large pair of frosted windows; the whiff of cumin and barbequed meat wafting up from a kitchen somewhere. Down below, a man in a long green robe and a white turban was selling oranges from his donkey and cart; two young boys throwing stones at one another in, what appeared to be, some kind of game. Walking in pairs, veiled schoolgirls chatted on their mobile phones and a few gangly teenage boys with darting eyes leaned against a wall smoking cigarettes. Over the road a woman beat a rug with a broom, a bearded man in a gallabiyah and skullcap bore a tray stacked high with flatbread and a mother in a niqab bent to scold her son; the odd car, Egyptian pop songs blaring from its open window, tooting as it wove its way through heedless pedestrians and a minefield of sandy potholes. I immediately claimed the room as my studio. Delighted to have been invited to participate in an Art Biennale in Turkey before leaving Australia, I decided it was a perfect space to do the work.

Although Gamal would have begged to differ, I didn't consider myself to be a delicate and easily breakable 'biscuit'—the Egyptian term for what we in the West call a 'princess'. My stint as a hard-core hippy in the Australian bush had trained me for such basic living conditions. But since then I'd become a bit soft, preferring, wherever possible, not to forgo my creature comforts. I began to write a mental list of the items I'd need to make the apartment liveable for the next two months.

Top priority was a decent mattress. There was no way my back was going to handle eight weeks of sleeping and other activities on the rollicking hills and deep valleys of the clapped-out piece of foam on the bed—I'd be a cripple in a week. I needed some candles as a substitute for the interrogation-room lighting, to create the romantic ambience a woman of a certain age requires, especially when entertaining a gentleman half her age. Incredulously, there was only one power point in each room, so a power board was essential. I definitely had to get another television set to replace the unwatchable piece of junk Gamal had dug up from God knows where. I also needed a worktable in the studio, an electric kettle and a mirror. I would've liked a rug on the ceramic tile floor but I realised I was getting carried away; my nesting instincts always try to get the better of me.

'You are so biscuity,' Gamal teased indulgently, patiently following me around the department store as I purchased my items.

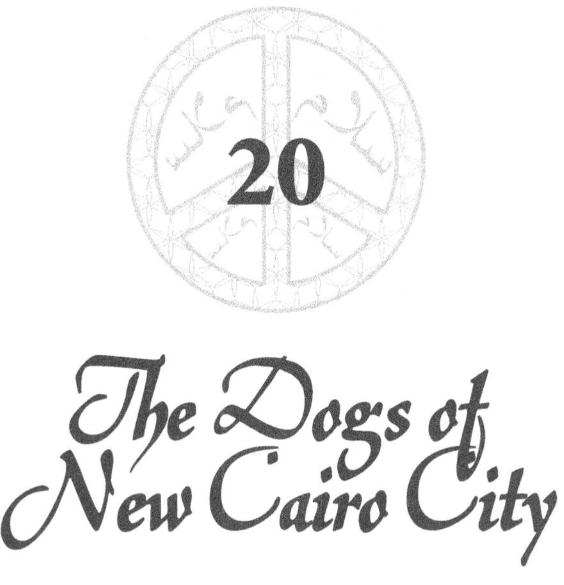

20

The Dogs of New Cairo City

Like a soldier in a desert war, the apartment block stood to attention at the edge of the desert when Abdul Bahar brought his young family to live in the satellite suburb of New Cairo City in the year of 1987. Its foundations dug deep, the five-story building held steadfast on the frontline amid a merciless blitzkrieg of sand. It wasn't until years later, when identical buildings positioned themselves all around it that it could drop its guard and stand at ease, knowing, as every war-weary warrior knows, there is safety in numbers.

'*Come*! Hurry up,' Gamal's father growled. With a baby on each hip and wary of aggravating her prematurely greying husband's permanent state of irritation any further, Naheema quickly shepherded the tottering Gamal into the tiny lift and slowly and laboriously the family rose to the apartment on the top floor. As an adolescent, Gamal would ride the lift alone, scrutinising himself in the mirror on the back wall of the airless cubicle—sucking in stomach muscles, expanding pectorals and flexing burgeoning biceps on the way up; checking nostrils, patting down curls and counting chest hairs on the way down. There was never a need to inspect his perfect white teeth.

✖ ✖ ✖

Naheema hung the 'chocolate box' painting on the wall above the red velour couch; three-year-old Gamal was entranced. Gazing at the picture from beneath, he'd find himself floating skywards and entering the idyllic scene—a rustic log cabin nestled beside a gentle stream on the fringe of an enchanted forest. There he would run through the emerald green grass, paddle in the bubbling brook or lie under the old oak tree looking up at the Constable clouds above. Deeper into the landscape, way beyond the bounds of the picture frame, he'd roam; through woodlands where fat rabbits hopped, birds flitted and a wolf stalked a pretty blonde-haired girl in a cherry-red chador. At the top of the hill, he'd scan the lush valley below before reluctantly making his way down the fragrant, flower-dotted slope and back to his life in the desert.

In those days, there weren't many shops or services in New Cairo City—just a bakery, a pharmacy, a grocery store, a hairdresser, a coffee shop and of course, a mosque. With the roads mostly empty of cars and people, Gamal could run wild with his friends: playing soccer or 'War of Stones' until inevitably one of the kids would sustain an injury, whereupon his mother would charge out of her apartment block and come looking for blood.

Grounded and confined to indoors after such incidents, Gamal would resort to playing war games with a militia of kitchen knives, spoons and forks. As a knife in one hand attacked a spoon in the other, the Commander-in-Chief of his Army of Cutlery would decide who would live and die. Infuriated with the sound of clashing metal, Abdul would abandon his prayers and storm from his room to reprimand his son. Gamal would then be forced to play the quieter yet no less intriguing 'Army of Cards' game where the chance landing of the King of Spades or the Jack of Diamonds decided the fate of the card soldiers and the outcome of the war. Bored with these solitary military operations and, careful not to provoke his father's wrath, Gamal would enlist his younger siblings to re-enact, in mime, a famous Egyptian movie. The plot an old family favourite in which an Egyptian national is arrested by the Security Force's Intelligence Agency and executed by firing squad for selling information to Israel.

On graduating from university, like most young Egyptian men his age, Gamal had no choice but to undertake his two years of compulsory military service in the army. Marching over the scorching hot sand dunes, assault rifle clutched in his blistered hands, yelled at this time not by his father but by his commanding officer, he would think back with fondness to those childhood games in the living room.

I'd been in Cairo for three whole days before I met Abdul, Gamal's father's daily routine making him difficult to encounter. At midday, he'd leave for the office, returning in the evening to eat the food prepared by his daughters before taking a nap in his room. Next, he'd rise, walk around the corner to the local coffee shop to play backgammon or chess and then come home to pray until dawn. After a few hours' sleep, it was time to get up and go to work again.

With eyes respectfully downcast (the proper way to receive a woman according to Egyptian custom), Abdul bent at the waist and extended his hand in greeting. It was then that I noticed the tell-tale 'prayer bruise' of the devout staining his brow.

'Hello. How are you?' he said gruffly, his thin lips trying their best to form a smile but not quite getting there. Perhaps that was the extent of his English or maybe he disapproved of my presence, because with another small bow Abdul excused himself and left the room.

Although Naheema and Ibrahim would occasionally invite me for afternoon tea, and the girls, when I bumped into them, would engage me in polite conversation, that was the extent of my interaction with Abdul for the entire two months of my sojourn in Cairo. Even when I turned on my renowned charm, on the rare occasions I saw him, I was unable to coax any blood from that man of stone.

One evening, as Gamal and I lounged on the couch watching an old black and white Egyptian movie on TV, Abdul burst from his bedroom demanding that Gamal tell Safiya not to go in there while he was praying.

'How come he doesn't tell her himself?' I asked Gamal when the disgruntled fellow had retreated. 'Why do you have to do it?'

'I am the eldest son. It is my duty,' he replied.

Over the next few weeks, I was fascinated to observe the family dynamics in action. Expecting neither rent nor board, Abdul provided for his offspring and would do so until they married and left home. Halima and Safiya did all the shopping, cooking, washing up and laundry, but a maid came once a week to clean the apartment, beat the rugs and change the bed linen. My thoughtful host would enquire if I'd like a cup of tea, then ask his sisters to make it. If the doorbell rang, Gamal would call the girls from the other end of the apartment to answer it despite the fact he was sitting a metre from the front door. Having eaten his dinner, Gamal would sit back and watch TV or go out without a thought to the dirty dishes left in his wake. Maybe he believed a genie came in the night and that food miraculously appeared in the fridge and cupboards—everything cleaned, cooked and washed as if by magic.

He's in for a shock if we ever live together, I thought. There was no way I'd be waiting on him hand and foot. Like most Western men in this day and age, he'd have to pull his weight on the domestic front.

But Gamal's sense of entitlement wasn't entirely his fault. On producing her children, Naheema returned to work; the task of raising her cluster of dark-haired cherubs falling to Gamal's portly, illiterate, salt-of-the-earth grandmother. In her eyes, her grandson was on a par with the Egyptian Sun God, Ra and she indulged his every whim and desire. If Gamal felt like skipping school he had only to sidle up to his grandmother's wide and sheltering side, bat his long lashes and feign frailty, the old dear straight on the phone to her daughter telling her the boy was too sick to go. Although suspecting foul play, Naheema would be forced to acquiesce, knowing she couldn't argue with the matriarch of the family. Should Gamal want a new game or a book his grandmother would instruct her daughter to purchase them. When he needed money to buy sweets or a Coke, his adoring *teta* would not deny him. If he was hungry for pizza she would make his sisters go out and buy it. When his grandmother died, it was Gamal who carried her large, muslin-wrapped body into the family tomb to lay it tenderly on the ledge beside the parched bones of his ancestors.

The getting of religion, however, fell to Gamal's father. When Gamal turned five Abdul gave him a copy of the Qur'an and his own little prayer mat; teaching the boy how to prostrate, pray and focus his mind on Allah the Merciful. Every Friday, answering the call to prayer emanating from the balcony of a minaret across the district, hand-in-hand father and son would make their solemn weekly pilgrimage through the sandy streets to the local mosque. Standing proudly with the other men and boys in the spacious and muted atmosphere, Gamal felt he was in the presence of something Big and Special. But at home, his practice was sporadic. His father never forced him to observe his spiritual duties so it wasn't until early adolescence, at that highly receptive and often self-righteous age when it all seemed to coalesce and Gamal began, of his own volition, to read the Qur'an and pray in earnest.

Gamal wasn't just a spoilt child, he was naughty too. Some nights, when everyone was asleep, he'd scramble out of bed, slip on a T-shirt, tracksuit pants and a pair of thongs which the Egyptians call flip-flops—like the rest of the world. Avoiding the clunky lift, he'd sneak down the internal stairwell to steal his mother's car, cousins Mohammed and Ahmed waiting for him in their mothers' cars at the agreed rendezvous. Together, the seemingly driverless vehicles— as the boys could barely see over the dashboard—would set off in a meandering convoy to patrol the deserted streets of the slumbering suburb.

Past the boarded-up tobacco stand on the corner, the domed mosque luminescent in the moonlight and the open-air coffee shop, its flimsy plastic tables and chairs stacked under the striped canvas awning, they'd cruise. Past the communal rubbish heap where emaciated cats with tails bent at abnormal angles (betraying some prior hellish suffering) poked gingerly around in the putrid contents of the disembowelled plastic bags, the wretched feline descendants of a once glorious era unaware of their former god-like status. Past the hairdresser-cum-beauty salon where a faded billboard of a swinging sixties Middle Eastern belle with a coiffed bob and a blue velvet headband glowed under the weak fluorescent light, they'd drive.

In the dead of the night, the empty streets became the domain of The Dogs of New Cairo City. Fierce territorial battles, heard but not witnessed by the human residents raged as rival packs of canines fought for supremacy, the mangy creatures slinking off as the boys' cavalcade approached. Perched high on the edge of their seats, their feet barely reaching the accelerator pedals, the dark locks on their angelic heads scarcely protruding above the arc of their steering wheels, the eight-year-old car thieves would imagine themselves to be soldiers in the legendary Egyptian Army on the hunt for Zionist insurgents. After parking the car precisely where his mother had left it the day before, the young hero would creep back to bed, clutching his toy pistol as he drifted off to sleep.

Even greater opportunities for entertainment than Gamal's regular activities were provided at the conclusion of Ramadan, *Eid Al Fitr*—the fast-breaking-feast—where the whole family would come together to eat *kahk*, an icing-sugar-dusted, honey-filled semolina cookie traditionally eaten with cups of tea at the end of the fast. Hiding on the balcony of the Bahars' fifth-floor apartment, pockets bulging with firecrackers, Gamal and his car-thieving cousins had a bird's-eye view of the street and the arrival of their relatives below. Before anyone had a chance to enter the lobby, a shower of exploding firecrackers would rain down from above, aunties and uncles whooping and squealing, leaping on each other to avoid the detonating bungers. When the smoke became too much to bear, one of the aunties would lose her cool and call for a ceasefire. Upstairs the victory cries of the little assailants rang out over the neighbourhood.

'*Allah Akbar*!' they would yell. 'God Is Great!'

✕✕✕

I began to call my boyfriend 'The Little Prince'.

'What do you actually *do* to contribute to this household?' I asked one day, sounding like a typical Australian mother, as opposed to an Egyptian mother who would never dream of questioning the imperial-like privileges of her eldest son. What was I thinking behaving like a mother anyway? I brushed away the uncomfortable observation.

'I do a lot,' Gamal confidently replied.

'Like what?' I prodded.

'I am here to protect my sisters,' he responded haughtily.

'If the family car needs servicing I take it to the garage,' he continued.

'Sometimes I buy bread on the way home from work. I, I…' he faltered, grasping at papyrus stalks.

'Is that *it*?' I goaded him, unable to help myself.

'I do a lot,' Gamal repeated with that winning, lopsided and wolfish grin he no doubt employed to charm his grandmother and all the other bewitched and bedazzled women who fell under his spell. He knew full well he had the better end of the deal. Always had, always would.

'Come. Give me a kiss,' he said, pulling me roughly to his bear-like chest and engulfing me in his beefy arms.

One evening, after he got home from work, Gamal explained the Islamic system of inheritance.

'In my family, where there are two sons and two daughters, Tarik and I will receive one third each of the inheritance and Halima and Safiya will share the balance. In a family where there is one son and one daughter, the son receives two thirds, his sister one.

'What's the reasoning behind this arrangement?' I enquired with barely disguised polite restraint.

'It is a very clever and sensible system,' Gamal replied with supreme self-assurance. 'In our society, when a son marries, he has all the responsibility and must provide for his wife and children. When my sisters marry, they will not need the money my brother or I will need to support a family. It is obvious,' he said.

'But what if the girls don't want to get married or nobody wants to marry them,' I asked.

'If my sisters are not married by the time my father dies, it is my responsibility to take care of them. There are laws to make sure I do this.'

So even if you're married, they'll come to live with you, I was about to ask before Abdul called out to Gamal from his room, wondering, as he went to see what his father wanted, how that arrangement would work for his wife.

Apart from work, university or wandering around shopping malls with their mother, Safiya and Halima rarely went out. They seemed to spend a lot of time in their bedroom, propped up in bed with their laptops—surfing the net, chatting on Facebook or watching Turkish soap operas online; rising intermittently to throw on a hooded, sack-like, flower patterned 'prayer dress' over their clothes and pray. Despite their prettiness and other charming attributes, there was no one banging down the door to get to them as far as I could see. I couldn't imagine how on earth they were ever going to meet someone and get married.

One day, I suggested to Gamal that we invite his sisters to join us for a day out. The girls jumped at the opportunity and early on a Friday morning we set off for the 14th century Khan El Khalili souq in Old Islamic Cairo. Entering the souq through an archaic and ornate stone arch, we stepped into a bygone world; exotic; mysterious; Middle Eastern. My skin prickled. I could feel the buzz and excitement of the place, drawing me towards the countless treasures within.

Far bigger than the market in Luxor but with the same aromatic scent, the bazaar was a fascinating and confusing labyrinth of twisting alleyways swarming with Egyptians and tourists alike. Stalls laden with gallabiyahs, painted glass water pipes, bright coloured headscarves, prayer rugs, essential oils, carved and inlaid timber boxes, metal pinprick lanterns, papyrus paintings, hammered brass plates and belly dancing outfits glittering with sequins and hand sewn metal coins, were punctuated with restaurants, spice merchant stands, coffee shops and traditional ateliers where goldsmiths and metal workers nimbly plied their craft; their finely-honed skills passed down from father to son since the Middle Ages.

After two hours, I needed a break. Gamal led the way through the crush, hubbub and clammy heat to an oasis—the famous two-hundred-year-old, mirrored and smoke-enveloped El Fishawy coffee shop. I'd had three glasses of sweet mint tea before the coals in Gamal's apple-flavoured sheesha died and, as we wandered back out into the bazaar, the call to prayer began blaring from the minaret of a nearby mosque—four loudspeakers, pointing in four directions to ensure no Muslim within cooee could miss it. Simultaneously and without a word, Gamal and his sisters turned and began walking towards an ancient stone-walled mosque on the corner. For a moment the girls disappeared, quickly returning with a headscarf they'd bought for me to wear so I could enter the building and observe the proceedings. I followed Halima and Safiya to the back of the cavernous edifice and stood silently to one side as they bowed, prostrated and prayed; their brother joining a small congregation of stooping and kneeling men at the elaborate front end of the building. To witness such devotion in such a sacred place was a humbling experience, bringing my own lack of spiritual conviction into stark contrast. When the girls and I came out to wait for Gamal, I was still wearing the headscarf; my lover's face, when he appeared from the shadows and caught sight of me, a picture. I thought he would melt.

Unfortunately, attempting to explain his family dynamics was about to become the least of Gamal's concerns. Since the Arab Spring uprising, like many Egyptians, he hadn't been paid; employers were using the revolution as an excuse to withhold wages. Then when his anchor-woman's television show was axed, she being seen as a hated puppet of the former regime, Gamal lost his job. Barely able to exist on his meagre income from the Ministry of Culture, the position also vulnerable due to the volatile political situation, his immediate prospects looked grim.

Despite his faith in God's will, Gamal was embarrassed to be in such a predicament. Although I assured him I didn't mind covering our costs while I was in Cairo it was unacceptable, he said, for an Egyptian man to take money from a woman.

'What must you think of me,' he said dejectedly. 'I am hopeless.'

'Are you crazy?' I chastised him. 'It's a temporary setback. With your qualifications and experience, you're bound to get another job,' I added encouragingly, dragging him to his laptop to look online.

Miraculously, without even having to ask the Arabian genie, we found something—a newly advertised position with a multinational media organisation in Cairo. It was the pot of gold at the end of every journalist's rainbow. Despondent and disheartened at that low point in his short life, Gamal allowed me to nag him, as would any good Egyptian wife, until he submitted an application.

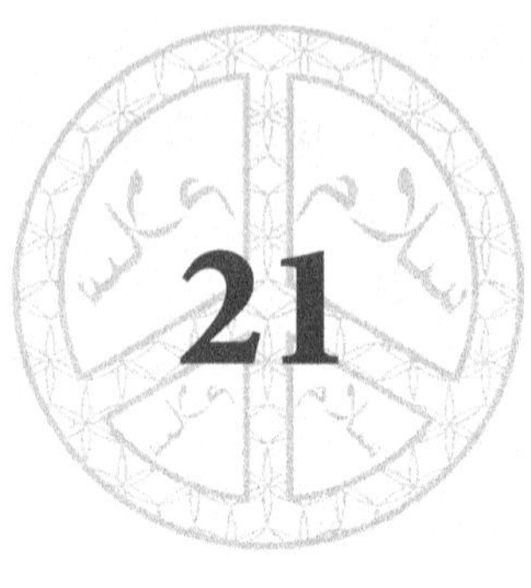

21

Camelot

'It was terrible, Katherine. I dropped you off at the airport and went back to the apartment and lay on the bed till it was time for prayers,' Gamal said mournfully when we recommenced our Skype routine within hours of my return to Melbourne. 'I could smell you on the pillow and I wanted to die. It is much harder for me than for you. I am the one who is always left behind.'

But had he been there to see me walk through the front door and into my flat in Melbourne following a miserable flight home, standing there alone and desolate with my suitcase and a sinking heart, he may have thought differently. I missed him like a lost limb.

Back in Australia, I set about organising my life so I could return to Egypt as soon as possible. Gamal and I agreed we'd try to see each other every two or three months until we worked out a strategy for being together on a more permanent basis. Once again, I faced family and friends concerned about my welfare—fearful of my forays into such a volatile region and alarmed that I was getting serious about someone living on the other side of the world; my mother concerned that I'd dipped into my limited savings and lost focus on my career in chasing my heart across the seas. Thinking I'd have come to my senses, she assumed that by now I would have decided against pursuing the relationship. No one could get their head around the age-difference thing and admittedly, I was tackling my own fears regarding that issue.

I tried to think of someone in similar circumstances: uber-cougar Madonna being the only name springing to mind. I recalled the movie *Harold and Maude*—a dark comedy from the seventies portraying a love affair between a dour young man and a spritely, much older woman. And I remembered that night at the Nubian restaurant in Luxor. Alone at a table adjacent to ours sat a po-faced, stocky middle-aged woman. I think she was English. With her plump forearms resting on the table, her chubby hands clasped around a sweating glass of Coke, the woman seemed indifferent to the lively performances of shimmying belly dancers, whirling dervishes and drumming Nubians. Instead, her eyes were fixed on the entrance to the restaurant. After a while, a lean, sullen-faced boy, he couldn't have been more than fifteen, accompanied by an elderly twig-thin man in a turban and gallabiyah, entered the room and approached the woman's table. The older man made some introductions, signalled to the boy to take a seat next to the woman and quickly left the restaurant. Focusing their attention on the floor show, the odd couple sat stiffly in silence. From where I was sitting I could see the boy's eyes. They reminded me of something I'd witnessed back in the Australian bush—the wild orbs of a terrified possum caught in a trap.

'What's going on there?' I asked Gamal, gesturing discreetly in the direction of the woman's table. He'd noticed the unfolding scene, too.

'The family of that boy will be poor,' he replied. 'The boy will have sex with the woman and she will pay his father a great deal of money. She will buy a temporary marriage certificate to make it legal and he will stay with her in her hotel room for a few days. Afterwards, the woman will buy the divorce papers and go back to her country.'

'Is this common?' I inquired.

'It is,' Gamal answered. 'Many older Western women come to holiday resorts like Luxor and Sharm El Sheik on the Red Sea to have sex with young Arab boys.'

I knew I wasn't paying for sex with an Egyptian boy; nevertheless, the thought of that woman and her tragic liaison left a disturbing impression.

✕✕✕

Another memory added to my reservations. Following the upheaval and trauma associated with my father's suicide, Mum felt and looked a wreck. Deciding to treat herself to a facelift, she found a reputable cosmetic surgeon in Melbourne to perform the procedure. Good on her, I thought, she'd been through hell. By that stage, I'd left home but one Friday night, soon after the operation, I went back to Bairnsdale for the weekend. I was making breakfast next morning when Mum woke up.

'Make us a cup of tea, will you, love,' she called from the bedroom. 'And bring my cigarettes,' she added.

By the time I brought in the tea, Mum was asleep again. Placing the mug and ciggies on the bedside table, I looked down upon her slumbering form and noticed the scars, like a line of tiny mouse tracks, behind her right ear. Other than that, my mother's transformation was miraculous; twenty years of time and stress erased from her face. Before long, my rejuvenated mum had a young boyfriend who seemed to genuinely love and care for her, even asking her to marry him. But Mum couldn't cope with the age difference and twelve months later, crazed with jealousy, she ended the relationship, never to go down that path again.

✕ ✕ ✕

With airfares to Egypt too expensive at the time, the next rendezvous with Gamal, three months since my last trip to Cairo, was in Vietnam. It was there I was confronted, like a smarting slap in the face, by the huge difference in our age. On our first day in Hanoi, Gamal and I took a cyclo to the French quarter.

'Where you from?' our wizened driver asked when I'd settled into his carriage.

'Australia,' I replied.

'Where *you* from?' he asked Gamal.

'Egypt,' Gamal told him.

'*You*, how old?' the man boldly inquired as he looked me up and down.

'Old,' I answered with an embarrassed chuckle.

'*You*, how old?' the man repeated his question to Gamal.

'Young,' Gamal tersely replied.

'You mummy?' the cyclo driver asked, looking directly at me as he stabbed his bony finger in the air at Gamal.

'*No!*' Gamal and I responded in unison, laughing at the audacity of our chauffeur's brazen interrogation. But I, for one, was not amused.

That evening, back at our hotel, Gamal noticed that I was quiet.

'Tell me,' he said, applying a communication technique we'd devised if one of us was out of sorts.

And it all came out.

I was too old for him, I blubbered. How can our relationship possibly survive, I asked? He should leave me and marry a good Muslim girl and have babies, I insisted.

Gamal listened patiently to my concerns, a deep furrow forming between his eyes before dismissing them out of hand.

'*Leave* you!' *Oh, my God!*' he exclaimed, his voice rising to a mezzo-soprano pitch. 'What are you saying? Do you think I am that kind of man? If you were in a car accident and became paralysed do you think I would leave you?'

'No,' I said tearfully, not doubting his sincerity, but at my age, with a lifetime of broken promises and disappointments under my belt, not altogether convinced he'd be there till the end.

'Then why would I leave you just because you became old? Please do not mention this again.' I sat quiet, trying to believe these noble sentiments, truly wanting to believe them, but a niggling doubt kept pecking away at the edges.

'Kathy,' Gamal said, gently pushing the hair out of my eyes, 'the longer we are together the more value you will have, the more history we will share and the closer we will become. Our relationship has gone beyond the physical. It is much more than that. I love you and, Insha'Allah, we will be together forever. Can I be frank with you?' he asked.

'Of course,' I said, blowing my nose into a soggy tissue.

'You have no idea what you represent to me,' he continued, handing me a clean one. 'You should know you are and always will be the most significant love of my life. You are the woman by whom I will measure all women. For as long as I live, I will not find anyone like you. Before we met, I would think about my ideal partner and what she would be like. It is true, I did not imagine she would be older than me. But then I found you and your age is irrelevant. I love you because you are Katherine not because of how old or how young you are,' he said, now dabbing my cheeks with a monogrammed napkin.

Though how could I believe him? I knew he meant what he was

saying, was being completely and utterly truthful about his feelings and intentions at that moment. But he didn't have the long view of a full and sometimes disheartening life, a life imbued with its necessary and innumerable experiences that give the farsightedness that troubled me now. He had no idea how things worked. Yet that was his saving grace.

Despite Gamal's reassurances, I became haunted with images of us in, ten, twenty, even thirty years' time. I began to feel as if I had a terminal illness called 'old age' and that our life together was limited. Like a scene in a movie, the camera would zoom in for a close-up (maybe not too close!): Gamal sitting at my hospital bed holding my gnarled, arthritic little hand, guaranteeing that after death we'd be together in Paradise for eternity. As my looks continued to deteriorate and I saw the passion die in my young lover's eyes, would I try to push him away? How could I bear to watch him watch me become frail, withered and possibly even senile? What sort of life would that be for Gamal? Am I being selfish? Should I let him go so he can find a younger, more appropriate match? What if he wants children one day? I'd ask myself, wrestling a host of loud and persistent demons.

'I understand why you are concerned and of course we can talk about it as much as you want,' Gamal said when I continued to dwell on the subject. 'But for me it is not an issue. Besides, I think it is the least of our worries at the moment,' he said dissolving my fears with that smile.

'Get over it, Mum,' I'm sure my hard-headed daughter would've said if she hadn't been so mortified by the age difference! I knew I was in danger of sabotaging what I had with Gamal if I became obsessed with the issue so I endeavoured, as much as possible, to stop fretting about what may or may not happen in the future and enjoy being in the relationship for however long it lasted. Reaping at least one benefit of the aging process, I tried to cultivate a philosophical approach. Nothing is permanent—thoughts, feelings, things; us, I reassured myself. Whatever the nature of a relationship, sooner or later someone will leave, get sick, become old, lose their wits or die.

By the same token, I was getting angry. Why, in our society is it considered unseemly for a woman to be with a younger man, when men are positively applauded for being with younger women? Who wrote that rule, I wondered? Differences in age, gender, race, culture, distance, religion, size, weight or anything for that matter—what did that have to do with love? And anyway, why Gamal wouldn't love me? After all, I was intelligent, funny, talented, attractive, a good person and, so I'd been told, great in bed. But I was also impetuous, hot-headed and many would say, especially in regard to my impossible love affair with Gamal, irrationally optimistic.

'Age is an issue of mind over matter. If you don't mind it doesn't matter,' said Mark Twain; and I tried to focus on those words of wisdom as I stood in front of the bathroom mirror slathering my face and décolletage with L'Oréal's Revitalift Laser X3 Power Serum.

✖ ✖ ✖

I was ten years old when I saw the musical *Camelot* at the Moondale Drive-in, a gigantic screen straddling a windswept paddock on the outskirts of Bairnsdale. Sitting in the back seat of the EK Holden in my flannelette nightie, chenille dressing-gown and fluffy pink slippers, sipping Fanta and sucking all the chocolate off my Maltesers, I faced a dilemma. It was impossible to choose between Franco Nero's young, gallant and zealous Sir Lancelot and Richard Harris's older, wiser and kind-hearted monarch, Arthur. I fell madly in love with them both.

'Oh, no, not in springtime, summer, winter, or fall. No, never could I leave you at all,' the ardent French knight serenaded his royal lover in her bed chamber.

'The way to handle a woman is to love her, simply love her, merely love her, love her, love her,' sang the cuckolded king alone in his castle tower.

I longed to be the object of their affection—Vanessa Redgrave's sorrowful and statuesque Queen Guinevere, who was, in my opinion, the epitome of womanhood and who, unbeknown to me at the time, was having a torrid off-screen affair with Nero while making the movie. At the end of the film, when they lopped Ginny's auburn locks and sent her packing to live out her celibate days in a nunnery, I was gutted.

A composite of my childhood idols, Gamal was different from anyone I'd ever met; far different from the Australian men I'd known. Young Aussie men would rather eat cut glass than be romantically involved with a woman my age. Furthermore, once having made the effort to land a girlfriend or get married, they seem to prefer to hang out with their mates, drink beer and watch footy. It's the Australian way. Despite their physical appeal, many have the emotional intelligence of a ferret and are about as romantic as … well … older Aussie blokes and/or ferrets (apologies to ferrets and the exceptions in the Australian male population for this gross generalisation). But generally speaking, I wasn't interested in young Australian men and they were certainly not interested in me.

I knew I still bore the scars from my relationship with my father and from what happened with John and Vicko. Reared on a diet of Grimm's fairy tales, romantic Hollywood movies, Top 40 love songs, Jane Austen and the Bronte sisters, I was aware that my understanding of the perfect man was based on a fantasy. I could see I was captivated, like many European women, by the idea of a passionate affair with a tall, dark and handsome Middle Eastern man. But it was too late for psychoanalysis now. I was in love with Gamal, not just with how he looked and spoke but also with who he was; with his sweetness, humility and constancy; with the way he loved me.

I don't know whether it was his formality of speech, his impeccable manners or his protective demeanour, but I often felt as if I was in the presence of someone from a past century. All he needed was a horse and a lance. At times, he seemed, in attitude if not in appearance, to be the grown-up in the relationship—me, the vivacious, impulsive, impatient and volatile one, him all pensive, earnest, steadfast and self-composed. My lover's devotion would've been legendary had we lived in the mythical, mediaeval Camelot and, after so many years an old wound was healing; my faith in the male of the species little by little, restored.

'What do you did to me?' Gamal would often exclaim, referring to the moment we met; often charmingly transposing the conjunction of the verb 'to do'.

And who knows, maybe we knew each other in a past life; reunited in a stand of fake palm trees in the brassy foyer of the Hotel Pyramisa. We could have been hummingbirds hovering over honeysuckle in a mountain meadow in Chile or frill-neck lizards running helter-skelter across the central Australian desert or once, early on in the interminable cycle of life and death, we may have been single-celled amoebae, clinging side-by-side to a slime-covered rock in a murky, primordial pool.

'Have you any idea what I have to do to stay looking good for you?' I'd rib my impatient boyfriend whenever he'd complain about how long I was taking to get ready to go out.

Basically, most men can shower, throw on some clothes, brush their teeth, run a comb through their hair and they're out the door. For women, those who choose to buy into the insanity of trying to keep up appearances for the opposite sex, it's a whole different ball game. Dieting, exercising and shopping for clothes, shoes and accessories aside, there's the plucking, manicuring, pedicuring, exfoliating, cleansing, toning, moisturizing, depilating, eyelash tinting and make-up applying; not to mention the hair dying, conditioning, blow drying and styling; fashion and beauty industries working around the clock to make us feel imperfect, inadequate and ashamed in order to sell their products. For me, the quest to remain attractive was becoming a time-consuming occupation and then there were the costs involved.

So far I hadn't been tempted to submit to the knife—the mere thought of it filled me with dread—but if our relationship endured, my insecurities might just push me to entertain the possibility; to follow my mother's example. Although Gamal assured me he didn't mind what I did to keep the advancing years at bay, I knew that ultimately, I was fighting a losing battle.

There was, however, one no-go zone I had to promise not to touch.

'Please do not do anything to these,' he said, stroking my breasts. 'They are perfect, and they belong to me.'

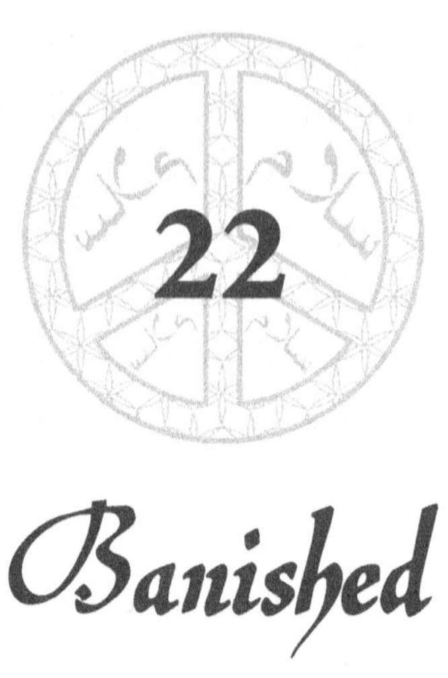

22

Banished

It was August the next time I flew to Cairo, stepping off the plane into a furnace. The following day I had an air conditioning unit installed in Gamal's apartment, knowing I wouldn't survive the next four weeks without it. Even for an Australian, an Egyptian summer is insufferable: no hope of a storm on the horizon, a refreshing downpour or a cool breeze blowing through an open window in the late afternoon; certainly no Fremantle doctor, or one of Melbourne's famous cool changes that can transform a parched and frazzled city into one awash following a thunderous deluge.

Instead, plastic bags filled with rotting rubbish sat in reeking heaps on the broken-up pavements of rubble. A poisonous infusion of exhaust fumes marinated the air; a grey film of dust coating every conceivable surface including skin, hair and teeth. With no desire to languish in Abdul's stifling apartment across the road or, unless absolutely necessary, endure the inferno on the streets, I tried, as far as possible, to stay indoors during daylight hours. As a consequence, although our paths occasionally and cordially crossed, I saw little of Gamal's family that trip.

Gamal and I did, however, manage a foray into the great outdoors during that stinking hot month—flying to the Sinai Peninsula to go snorkelling in the Red Sea. It was our first proper holiday and the first time we'd spent the entire night together. It was an expensive exercise, however. At the Sharm El Sheik Four Seasons Resort, graced with its own coral reef, we were required, as an unmarried couple in which one of us was an Egyptian national, to book separate rooms. From the hotel manager to the bellhop, everyone knew we'd be sleeping together in just one room. But that was irrelevant. As long as Gamal and I had checked in separately, the hotel was covered in the event of an Adultery Police raid.

Gamal had never experienced such luxury, never slept in a king-sized bed or even had a bubble bath. Mucking around in the spa, we made soap-sud beards, koala noses and frothy bras; giggling like kids in our fluffy white bathrobes as we wrestled on the over-sized and luxuriously soft mattress.

'Look at this!' my delighted lover exclaimed, his arms and legs flapping in windmills as I lay panting and defeated on the far side of the bed. 'It is so big we do not touch!'

One day we hired a chauffeur-driven car to take us snorkelling in the Ras Mohammad National Park, arriving an hour and a half later in an arid and alien landscape. We climbed out of the vehicle and stood on the gravel shore. The blistering sun bore down on the burnt orange earth; behind us a shimmering range of dusky purple mountains, before us the deep blue and sparkling Red Sea. I'd crossed the Nullarbor Plain in Australia but this was something else; no trace of vegetation or a sign of anything animal or human. Strangest of all was the silence. We were utterly alone. With a promise to return in four hours, our driver unloaded our gear and sped off in a cloud of grit.

Although I'd lived most of my life within easy reach of the Great Barrier Reef, I'd only ever seen coral in an aquarium.

'I'm going to be a while,' I warned Gamal as I adjusted my mask and flippers. 'I've wanted to do this my whole life.'

Already putting him out of my mind, I dipped into the tepid water and began snorkelling towards the infinite expanse of ultramarine some hundred metres away. With the sound of my beating heart and laboured breath resonating in my ears, I passed over the coral cliff and into another realm, weightlessly suspended in an ethereal LED-like blue light void. Turning to look at the reef that dropped to an unfathomable depth below, I came face-to-face with a wall of psychedelic colour; an immense and throbbing city built entirely of domed and branching castles of fuchsia, tangerine, turquoise and lemon, so vivid you could have sworn it was a high definition digital animation. Any second, I expected Nemo to pop out from behind a coral polyp to say hi. In the blinking Impressionist light, a kaleidoscope of thousands of pinstriped, polka-dotted, herring-boned and highly accessorised fish, some right on trend, choosing to colour block in primaries, flitted in, out and over the aquatic metropolis.

'Oh, my God, this is *awesome*!' I screamed into my mouthpiece as I propelled myself along the reef, uttering a term I'd never use on dry land. Now I knew the secret to Kandinsky's brilliance: the guy was clearly a snorkeller!

After a while, I surfaced to check on Gamal. Astonishingly, my diving buddy had deserted me, having made his way back to the beach—the call of the wild proving too much for the city slicker from Cairo. I couldn't believe he didn't want to spend every second in the water. But I had no time to worry about what he was doing. With a trillion fish and acres of coral to see before our driver returned, once more I duck-dived down into the crystal-clear depths.

Eventually emerging from the underwater wonderland, I swam towards my lover as he waded about in the shallows.

'Hey, let's skinny dip,' I called out as I came closer.

'*What*?' he yelled back, his chest expanding in indignation, his hand gravitating towards his groin. 'Why you are calling me a skinny dick?'

'Skinny *dip*, not *dick,*' I said laughing as I reached his side. 'We take off our costumes and swim naked,' I explained. 'Wouldn't you like to feel free and be at one with nature?'

'Are you *serious*? We cannot do *this*!' Gamal exclaimed. 'What if someone sees us?'

'Are you kidding?' I replied, cupping my brow, squinting as I pretended to scan the horizon. 'Don't be so silly. We're in the middle of nowhere,' I said as, ignoring the horrified look on his face, I took off my swimmers and flung them in a careless arc onto the sand before gliding into the water to float spread-eagled and bare-breasted in the warm and buoyant sea.

It took a few minutes to convince Gamal to strip, but I knew he was only doing it to please me as, reluctantly, he removed his shorts and bobbed around miserably in the water for a moment before hastily getting dressed again.

✕✕✕

We were packing for the flight back to Cairo when Gamal received a text message.

'I've been shortlisted for that journalism job. The one I applied for, months ago,' he calmly announced, never one, when it came to the cutthroat world of his profession at least, to get his hopes up.

'And?' I asked, knowing that if he got the job it would dramatically change the course of events; wondering about the implications for our relationship.

'I have agreed to attend the interview,' he replied. 'We will see what happens.'

At home, Gamal had found full-time work as a political analyst in a media monitoring company and, having negotiated a deal with another TV station, his former anchor-woman boss, ex-puppet of the Mubarak regime, was back on air, hiring Gamal to work for her again; the arbitrary nature of the machinations of contemporary Egyptian life, a mystery to me.

Before I left Egypt, we'd arrived at a major decision. I'd return to Australia, pack up my life and come back to Cairo to marry Gamal. Apart from the polite but uncommunicative Abdul, the rest of the family, despite the fact I hadn't spent a great deal of time with them, seemed quite fond of me. When Gamal assured me that they had no objections to us marrying, I breathed a sigh of relief. I was apprehensive at the thought of leaving my family but I consoled myself with the knowledge that I'd fly home as often as I could to see them. Marriage was something I never expected to commit to again. I read all the online forums and accounts written by Western women who'd married Egyptian men, some tales of horror and woe, others stories of love and devotion. But with de facto relationships *haram* (forbidden) for Muslims, I swallowed my qualms. Unless we were married, there was no way Gamal and I could live together in Egypt. As an artist, I figured I could work anywhere in the world. It would be less detrimental for me to uproot my existence than for Gamal to abandon his emerging career in Cairo. At the critical beginning of his working life, he'd be taking a huge risk coming to Australia where he might wind up cooking kebabs for a living. I did *not* want the responsibility of jeopardising his career in journalism before it had even properly begun.

Back in Australia after the now familiar, heart-wrenching farewell, exacerbated by the prohibition on expressing it openly at the airport, my life went into overdrive. I had two months to prepare for an exhibition in Los Angeles, pack and freight the work, move out of the apartment I was renting with Lisa, sell my furniture, car and all my possessions, find storage for all my unsold, unfinished paintings and bid farewell to my family and friends. I promised my mother and Eva I'd come back at least twice a year to see them, to make work for my representing galleries in Australia and fulfil my exhibition schedules.

Nevertheless, it was a big move and I was aware that once again I was taking a giant leap of faith. What if it doesn't work out, I wondered. How would I cope so far away from all my support networks in a culture I had barely scratched the surface of, without even knowing the language? What have you got to lose, some said? Including my mother. Follow your heart. You only live once. You'll never know unless you go. You can always come home, she counselled.

Do I love him enough to take the risk, I asked myself? Yes, you do, my quivering heart replied; as always, my heart winning when it came to an argument with its more logical associate, my mind. Besides, I assured myself, it would be a temporary measure. Once Gamal had more work experience under his belt, he'd be in a better position to find a good job if and when we returned to Australia on a permanent basis.

En route to Cairo to start my new life, I flew to Los Angeles for my exhibition; a group show including two other Australian artists and three from LA. I was conscious of an undercurrent, a twinge of uncertainty—or maybe it was panic. But too overwhelmed and preoccupied to pay it much heed, I focused my sights on being with Gamal finally and permanently, and on doing whatever was necessary to make it happen. In retrospect, I should have taken more notice of my gut intuition, or was it a tiny part of my analytical brain desperately trying to reason with its lusty reptilian counterpart.

✗ ✗ ✗

219

It was late at night when Gamal picked me up from the airport. He didn't look at all well: his face was pale and pinched and he seemed to have lost weight. While I was preparing to leave Australia, he'd had the task of finding us a place to live. I'd mentioned I didn't want to stay in his bleak little apartment in New Cairo City and had asked him to look for something nice in Heliopolis, an upmarket and prettier suburb nearby. On a previous visit, we'd spent a pleasant afternoon traipsing around the old residential area which I'd loved: the nineteenth-century architecture, the streets lined with shade-bearing trees, scented jasmine and sprawling hot-pink bougainvillea. As we'd strolled through the district, stopping at Groppi's, a trendy coffee shop situated across the road from the Presidential Palace, I pointed out the sort of thing I imagined us renting if ever I came to live in Egypt.

Envisaging Gamal had found an apartment similar to those we'd looked at that day, I was keen to see what he'd leased. So, when the car pulled up in a drab, unvegetated part of town outside an ugly and poorly maintained, twelve-storey apartment block, I was already in shock. Gamal grabbed my suitcases from the boot and we entered the entrance hall of the building. We didn't get far, however. Materialising from out of the shadows, a beefy, surly-faced super-visor stepped defiantly in our way, blocking our passage. Immediately, the two men began to argue. Unable to understand a word, I stood apprehensively on the sidelines watching as the altercation intensi-fied. Eventually, baksheesh changed hands and the irate man, eyeing me with distaste, let us pass.

'What was that about?' I asked Gamal.

'He thinks something is going on,' he replied through clenched teeth. 'We do not have the marriage documents so he assumes we are doing something illegal and that you are a prostitute.'

'Welcome home,' I thought, my unease mounting.

We took the lift to the top floor. Gamal opened the door to the apartment and together we entered the unlit room. Instantly, I was hit by a wave of something malevolent.

Run, get out! The words seemed to scream in my mind. Or was it someone crying out from another plane of existence?

Gamal turned on the light and as I took in my surroundings, my heart sank. It was terrible. Worse than anything that I could ever have imagined. Taking a deep breath, I walked further into the flat. But as I went from room to room, becoming more despairing with every step, I wanted to weep.

'How on earth did he think I could live here?' I whimpered to myself. 'I've left my beautiful home and country to come to *this*?'

In the musty and airless living room, the smell of mould had been disguised with the cloying scent of cheap air freshener. Painted an eerie green and stuffed with a collection of crushed and grubby floral-patterned sofas and armchairs, a vase of decrepit plastic flowers and faded-beyond-recognition prints failed miserably in their attempt to decorate the space. Worn carpet of an undecipherable colour covered the floor. As I parted the shabby damask drapes to get a glimpse of the bleak view outside, dust motes rose in a cloud. The kitchen was a dungeon with no natural light; a scratched single basin sink sat in a sticky faux granite Laminex bench above a bank of heavily varnished wood cupboards. I couldn't bring myself to open the battered-looking fridge in the corner and, almost gagging from the odour of cooked dinners past, I fled the room. In the bathroom, a weak arc of tepid water sprang from the reedy spout as I turned on the tap in the warped Formica-lined shower cubicle. The most depressing room in the apartment was the bedroom. A chunky, colonial-style bed spread with old and odiforous blankets that had never seen the inside of a washing machine, supported an ancient foam mattress embalmed in other people's juices; a pair of humanoid shaped indents lying in state. A massive wooden wardrobe filled an entire wall, leaving barely enough room to swing what would surely be in these circumstances, a mummified cat.

The dingy flat overlooked a military cemetery where hundreds of British and Commonwealth soldiers killed in the Western Desert during the Second World War lay buried; rows of white crosses and headstones glowed spookily in the moonlight. Outside, a ghostly wind began to whistle and with every creak and rustle in the apartment my hair stood on end as I imagined the soldiers with their gory injures and missing limbs materialising like zombies from the ceiling. Goya would have wanted a five-year lease.

Half-heartedly we made love, afterwards trying to sleep, clinging to each other in the darkness. But it was a fitful night for both of us and at first light, I shook Gamal awake.

'I'm not spending another night in this place,' I declared. 'How on earth did you think I could live here?' I asked, voicing my thoughts from the previous night.

Gamal sat up, rubbed his eyes, raked his fingers through his matted curls and breathed a sigh of relief. Having spent two nights in the apartment alone before I arrived, he was even more affected by the atmosphere than me.

'*Al-ḥamdu lillāh*,'[3] he said in a small voice. 'I do not want to stay in this place either. I thought we could live here temporarily until we found something better. But I think this building is haunted.'

We packed our bags and left, our bond and one month's rent lost. In his haste, Gamal left his favourite shirt in the wardrobe but thankful to get out of that house of horrors alive, he never returned to claim it.

Dazed and in shock we drove to his flat in New Cairo City and,

---

3   Thank God.

relieved to be in a familiar and safe environment, we crawled, like wounded dogs, into bed, instantly falling asleep.

'So now what?' I asked Gamal when we woke a few hours later.

'We will stay here for now. Until we decide what to do,' he replied. 'But we will not turn on the lights at night. My family do not know that you are here yet. They know only that I have gone away for two weeks. I wanted to settle into the apartment in Heliopolis and get married. I was going to tell them then.'

Too frazzled from the events of the previous forty-eight hours to query this information, I dismissed it from my mind.

For the next few days, the arrangement worked well. No longer returning to his father's apartment to sleep, Gamal was able to stay all night with me. We were living as a couple—cooking, cleaning, talking, arguing, washing, laughing and making love as much and as often as we liked. But our experiment at playing house was short-lived; a seemingly innocuous action diverted the course of our lives in an instant.

On the fourth morning, when Gamal had left for work, I did some handwashing in the kitchen sink, hanging the wet items on a make-shift clothesline I'd rigged up in front of the frosted glass windows. That night, as we lay together in the dark there was a loud and insistent knock on the front door. Gamal sprang out of bed, slipped on his gallabiyah and hurried to answer it. From under the covers, I could hear a woman shouting angrily on the landing whilst Gamal did his best to placate her. I recognised the voice of his mother, Naheema.

Next minute, the door slammed shut and Gamal was back, his face as bloodless as a cadaver on a mortuary slab.

'What's going on?' I asked, my heart in my throat.

'My mother saw the shadow of your washing in the window. She thought someone had broken in. Now my family know you are here,' he said burying his head in his hands as he sank down to the edge of the mattress. And just as I was getting up to go to him, his mobile rang, the ringtone *I Can be Your Hero* reverberating off the tiled floor and plaster walls.

'It is my father,' Gamal said, looking at the screen. 'I am so sorry. I must go and deal with this.'

'*Go, go!*' I said, without hesitation, feeling my stomach begin to churn and my hopes and dreams falling in shards at my feet. And he was gone, leaving me to the deathly silence of the apartment.

Huddled under the blankets, I tried to imagine the terrible scene that was surely unfolding across the other side of the street. Two hours passed and Gamal returned, his face now a ghoulish avocado flesh green.

'Tell me,' I said leaping from the bed to greet him. 'What happened?'

'I told them I want to marry you,' he said.

'And?' I inquired anxiously.

'They said if I married you I would be dead to them. I will not be welcome in my father's house and he will disown me. They said they will come to my work and make trouble.'

'*Oh God! Oh God! Oh God!*' I repeated like a demented pious parrot, clasping my scalp as I began to pace back and forth across the room. I wanted to throw myself off a bridge. At one point, I caught sight of myself in the mirror, Edward Munch's *The Scream* staring back.

'Katherine, I am so sorry,' my distraught lover cried as he followed me to and fro. 'I am *so, so* sorry.'

'But I thought your family knew we were going to get married. You told me they were okay with it,' I exclaimed accusingly, desperately; now realising that he hadn't been honest with me.

'I thought they were,' Gamal replied miserably. 'I told them many times that I was going to marry you, I swear. Obviously, they did not take me seriously. They are in shock. They did not know you were here and now this has happened. I wanted to break it to them gently, not like this.'

'What are their main objections?' I asked, as if I hadn't already guessed.

The fact that I wasn't Muslim notwithstanding, a divorced, foreign woman twice his age who was past bearing children was not exactly ideal marriage material for any young man. I understood that for Gamal's parents and for the overwhelming majority of parents all over the world, I didn't tick any boxes. Clearly, they hadn't been made aware of my imminent arrival in Egypt and the reason behind it. No wonder they'd reacted like this. Why had I believed him so implicitly when Gamal insisted that his parents had no objection to us marrying? It hadn't occurred to me that he'd lie about something that could have such a significant and devastating impact on both me and his family. Still, in spite of the fact that I was blinded by love and lust, I should have seen it coming. If I had, I would never have contemplated relocating to Egypt to marry him.

I could feel the anger well up like molten lava to my face. While Gamal had obviously misled me, I felt like a fool; stubbornly sticking my head in the sand of denial and avoiding entertaining any commonsensical thinking about the future of the relationship. I knew I wasn't alone. I was only human after all; most of us fall prey to some such foible at some point in our lives, especially regarding matters of the heart. But right there and then, my valiant effort to justify my actions was of little comfort.

'So, what are we going to do now?' I asked for the second time that day, getting more and more agitated by the minute.

'I do not know,' Gamal sighed, exhausted. 'We will sleep and in the morning, we will decide what to do.'

That night, as I lay awake and waiting for my anger to subside,

I was overcome by a wave of compassion, not motherly love exactly but definitely something resembling it; the unconditional love kind of feeling that compels a mother to make excuses for her child's rash behaviour. He was so young to be dealing with such stress. He had no experience of relationships. He was doing the best he could. Yes, he'd made a monumental cock-up of things, but I could see there'd been method in his madness. His plan, ill-conceived and doomed to failure, foreseeable if he hadn't been so blinkered by passion and had taken a moment to think things through, had involved getting me to Egypt, marrying me and presenting the marriage to his family as a *fait accompli*; their acceptance, he'd hoped, just a matter of time. The dire predicament in which we now found ourselves wasn't all his fault—youth and inexperience were partially to blame. What was my excuse? I asked myself.

Next morning, before we'd had a chance to talk, Gamal went to work; leaving me at home to stew, which basically meant pacing from room to room or lying curled up in a ball on the bed. In between, I scrubbed the bathroom and mopped the floors, wiping the dust from any surface or object that crossed my path. Gamal rang at regular intervals to check on me. But with no opportunity to continue the conversation of the previous night or reach some kind of resolution, I was at my wits end. I couldn't go out, I hardly ate. I can't remember if I washed. I was a nervous wreck; any moment expecting Abdul or Naheema to come barging in with orders to leave the apartment. I wanted to ring my mum but with the nine-hour time difference I knew she'd be sound asleep. By the time Gamal walked through the door that evening, I was a mess and he was shattered, his family having harassed him with a barrage of hostile and threatening phone calls throughout the day. On the way home, he'd called in to see Uncle Ibrahim to get some advice.

'If you want to marry Katherine, you cannot do it in Egypt,' Ibrahim told him.

'My uncle is right,' Gamal conceded. 'My family will not give us a moment of peace if we remain here. They will destroy our relationship. They had the chance to keep me in Cairo but now they are forcing me to leave. They will regret what they have done and I will take my revenge,' he snarled, his body stiffening for attack.

Although there was something comical in his histrionic superhero statement, I sensed Gamal was deadly serious, his outrage based on defending my honour and my heart tightened at his devotion.

Within two weeks, having had no further contact with Gamal's family, I was on a plane back to Australia. But Lisa had let go of the flat we'd shared in Melbourne so I no longer had a home to return to. Licking my substantial wounds, I did the only thing someone in my situation could do: I went home to my mum who, not surprisingly, was delighted with the turn of events that had brought about the sudden and unexpected return of her daughter.

Regrouping, Gamal and I looked at our options. The Prospective Marriage Visa allowed successful applicants to emigrate to Australia and marry an Australian citizen within nine months of the visa being approved. It was an expensive exercise and required an enormous amount of supporting documentation, but it looked to be our only alternative. We realised we should have done this in the first place.

'I did not want you to think I was interested in you only because of the visa,' Gamal explained. 'But actually, everyone is trying to get out of Egypt, not the other way around,' he said laughing. 'We were crazy.'

To be honest, once I'd recovered from the shock, I was sort of pleased to be back in Australia and almost glad that Gamal's family had overreacted so magnificently, prompting my swift flight from Egypt and making it impossible for me to live there. I'd been willing to give it a go for Gamal's sake but I think I'd have had trouble living in Cairo for any length of time. Although I was fond of the Egyptian people I'd met, reminding me of their warm and passionate Italian 'cousins' across the Mediterranean, I found the heat unbearable, the gender restrictions oppressive, the traffic horrendous and the piles of rotting rubbish and pollution abominable. Maybe it's my artistic sensibilities or because I really *am* a spoilt Western woman but, apart from the Nile, the treasures in the Egyptian Museum, the Pyramids of Giza, the mosques and heritage architecture—once giving Cairo its title the 'Paris of the Middle East'—I found it difficult to fall in love with Gamal's hometown.

Perhaps I'd have been overwhelmed with a longing for green, for paddocks of knee-deep grass swaying in the breeze (when there's no drought) and bushland as far as the eye can see (when it's not on fire). I assured myself I'd have missed the moodiness of clouds, the sound of rain on the roof (when it isn't flooding) and the smell of the ground after a downpour. I'm sure the relentless blue of the Egyptian sky, the barren, featureless desert, the permanent aura of repression, the dearth of opportunities to communicate in my native tongue and the poverty coupled with the political tension would have got to me in the end. I began to realise, even with no knowledge of the horrific wave of violence that would shortly spread across the nation, some targeting foreigners, that Gamal's parent's reaction may have saved my life.

But taking refuge in my mother's house, shaken by the upheaval and trauma, and uncertain about the future, I was overcome by bouts of weeping. I felt foolish and ashamed that, at my age, I'd put myself in such a position. I should have known better. I was embarrassed to contact my friends. I knew I was in for a pasting with Eva. Gamal listened patiently to my outpouring of grief. Not fair, I know; he was struggling too. Valiantly, he tried to cheer me up.

'It will be all right. Everything you had, can be replaced,' he'd say encouragingly on Skype.

And then he'd fall in a heap. 'This is all my fault,' he'd lament. 'I feel terrible. I have failed you. I do not blame you if you want to leave me.'

But how could I blame him, knowing I was also to blame. Assuring him I didn't want to leave him, I focused my thoughts and energy on getting him to Australia, instead.

23

Terminal Blues

Despite the odds against us and aware that the Australian Department of Immigration and Citizenship[4] (as it was called then) may find it hard to believe our relationship was genuine, we filled out the reams of paperwork and gathered the necessary documentation attesting to our ongoing and committed relationship; Gamal ready to lodge the Prospective Marriage Visa at the Australian Embassy in Cairo even if it meant being ostracised by his family.

'It is my life and I will do as I wish,' he said, still furious about his parent's reaction to our marriage plans. 'And anyway, they will become used to it. They care only for what people think. As long as we do not get married in Egypt, they will not object,' he added, more optimistic than realistic, in my view.

However, just as we were getting excited about being together at last, the goal posts shifted yet again. Out of hundreds of applicants,

---

4 Now called the Department of Immigration and Border Protection – a government department that ironically welcomes some arriving in Oz whilst at the same time ejecting others.

after multiple examinations and following numerous interviews, Gamal was informed that the job application he'd submitted to the multinational media organisation in Cairo when he was unemployed and in despair in the aftermath of the Egyptian Revolution, had been successful. For an ambitious early-career journalist, it was equivalent to winning the lottery.

'You have to take it,' I told him, knowing it would mean he'd need to remain in Egypt for the foreseeable future and already feeling anxious about the implications.

'Yes, I know,' he said earnestly.

Quickly changing tack, we revised our plans: a. Gamal would stay put in Egypt for twelve months, b. Having proved himself in his new position in the Cairo office, he'd apply for an attachment to London, c. I'd join him there. Our back-up plan? Gamal would remain in Egypt for another year before coming to Australia; his enhanced resumé hopefully improving his chances of finding decent employment.

But we both knew what this entailed. In order to see one another and maintain our relationship it would require, on my part at least, a Herculean effort and I wasn't sure if I was up to the task. I would have to fly to Egypt every two or three months and then find somewhere to live while I was in Australia. Clearly, I couldn't stay in Gamal's apartment when I visited Cairo. The family's reaction to my presence there had surely put the kibosh on that. While Gamal stayed at his father's flat, I'd need to rent a furnished apartment or stay in a hotel when I was in town.

'You cannot be in an apartment alone.' Gamal said. 'It is out of the question. It is not safe. I would be too worried about you. You are my responsibility.'

So, we came to an arrangement. I'd pay for my airfares to and from Egypt; Gamal would pick up the bill for my hotel accommodation.

The Hotel Longchamps, a quiet oasis situated in Zamalek—a small island in the middle of the Nile—became my home away from home. Gamal was happy in the knowledge that the Longchamps provided around-the-clock security for my protection. I didn't have the heart to tell him that security consisted of a stooped, frail, walrus-moustachioed old gent in a brass-buttoned, bottle-green uniform who, stationed outside the antique lift, looked as if he'd be bowled over by the first flutter of a papyrus fan.

Many ex-pats and upper-class Egyptian families live in Zamalek; embassies, boutiques, jewellers, art galleries, beauty parlours, restaurants, bookshops, museums, antique dealers, cafes and bars jam-packed into the tiny district. Described as 'a teeny slice of Europe' the leafy suburb is graced with an abundance of magnificent nineteenth-century mansions and art deco apartments; winking glimpses of the Nile and *felukas*[5] languidly sailing by at the end of every street.

Despite some kind of political unrest that seemed to be brewing while I was in Cairo I never felt unsafe in Zamalek. Admittedly, a lot of the time, I was on the arm of my own personal and very handsome bodyguard. But while Gamal was at work, I'd venture out alone to wander down narrow lanes and alleyways, stopping to buy a freshly squeezed pomegranate juice, take photographs, visit a gallery, browse an English-language bookstore or rummage through a shop full of dusty antiques. I'd take walks along the Nile, resting at an open-air waterfront cafe to drink mint tea or enjoy a delicious and sticky slice of apricot *kanafa*[6]. Lunch times, I'd sit on a bench in the park eating my flatbread, falafel and pickles as I watched the animated interactions between the Faculty of Fine Arts students from Helwan University. Back in my hotel room, I kept myself

---

5 An old-fashioned sail boat.
6 A Middle Eastern cheese pastry soaked in sweet, sugar-based syrup.

busy—reading, surfing the net, learning Arabic, manipulating my latest batch of images in Photoshop, emailing friends and family in Australia and writing in my diary. I practised belly dancing in front the wardrobe door mirror—working on my snake arms, shimmies and belly rolls; planning to entertain Gamal with a surprise performance once I'd mastered the moves and mustered the nerve.

Flying to Cairo every few months was expensive. There was no way I could afford to rent an apartment in Melbourne as well. Having no idea where I was going to be from one month to the next, I was reluctant to take on a lease when I might be forced to break it before it expired. Someone suggested I house-sit during the periods I was in Australia; so registering with an agency, I found that as a single, mature-aged woman (in years if not always in actions or thoughts) I was in demand. There are some perks to approaching the autumn of your life!

I fell into a strange, unnerving and exhausting routine living between Cairo and Melbourne; struggling not just with the logistics of my transient existence but also with my escalating anxiety. Established in secure and stable environments, their mortgages paid off and superannuation accumulating, most people I knew were surrounded by a life-time collection of 'stuff'. By contrast here was I, dispossessed and homeless, recklessly following my heart; traipsing across the world like a middle-aged, couch-surfing nomad. Although my gypsy lifestyle was adventurous and my lack of material possessions was liberating, I hadn't provided, in any shape or form, for my rapidly approaching old age. I made a pact with Gamal. I'd handle the arrangement for twelve months; then I wanted somewhere to settle.

However, there was another problem Gamal and I needed to address. How on earth did one get laid in the 'Mother of Cities'? Where did you go to know each other in the biblical sense when your efforts were thwarted at every palm tree? I was hoping Gamal could visit me in my room at the Longchamps.

'Madam, it is hotel policy that visitors are not allowed in the rooms,' said the concierge with a barely disguised look of disgust. 'You infidel whore,' I could almost hear him think.

Refusing to let a ban on bonking ruin my love life, I hastily devised a plan:

1. Gamal would pick me up outside the hotel after work
2. We'd grab some spicy sausage sandwiches to take away or eat at the Pigeon Restaurant—three pumping and packed-to-the-rafters floors of Cairenes gorging themselves on the delicious stuffed and roasted birds
3. We'd drive to New Cairo City
4. We'd sneak into Gamal's vacant apartment
5. We'd make love
6. We'd make love again
7. Gamal would return me to my hotel in Zamalek

Although it was an inspired solution to our sexual dilemma, unfortunately, it entailed driving in Cairo at peak hour. Inching our way over the Sixth of October Bridge in bumper to bumper traffic, I'd study number plates; most plates in Egypt display English letters and numbers above the Arabic script—handy when you're trying to learn the language. Some evenings, Gamal would serenade me with Egyptian love songs, occasionally breaking into English to give me hopelessly out-of-tune renditions of Kenny Roger's *Lady* or his all-time favourite, *I Can Be Your Hero*.

'I can be your hero, baby. I can kiss away the pain. I will stand by you, forever. You can take my breath away,' Gamal would warble with such unabashed sincerity he took *my* breath away.

When we finally reached our destination, Gamal would park in the street behind his apartment block and after racing inside, we'd scurry up the stairs and slip into his flat, mindful not to turn on the lights and alert his family to the clandestine coupling across the street.

It didn't seem to matter how careful we were, however—we could always count on getting busted by Gamal's younger brother, Tarik. Lurking in the dark, the beanpole of a young man, dressed in a hoodie and low-cut baggy jeans, looked as if he'd just walked out of the Bronx. Practically living on the streets, smoking cigarettes and, who knows, maybe hashish, he'd spend his nights hanging out with his friends before returning to his father's apartment to sleep for most of the day. It was taking Tarik forever to complete his university degree and his parents, who were funding his indolent lifestyle, were concerned that he'd never amount to anything.

'Have you ever heard of a concept called 'tough love'? I'd asked Naheema and Ibrahim one day over afternoon tea, prior to my ignominious excommunication. Gamal was translating and they'd been discussing Tarik and what could be done to motivate him.

'You're not doing him any favours by giving him money,' I said when they sought my opinion. 'You're crippling him. If you want to help him you need to let him face the consequences of his behaviour and then maybe he'll get his act together,' I added, getting the distinct impression that they thought my suggestion, although politely acknowledged, was a crazy idea. As far as I was concerned, the young freeloader needed a rocket up his arse but when Gamal admitted that he and his sisters were forking out, too, I gave up in frustration.

With a sly grin and a knowing glint in his eye the lanky Tarik would saunter over to meet his older sibling at the car, shaking his hand before bending to greet me warmly through the open window. Fortunately, brotherly loyalty ensured that Gamal's illicit love life was never revealed to his parents by the street-smart Tarik—especially when a little baksheesh changed hands.

XXX

Breakfast at the Art Nouveau period Hotel Longchamp was a delectable and delightful affair. One could have imagined Isadora Duncan with her trademark flowing silk scarf breezing through on her way to see the antiquities at the Egyptian Museum. Laid out on the starched linen tablecloth, cut glass jugs of freshly squeezed orange juice and china plates piled with fresh dates, figs, peeled hard boiled eggs, sliced watermelon, mango, cucumber and tomato sat amongst vintage silver plate trays of sticky French pastries and still-warm-from-the-oven flat bread; clay pots of creamy homemade *labneh*[7] and glossy black olives placed here and there. Orders of felafel, *ful medames*[8], spicy beef sausages and scrambled eggs, trailed by their fragrant Middle Eastern aromas, were delivered periodically from kitchen to table; tulip glasses of Turkish coffee and porcelain cups of Earl Grey tea topped up by a slick-haired, bowing and scrupulous waiter. Each morning, book in hand, I'd make my way to the dining room to enjoy an unhurried and lingering first sitting.

One day, I got chatting to one of the elderly and long-term guests. Dressed in a baggy cream linen suit—a carved ebony walking stick, Panama hat and a book about the female pharaoh Hatchepsut on the bench seat beside him—I learned that the sparkly-eyed, bespectacled octogenarian English gentleman was a retired Oxford Professor of Egyptology. After picking the old man's sharp and scholarly brain, I'd compiled a comprehensive list of Cairo's lesser known museums. One, in particular, took my fancy—the Gayer Anderson Museum, former residence of an 18th-century British

---

7 Strained yoghurt.

8 Cooked fava beans with spices, traditionally eaten at breakfast.

officer and Orientalist, which was apparently a treasure trove filled with antique Middle Eastern furniture, carpets, silks, crystal, glassware and embroidered Arabian costumes. I couldn't wait to ask Gamal about it and plan our visit that weekend.

'Who is this man?' my jealous lover demanded angrily when I brought up the subject. 'Why you are speaking to him? He does not know Egypt. You should ask me these things, not this Englishman. Who else you are speaking to at the hotel?'

I was furious. How dare he jump down my throat when, in my opinion and no doubt practically every other Western woman in the world, I'd done nothing untoward? I would not put up with his possessive and domineering behaviour, I declared. I'd speak to whoever I wanted to. In my country it wasn't a crime to talk to a member of the opposite sex, I said sarcastically. I didn't have to justify or explain my actions to him or to anyone else. He was being an arsehole, a child, he was living in the Dark Ages, on another planet, etcetera, etcetera.

I'd experienced Gamal's jealousy before; his 'death stare'; the glowering look and sullen demeanour if he thought I'd been overly friendly with a male shop assistant, too chatty to a male tour guide or a tad flirtatious with a male waiter. It drove me crazy. John had been prone to outbursts of jealousy on social occasions but Gamal was taking things to a whole new level.

Not wanting to spoil the brief and precious time we had together I would try, not always successfully, to look past, what I believed to be, his manipulative and controlling behaviour.

'Stop acting like a teenager,' I'd say whenever I lost my patience. 'You're being ridiculous.'

Yes, it was troubling, but ever hopeful we'd work things out— please let it work out, I'd pray to a god I didn't believe in—I felt confident, albeit naively, that we could move beyond this disturbing and annoying glitch in our relationship. He was young and malleable and crazy about me. Eventually, he'd see the error of his ways and realise that I was faithful and trustworthy to a fault and that he had no need to be jealous.

If there was one thing I was learning about long-distance relationships, it was that they required a great deal of nurturing. For love to transcend oceans and continents you need to have plenty of contact. Thank goodness for technology! From the mundane to the noteworthy, we were able to discuss the latest news, a movie we'd seen or weird and wonderful facts about our respective cultures; Skype, Viber, emails and text messages kept us connected and made our time apart almost bearable. Whether it was the Klu Klux Clan, John Lennon, mojitos or Aussie slang and football, I delighted in telling Gamal about things he didn't know about the West and my country. In return, he had seven thousand years of Egyptian history, the life and times of The Prophet and the entire Middle East to talk about, not to mention the family gossip.

Our exchanges were intense; sometimes heated, sometimes hilarious. I was shocked to learn for instance, that most Egyptians are Holocaust deniers; he was appalled by my pro-choice stance on abortion. I'd express outrage at what appeared to me to be the dictates of a vengeful God; he was saddened by my inability to, as he put it, let Allah into my heart. But whenever we got onto the topic of health, the conversation would go from the sublime to the ridiculous. While Gamal tried to convince me that you could catch a cold from eating a bad mango and that you shouldn't eat fish when you had the sniffles, I extolled the virtues of fish oil, which in my opinion prevented everything from bipolar disorder to the bubonic plague.

He believed that antibiotics were the universal panacea for every ailment known to man—from a headache to a stomach bug to a stubbed toe. My response when he declaimed his views on medical science, was to give him a lecture on the scourge of antibiotic resistance, admonishing him for taking the drug unless he had a serious infection (NOT A VIRUS!) and was on death's door. You can imagine what I had to say when I discovered that Egyptians don't require a prescription to buy antibiotics, purchasing them over the counter like bags of lollies.

I asked him about the violent verses in the Qur'an, not dissimilar to those in the Old Testament, which advocate the wholesale massacre of non-believers—I was taking them out of context, I was told. Then there was the four-wife rule which seemed like a legalised form of cheating. You can't tell me that when a married man gets to the point of taking a second wife, there's been no scheming and deception beforehand.

'In Egypt, the first wife can accept her husband remarrying and retain her financial security and position in society or she can choose to get a divorce. It is a fairer and more compassionate system than what you have in the West. In any case, you have to be rich to support more than one wife. For the majority of Egyptian men it is not an option.'

I took a deep breath. Clearly, we weren't going to agree on some basic fundamentals and although I was determined not to let our respective cultural differences come between us, I was beginning to feel uneasy. It wasn't such an issue being so far apart, it made for some interesting discussions but how would these differences play out when we lived together?

'And what about the seventy-two virgins in the Afterlife?' I asked, changing the subject. 'How does that work? Are they turned back into virgins once they've been fucked or does every guy get a fresh batch? How are women rewarded? Why don't they get seventy-two spunky young men? It's discrimination,' I joked but not really. I can't recall Gamal's response, no doubt because it was as farfetched as the original premise and to my mind, didn't bear scrutiny.

Although there were advantages to instant communication technology, there was one drawback, like when I didn't respond immediately to Gamal's text messages.

'You did not answer my text,' he'd reprimand me when I saw him next on Skype; and this after I'd been looking forward to seeing him, waiting all day for him to wake up and let me know he was online.

'Where were you? What were you doing?' he'd demand, his face like one of those surly marble portraits in the corridors of the Uffizi Gallery in Florence; obviously convinced that the minute I stepped out the door I'd be hit on by every man within cooee.

'So?' I retorted angrily following one such flare-up. 'I didn't reply to a fucking text message. For Christ's sake, Gamal, you've got to stop this. You're freaking me out. If this is how you behave over something so minor, what would you be like if I actually did the wrong thing?' I said in exasperation and with genuine concern. I understood that it was difficult for him with us being on opposite sides of the world and I knew how anxious he became if he wasn't able to contact me. I'd become hyper-vigilant in responding as quickly as possible to his messages, as well as letting him know where I was and when I'd be home; desperately trying to ignore the red flags waving in front of my eyes.

'I was worried about you,' he'd say, attempting to deflect my anger after his initial accusatory tone. But we both knew there was a lot more to it than that.

✕✕✕

'My cousin is divorcing her husband,' Gamal announced one day on Skype.

'Oh, my God!' I replied. 'What happened?'

We'd attended their wedding party (when I was still in the good books with Gamal's family) less than twelve months ago. While

240

many poorer Cairene newlyweds make do with driving around in their cars post the marriage ceremony—yahooing, blaring their horns and stopping traffic, this upper-class reception had been a lavish and flamboyant affair. The couple, both doctors, who'd officially married at a sombre service at a mosque earlier in the week, made their entrance down the winding, flower and ribbon festooned reception centre staircase, accompanied by a deafening cacophony of bagpipes, Nubian drumming and the customary primal ululation of female relatives below. No Adonis, the bespectacled, penguin-suited groom with a receding hairline and a substantial overbite appeared nervous; the bride, effervescent in a fluffy confection of head-to-toe white sequins and lace; the veiled women guests—a dazzling kaleidoscope of colour and bling. Perfumed fog billowed from vents in the floor, metallic glitter fell unceasingly from the ceiling as strobe lighting bounced off every surface. On one wall, larger-than-life childhood photographs of the happy couple were projected in a continuous loop. Dancing troupes, boy bands, opera singers, DJs, stand-up comics, belly dancers, classical musicians, crooners, drummers and swirling dervishes performed, well into the night. Apart from a few dowagers sitting stoically on the sidelines, everyone hit the dance floor. All this, without a drop of alcohol in the house.

Halfway through the evening the guests, rising *en masse* from their seats, made their way to the heavily-laden banquet tables in the foyer. Thirty minutes later, having devoured every last morsel of *hamam mahshi*,[9] *shawarma*[10] and *fatoush*[11] and leaving a virtual wasteland in their wake, everyone headed back to the reception room to watch the grand finale—the cutting of the wedding cake.

---

9 Stuffed squab.
10 Rotisserie-cooked meat.
11 Bread salad.

The lights dimmed and for a pregnant moment we sat silently in the dark until suddenly someone switched on a spotlight. There, centre stage, in all its illuminated glory stood the sparkling, metre-high snow-white marzipan and fondant edifice. Appearing from the wings, the bride and groom cut the monster cake and, to the accompaniment of Bryan Adams' *Everything I Do, I Do It for You*, slow-marched to the end of the organza and garland-draped catwalk where a cluster of squirming young women waited in anticipation. Without further ado, the bride turned her back on her audience, flinging her bouquet over her head and into the jostling throng at her feet.

'It is a big scandal in our family,' Gamal said. 'The husband has a medical condition. He cannot get an erection so he cannot have sex. My aunts are very angry. They say he should have told my cousin about this before he married her. She will not be able to have children with this man, so she will divorce him.'

I was angry for his cousin too. As a twenty-eight-year-old divorcee she would find it hard to meet another man. Not only that, to add insult to injury, she was still a virgin. Encountering the ramifications of a patriarchal society first-hand was confronting and deeply frustrating and in Egypt I seemed to be coming across such inequities on a regular basis.

✖ ✖ ✖

Occasionally, I would ask Gamal about his sisters. I was concerned for them as they weren't getting any younger and nothing seemed to be happening on the 'salon' marriage front, as far as I could tell. It had been four years since a young, bearded man had come calling on Halima with his mother and father. On discovering the parents of his prospective wife had been divorced not once but twice, the family objected to a marriage between the couple, so Halima never saw the fellow again. The beautiful Safiya had also been interested in someone—a strapping young officer in the police force introduced to her through one of Uncle Ibrahim's connections at his university. But on this occasion, it was Naheema who opposed an alliance due to the belittling way the officer's mother treated her potential daughter-in-law.

'I do not know what is going on with them,' Gamal said. 'They do not tell me anything and it is awkward for me to enquire. But I think they meet guys at work or through friends. They have learned their lesson. They will not bring anyone home unless they are certain he is the one.'

'What about your uncle?' I'd enquired, having a particular soft spot for this wise man who'd been the only family member to offer Gamal and I advice and support during the 'The Troubles'.

Ibrahim's health was delicate and I knew he suffered terribly from the cold. When Gamal was a child, his uncle would accompany the family on seaside holidays to Alexandria. Adored by his nieces and nephews, they'd tug at his sleeve and beg him to join them in the waves; Ibrahim fondly fobbing the youngsters off with excuses, preferring instead to remain fully dressed and rugged up in a blanket in his deckchair on the sand. With his health in mind, I'd bought the beloved uncle a present from Australia—a beautiful Merino wool scarf. He thanked me profusely for the gift but didn't open it at the time. In fact curiously, none of the family unwrapped their gifts on that first visit to the family home.

'How come no one opens their presents?' I asked Gamal later.

'It is customary in Egypt' he'd replied. 'It is so the person giving the gift will not be hurt or feel awkward if the person accepting it cannot hide their disappointment'

That's so lovely, I thought; moved by the thoughtful and kind-hearted sentiments informing the tradition. I'd been similarly touched when I'd watched the way Gamal gave money to the beggars on the streets of Cairo—always a discrete and courteous transaction, to avoid causing embarrassment, he said. If he didn't have any change or felt he'd given enough already, he'd bring his hand to his heart, bowing slightly when approached.

'What does that mean?' I enquired.

'I am letting the person know that I feel for them; that they have my respect and that I hope Allah will protect them,' he replied with a bashful smile.

My uncle's immune system is not good,' he told me during another session on Skype. 'After he was born, my grandfather became jealous of the attention Ibrahim received,' he said. 'He was very cruel and would not give his wife money to buy milk powder for her baby. So my grandmother, who for some reason could not breastfeed, fed Ibrahim on sugar and water. This has affected his constitution. He is very frail. Do you want to hear a funny story?' Gamal asked.

'Of course,' I replied, all ears.

'Once, when she had saved the money, my grandmother asked her sister to go to the shop to buy baby formula,' he began. 'On her return, the sister realised my grandfather was at home. She knew she could not bring the formula into the house. So, do you know what she did?'

'No,' I answered, wondering how this tale could possibly have a comedic ending.

'She dug a hole in the sand and buried the tin and next day, when my grandfather went out, she dug it up again,' he said chuckling.

Maybe it got lost in translation but I couldn't see the funny side of his anecdote. Depriving your child of adequate nutrition was an appalling thing to do, and noticing how his story had affected me, Gamal wiped the smile from his face.

'Ibrahim's family was extremely poor,' he explained before I had a chance to query his dark sense of humour. 'They did not have a toilet—just a room with sand on the floor. Every few days someone would scrape up the shit and spread more sand.'

This clarified a great deal. Through hard work and judicious saving Ibrahim had prospered and now lived in comparative luxury. But it seemed his excessively thrifty approach to life, often commented upon with amusement by his family, was rooted in a deep-seated fear of poverty.

Sometimes, I'd ask after his mother. 'Why she is so bitter and twisted about your father and his family?' I wanted to know one day.

'Ah yes, that,' Gamal said with a small smile. 'I will tell you.'

'My father's family is not sophisticated,' he began. 'They possess an 'Upper Egypt' mentality' (translated in Australian as 'red-neck' or 'bogan', I gathered).

'My parents were both twenty-eight when they married in 1983. My grandmother and her three daughters became jealous of my mother because she was beautiful and educated. She was a teacher. She was financially independent and my aunts did not like this. They realised they could not control her so they began to poison my father's mind against her. They treated her badly when she visited the family home, ignoring her and not offering her food or drink.'

I was incredulous. The whole thing sounded like something out of Cinderella to me, but keen to hear the rest of the story, I didn't interrupt.

'My father was foolish and listened to his mother and sisters. He was the only son, the youngest, and from the day he was born they were very controlling,' Gamal continued. 'Westerners think that Middle Eastern women are oppressed. They would be shocked if they knew the truth. Egyptian women … how do you say in English? They "rule the chickens".'

'Rule the roost,' I said laughing as I wiped the spluttered green tea from my computer screen.

'Anyway, the relationship between my parents became very bad,' Gamal went on; my correction an obvious dent to his manly pride. 'Many arguments. My father took Tariq and me to the mosque on Friday and supported the family financially but that was all. He would not come on holidays with us or take us to the doctor, and he never once came to see me practise karate. He is not a bad man. He is very kind, actually. But he was not a family man. That is why we love Ibrahim. He was like a father to us.

In 1996, when I was twelve years old, my parents divorced for the first time,' Gamal continued. 'After a few months, my mother decided she did not want to raise her children in a single-parent family so my father agreed to remarry her. But he had not changed and my mother had had enough. She had done her duty to her children and in 2008 she divorced my father again,' he concluded.

'So, she's resentful about her life and how she was treated by her husband and her in-laws and it's made her sick,' I surmised, wondering if Naheema believed her sense of self depended entirely on family expectations and why her work hadn't taken a more central and fulfilling role as it does for so many women in Australia of my generation. Was it something to do with her as a person or was there shame, rejection and betrayal at the root of her problems?

A few weeks later, Gamal announced that he thought his father had met someone and had secretly remarried.

'Some nights he does not return home. I think we should hire a private detective and have him followed,' he said with a snigger.

'And what if it's true?' I asked. 'Why hasn't he told you and your brother and sisters? How come he isn't moving his wife into the apartment? Don't you want to meet her? Aren't you happy for him? Why doesn't he sell up and go and live with her? So many questions.

'He would not dare move his wife into the apartment or sell it and he will never bring her here to meet us,' he replied sternly, almost angrily. 'He knows I would forbid it. He has a responsibility to his children. This is our home.' As if that was the end of the matter.

'But you're not children anymore!' I cried in exasperation. 'You're adults. You should be out fending for yourselves. Letting your father move on. He's spent his whole life providing for you all. Surely he deserves some happiness in his retirement.'

How is it that Gamal can forbid his father from bringing his new wife into his own home? Why can't Abdul be open with his family? Hasn't someone asked him about why he doesn't come home two or three nights a week? I didn't understand. Although I continued to press Gamal, trying to make sense of what he'd told me, in the end I had to accept that I'd never fully comprehend his family dynamics or know whether secrets and subterfuge were characteristics specific to the Bahar's or whether they were part and parcel of Egyptian family life. Either way, it was a cause for concern.

✕✕✕

On one of our reunions Gamal and I met halfway between Cairo and Melbourne, in Phuket when the wet season was in full swing. After settling ourselves into our hotel room, we hit the footpaths for a bit of sightseeing, where, to avoid the risk of certain blindness, I was obliged to explain the ins and outs of umbrella etiquette (not much call for one of those in the desert) in which an inexperienced *umbrella bearer* needs to be aware of the presence of his *shorter companion* and the proximity of *her eyeballs* in relation to *the spikes* on the *lethal apparatus*.

Revelling in being together and once more away from prying eyes, we swam, made love and canoed around the massive, sheer limestone karsts in the emerald-green waters of Phang Nga Bay; living on tom yum soup, pad thai noodles and green papaya salad. To my amusement, Gamal was intrigued but scandalised by the sleazy nightlife and the flamboyant and stunningly attractive lady-boys cavorting on Bangla Road.

Six months went by before we were able to see each other again, this time in London when he was sent there for four weeks to work. During this glorious month, it felt as if we were living something approximating a 'normal' relationship. We saw *The Lion King* in the West End, visited Westminster Abbey and marvelled at the dinosaurs in the British Museum. For the first time, my lover experienced throwing a snowball, eating fish and chips, drinking a beer and kissing his girlfriend in public. Hand in hand, we'd stroll along the banks of the Thames in Turner's translucent light.

On three occasions, Gamal tried to visit me in Australia. I was keen to show him my country and had visions of us catching the ferry across Sydney Harbour, petting a koala at Taronga Zoo and racing him into the surf at Bondi. Naturally, I wanted to introduce him to my mother, my rock of ages. Despite her initial misgivings, she'd become quite fond of my handsome young lover, having spoken to him on Skype during my visits to see her at the retirement village.

'How are you, darling?' he'd greet her online, rolling his 'r's' and giving her his most winsome smile; mum becoming putty in his hands.

Each time Gamal submitted his tourist visa, however, the Australian Department of Immigration and Citizenship saw fit to reject it. It was unbelievably exasperating. Why couldn't Gamal visit my country? His visa applications dotted all the i's and crossed the t's; his supporting documents were exemplary. Obviously, though, as a young Muslim male from the Middle East he must be terrorist material and, therefore unwelcome, no matter what his credentials.

I wrote to the Department asking for an explanation, complaining that Gamal's visa rejections reeked of discrimination and that they seemed to be extracting money (via the substantial application fee: three hundred dollars a pop) under false pretences. If the Australian government had no intention of allowing young Egyptian men into the country they should be transparent about it, I argued. Taking hard-earned cash from uninformed applicants who could ill afford to throw it away on what appeared to be a futile exercise was tantamount to extortion, I wrote. The Department acknowledged my frustration and explained that their position was based on a statistic called the Rate of Non-Return. The global Rate of Non-Return, where visitors don't return to their country of origin when their holiday visa expired, was less than one percent. In 2012, the Rate of Non-Return for Egyptians was almost ten percent. As the situation in Egypt continued to deteriorate I understood why people wanted to escape their homeland. Australia must have seemed like paradise by comparison. By the same token, if so many Egyptians were overstaying their welcome, it was no wonder the Australian government was knocking back applications. But as a journalist employed by a highly respected international media organisation, one would have thought that Gamal, at least, would have been able to visit Australia.

'Your government is *so* racist,' he complained as we luxuriated in a pool in Thailand.

'Don't blame my government!' I replied with a snort. 'It's all you wayward run-away Egyptians with a taste for the First World in your blood. If you didn't go AWOL all the time you'd be 'tossin' back a cold one' by now!'

'What does this mean, "tossin' back a cold one"?' he asked.

'Well, you know. You'd be "crackin' a tinnie", "suckin' on a syrup",' I retorted with a wet grin.

'What are you *talking* about?' Gamal demanded in frustration.

And splashing my bewildered lover in the face, I torpedoed underwater and made a hasty escape.

XXX

Thankfully, with the entire country in slow-mo, everyone either cantankerous or catatonic with thirst and hunger, my visits to Egypt never coincided with Ramadan. The closest I came to experiencing the annual month-long fast was to watch Gamal go through it on Skype. If we spoke after sunset when he'd finished fasting for the day, he was his usual lovely and loving self. But if he called *during* the fast it was a different story. As soon as I saw his face, I knew which was which. His fasting face—drawn and grey, looked like thunder; with bruise-coloured circles under his eyes and lips drained of colour. Slouched on the couch, he resembled a withering pot-plant in need of watering and was barely able to talk. Worst of all, he was extremely sensitive and tetchy.

'I'm just warning you now, for future reference,' I said at the end of one particularly gruelling, height-of-an-Egyptian-summer fast, 'I am never, ever going to be anywhere in your vicinity during Ramadan.'

'I understand,' he said laughing, almost choking with a mouth full of pita and felafel.

XXX

For most couples in long-distance relationships, parting isn't such sweet sorrow. It's pure misery. In an airport terminal somewhere in the world, the final departure call would be announced and tearing ourselves apart, Gamal and I would walk in opposite directions, catching a last glimpse of one another over our shoulders as we wondered if, how, where and when we'd be together again.

250

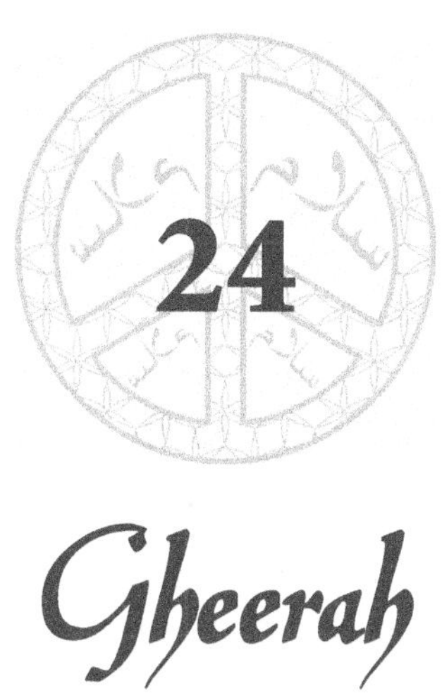

24

Gheerah

I'd always been a faithful partner to John and had never knowingly given him cause for concern. Nevertheless, my husband was a jealous man; his paranoia no doubt exacerbated by his excessive consumption of wacky baccy. Parties and barbecues were an ordeal and often resulted in a screaming argument in the car on the way home. Invariably during the course of the evening, some unsuspecting male would engage me in conversation and, eyeing me from the other side of a campfire or across a marijuana smoke-filled room, John would decide that I seemed a little too animated or attentive. Usually I was bored and feigning politeness, counting the moments until it was acceptable to leave without appearing rude. For someone apparently so sociable, I'd never much cared for parties and even today I dread my exhibition openings—all that meaningless and superficial small talk.

Like clockwork, John would appear at my side, proceeding to intellectually intimidate the poor sod talking to me who, once annihilated, would make his excuses and beat a hasty retreat. In the end, most men avoided me at social gatherings, scared off by the bullying tactics of my articulate and jealous mate. To make matters worse, John was offended by my lack of jealousy; it demonstrated that I didn't love him as much as he loved me, he'd grumble. But secure in myself and the relationship in those days, naively so in light of the fiery affair that ended our marriage, I didn't mind when I saw my husband flirting with other women.

Admittedly, I haven't always had a handle on the green-eyed monster. One day in England my mother came home to find me in my school uniform kneeling on the kitchen floor with my head in the oven, Harry Nielson's *I Can't Live If Living Is Without You* belting out from the record player in the front room. My boyfriend, Patrick (he of the 'pash rash' and ban-the-bomb pendant), had dumped me for a little English slapper, leaving me wracked with jealousy and anguish.

'It's natural gas, love,' Mum said as she sidestepped around me to put the kettle on. 'I don't think you can kill yourself with that.'

✖✖✖

When I'd fallen for Vicko on the rebound, I had plenty of reasons to be jealous. But if I challenged the Croat's outrageous behaviour, a bitter row would ensue. Somehow, the slippery and quick-witted architect would twist things around so that I'd come away reeling, convinced my feelings were ungrounded and that there was something seriously lacking in my mean-spirited character. Why couldn't I cope with being left at home alone while Vicko went out drinking with a female friend, only to stagger back to bed at 5 o'clock in the morning? What was I thinking objecting to him sticking his tongue down the throat of another woman at his fiftieth birthday bash? Surely, I shouldn't have been upset when on holiday in Bali I woke in the middle of the night to find him groping his brother's girlfriend? And how could I possibly mind when he'd disappear for hours during a dinner party to console a young, attractive neighbour who'd recently broken up with her partner? What was wrong with me and why on earth was I making such a scene?

But I wasn't the only member of my family to suffer when it came to jealousy. As an art student at RMIT, homesick and in need of some TLC from my mum, I'd catch the Friday night train to Bairnsdale; then head back to Melbourne on Sunday evening to attend classes the next day. One Sunday night, snuggled under the doona in the city, I was woken in the wee hours of the morning by a loud knock on the front door. I stumbled out of bed and went to answer it, only to find my mother on the porch, wild-eyed and beside herself.

'Where is he?' Mum demanded as she pushed her way past me into the flat.

'Where's *who*?' I asked, shaking myself out of my sleepy stupor. 'What's going on?'

Half crazed with jealousy, Mum had driven through the night after a well-meaning friend informed her that I'd boarded the train with her young lover, Ed. I had in fact boarded the train with Ed but we weren't 'together'. It was pure coincidence. Following an awkward greeting, Ed had made his way to the bar where, knowing his love for a drink, I assumed he remained for the rest of the journey. I was seventeen and he was thirty-five. I'd been immensely relieved that I hadn't had to hang out with my mum's boyfriend.

On realising her mistake, Mum was mortified. Resisting my appeals to stay and get a few hours' sleep, she jumped in her car and drove all the way home—a five-hour drive—turning up unwashed and dishevelled for work in the morning. Soon after that hideous and embarrassing incident, she broke off the relationship with the devastated Ed.

XXX

I loathe jealousy, both feeling it and being subjected to it. Here I was in a relationship with a person whose DNA was composed entirely of little green genes. With Gamal, I only had to mention the name of another man and it would cause his blood to boil.

'It gives me a fever,' he tried to explain one day as we discussed his unruly emotions. 'My ears turn red and it feels like my head will explode.'

'Oh dear,' I said gently teasing him as I tucked a dark curl behind his pretty ear, all the better to see it. The next day I got online and searched for one of those *Is Jealousy Destroying Your Relationship?* type of article, and emailed Gamal the link.

'Thank you,' he said later. 'I realise I am going down a very destructive path. It is like you have put up one of those WRONG WAY, TURN BACK signs. I will try to work on this,' he promised, earnestly.

But I knew Gamal was haunted by my past. While I was his first and only love, he felt he was merely the latest in a line (a very short line, I'd like to add) of the men in my life. Despite his good intentions, I suspected that old habits and years of social, cultural and religious conditioning died hard. God knows what it cost him to square his world view with the fact that I was, in the opinion of the entire Islamic world, damaged goods. After all, Egypt is a country in which virginity, for females at least, is sacred; where the state of a girl's hymen is not a private matter but a public concern and a national obsession; where, in the interest of protecting the integrity of that flimsy scrap of membrane so tied to a family's honour, many mothers prohibit their daughters from playing sport, inserting tampons, masturbating or washing their pink bits with the ubiquitous water hose used in lieu of toilet paper.

In Egyptian days of yore, a girl who was no longer a virgin would insert a blood-filled pigeon's giblet into her vagina in order to prove her purity on her wedding night. Nowadays, in a cheap but dangerous procedure, the vaginal opening can be sewn together a few days before the wedding, ensuring the husband will 'feel' his new bride's virginity and there's blood on the sheets the next morning. Until parliament banned their import, claiming it would promote sex before marriage, Egyptian women were able to buy fake hymens imported from China. However, well-heeled, deflowered brides-to-be can still get around this by paying for the construction of a brand-new hymen.

'I may be your first love, but you'll be my last,' I assured Gamal, trying to ease his torment.

Clearly, I needed to make a few adjustments if I wanted our relationship to work. I asked Gamal to list his expectations, a request that surprised him because he assumed that I would have known these things implicitly. See below Gamal's Great Expectations:

- I should dress conservatively, exposing neither cleavage nor thigh
- I should give up male friends and never flirt with, smile at or touch another man
- I should never be alone with another man
- I should have no contact, unless it is related to Eva, with John
- I should respond to text messages or missed calls immediately
- I should never swim naked in the sea

I was about to laugh and give him a joshing push to the chest, when I realised he was serious. I'd already 'defriended' him on Facebook for giving me a hard time about some bloke from Gdansk I didn't know from a bar of soap 'liking' my posts. I'd seen him pout when I mentioned that Javier Bardem was my favourite male actor; and watched his face darken if I talked about my past life with John.

More than once he'd adjusted a top I was wearing in order to conceal my cleavage. Then there was *The Strange Case of the Unanswered Text Messages* (see bullet point five above).

We were bouncing texts to each other across the world one day when he'd sent me a pet line:

'I love you much more than you love me. xxx ☺.'

'No way, José,' I replied.

'Who is this José?' he responded, quick as a flash.

I listed my sole expectation of him:

- He should chill out and stop being so Old Testament and ridiculous.

'You are in a relationship so, of course, it is natural to compromise,' he said, the paragon of patience ignoring my rude remark. 'It is the tax one must pay. It is not a question of culture or the fact that I am a Muslim. Most Western men would not approve of their fiancée or wife being alone with another man. It is a matter of respect.'

I'd like to be able to report, dear reader, that at that juncture I counted to ten, gathered my thoughts and, sticking entirely to the point, calmly and coherently explained to Gamal the facts as I saw them—that there were circumstances in which men and women in the West could be alone and that (surprisingly!) no sexual behaviour ensued, and that couples often remained friends after they'd separated or divorced. Instead, I'm ashamed to admit, I lost it, launching into a diatribe on topics including but not limited to the death of patriarchy, a woman's right to choose and female genital mutilation.

As a reasonably intelligent, strong-willed, independent woman in her fifties accustomed to the freedoms associated with single life in Australia, the concessions Gamal expected me to make were, in my opinion, unrealistic, unreasonable and, quite frankly, outrageous. I'm too old for this shit, I thought.

'I'm too long in the tooth and stuck in my ways to change,' I said when I'd calmed down a bit. 'Haven't you heard the English expression "you can't teach an old dog new tricks"? Wouldn't it be easier for you to modify your expectations and change your way of thinking?' I suggested, trying another tack. But Gamal wasn't fooled.

'The English word for jealousy does not properly capture the meaning of the Arabic word *gheerah*,' he went on to explain. '*Gheerah* is seen as an honourable quality. Men should have a strong sense of *gheerah* and feel responsible for their mothers, their wives, their sisters and their daughters. A good Muslim man wants the women in his life to be treated with respect. He does not want them to be harassed or looked at lewdly by other men. He should ensure that he is treating women in the proper manner. According to Islam, a husband must to try hard to make his wife comfortable and happy by providing for her and taking care of her needs.'

I remembered the time Gamal took me to a dentist in Cairo and that I'd had to banish him from the surgery. My boyfriend wanted to stand sentinel at my side, ensuring that as I lay helpless in the dentist's chair looking stunningly attractive with my decayed fang, a profusion of instruments sticking out of my gaping mouth and saliva drooling down my chin, the dentist, overcome by uncontrollable lust, didn't try to molest me.

'I'm not denying that aspects of the idea have merit,' I said, recalling how touched I'd been by his desire to protect me that day; torn between appreciating the seemingly benign and altruistic characteristics of the concept and being suspicious of its underlying, less benevolent implications.

'Treating people with respect is great. But can't you see that this *gheerah* thing is patronising to women? It assumes they're like children who need 'parenting' and protection by men,' I added, using finger quotes to emphasis my 'parenting' point.

But Gamal couldn't see that at all.

'You are the one being ridiculous,' he said tersely.

'So basically, what you're saying is that I shouldn't mind if you get jealous. That I should welcome it, in fact,' I said with more than a hint of derision.

'It is natural for a man to want to protect his wife. Muslim women also want this,' he replied coolly. 'They are honoured and proud that their husbands have a strong sense of *gheerah* for them. Married or engaged Muslim women do not have male friends because this sort of casual contact can lead to attraction and sexual relations.'

'Well bully for them!' I retorted sarcastically. 'But if you hadn't noticed, I'm not a Muslim woman.' And with that, I stomped off to the bathroom to run myself a bath.

It was evident that if it ever came to living under the same roof, this issue would be the biggest challenge in our relationship. As I lay stewing in hot water, I hoped to hell we'd have it sorted by then.

Of course, I wasn't the only one who would have to make compromises. According to Gamal, he was already bending over backwards to accommodate my laissez-faire, Western sensibilities. Over the decades, I'd kept in touch with my English ex-boyfriend Patrick, catching up with him and his wife whenever I was in the UK. Gamal and I were in London when the couple invited us for dinner and to stay the night.

At first, to my chagrin, Gamal refused to go. But unable to bear a woman's tears, he finally agreed to do something he'd been certain his principles would never permit: he'd have dinner with his lover's ex, and sleep overnight in his house. Despite his misgivings, Gamal promised to be polite and sociable, and not to embarrass me in front of my friends.

'Am I not good?' he asked sweetly. 'Do you see how much I love you and what I am prepared to do for you? See how I am very liberal compared to other Egyptian men.'

So, as the train rattled past the snow-covered rooftops on its way to Twickenham station, Gamal steeled himself for his impending ideological battle, and aware he was doing this for my sake alone, I kissed him and thanked him for the tremendous sacrifice he was about to make.

25

The Cold Feet

The Egyptian Revolution had come and gone. For the first time, democratic elections were held in Egypt. But given the lack of a credible or organised opposition, the Egyptian people had no choice but to elect the conservative Muslim Brotherhood's 'Freedom and Justice Party' into government; the very opposite outcome to the ideals of the Arab Spring uprising. It soon became apparent that the Brotherhood were as power-hungry and dishonest as their predecessors. Furthermore, having absolutely no experience, they were utterly inept at managing the country as so often happens when a dictator is overthrown. With worsening economic hardship and civil unrest, anarchy loomed as a real possibility. It seemed that every time we spoke, Gamal had another horrifying story to tell—reports of state-condoned rape of women in Egyptian cities, brutal bashings of citizens opposed to the new administration, violent clashes between the police and anti-Brotherhood activists, talk about the introduction of Sharia Law and animosity towards foreigners. By the end of 2012, Egypt was rated as one of the most dangerous destinations in the world.

'It is out of the question for you to come here, now,' Gamal said despairingly. 'There is no state or rule of law. Things are truly falling apart.'

Following the situation in our media as it was unfolding there, I knew that returning to Egypt was no longer an option. Pursuing their hard-line Islamic agenda rather than encouraging political reconciliation or developing policies addressing matters of critical national interest—economic or cultural—there was no telling what would happen while the Brotherhood remained in power.

Meanwhile, the country plunged deeper into economic depression and the tourists stayed away. When Gamal's regional manager flew in from London, the Cairo office arranged the mandatory outing to the pyramids.

'I could not believe it!' Gamal exclaimed afterwards on Skype. 'There was no one there. *No one.* We were the only people at the pyramids that day.'

I'd witnessed an example of the deteriorating situation for myself the last time I was in Cairo—a bedraggled line of dusty-robed men on the side of the road as we drove home from seeing a movie at the City Stars Mall.

'What's going on?' I'd asked.

'They are the poor queueing for bread,' he explained. 'Bakers are given subsidised flour by the state but they sell it on the black market instead of using it to bake bread. So now there is a shortage.'

It was obvious that Gamal was becoming depressed by his country's rapid decline. I felt helpless; unable to give him so much as a hug. Each time we Skyped, he'd report on the increasingly chaotic situation in Cairo: the traffic so congested that some nights it took him two hours to drive home from work where normally it would take an hour at most; essential services like electricity and water cut for extended periods; industrial strikes on a regular basis; the police, if they dared or deigned to show up for work at all, refusing to do their job. Rumours circulated that foreign interests were behind the shortages and disruptions; the aim apparently being to destabilise the country and incite the Egyptian people into yet another uprising. Who would know if that was just a ruse perpetrated by the government to take the spotlight off their incompetence and corruption.

'Can you believe it? Today our Prime Minister released a statement suggesting we sit around in our underwear when the air conditioning is not working,' Gamal said on one occasion. 'The government warned that this summer we should be prepared for at least two electricity cuts a day. Everyone is saying that if we miss the power cut in the morning not to be upset because the Muslim Brotherhood will ensure we enjoy another one in the afternoon,' he added mirthlessly.

One morning, I found him online looking decidedly unkempt.

'We have not had water all day,' he complained. 'No one can use the bathroom.'

The poor bugger, I thought, wishing I could swoop down, pluck him out of his appalling circumstances and whisk him off to a spa bath in a Four Seasons Hotel somewhere.

When we spoke the following day, he reported that a group of Coptic Christians was attacked and a young boy killed, while the police stood back and did nothing.

'I think there will be another revolution,' he said. 'But next time there will be much more spilling of blood.'

Sadly, returning to Egypt and my home away from, the Hotel Longchamps, was becoming an ever more unthinkable prospect, especially in light of the ruling party's attitude towards women. With a stricter interpretation of Islamic laws, many human rights groups were seeing a regression in freedoms for women. Opposed to a Muslim woman marrying a non-Muslim man, the Brotherhood also contested the right of a woman to lodge a legal complaint of marital rape. They rejected resolutions for equal inheritance rights as well as equal rights for the sexes; reasserted the requirement for a woman to obtain her husband's permission to travel or work; and opposed the provision of contraceptives for adolescent girls. Predictably, they severely criticised a UN recommendation supporting the legalisation of abortion and the right of a woman to choose the gender of her partner.

Since the Brotherhood's election, I'd become alarmed by reports of increased violence against women, including an upsurge of sexual attacks; some said the incidents were part of a state-organised campaign to discourage women from participating in the ongoing protests and in public life generally. The Brotherhood rejected a draft United Nations' document supporting the combatting of violence towards women, arguing it was not in accordance with Islamic principles and that it would lead to the breakdown of family values and thus to the disintegration of society.

Due to its criminalisation in 2008 and a campaign to educate the Egyptian population about its risks, female genital mutilation had been on the decline; Egypt's Grand Mufti even issued a legal opinion stating that FGM was against the Islamic value system. But since coming to power, there were reports that the Muslim Brotherhood planned to legalise it again and were sending mobile health clinics into rural areas to carry out the 'operation' free of charge.

Traditionally, female relatives are complicit in perpetuating the practice, often carrying out the procedure themselves; sometimes with fatal consequences. Typically performed in conditions of minimal hygiene, a girl's genitalia is partially or totally removed with a razor blade. In some cases, the entrance to her vagina is sewn together, causing chronic pain and infection when she begins to menstruate. And then horror of horrors, imagine her wedding night—her husband tearing apart her long-sealed passage in order to consummate the marriage.

I'd read shocking accounts of the practice including the results of a survey which estimated that nine out of ten Egyptian women aged 15 to 40 had undergone the procedure; that's over 27.2 million women. I'd ranted and raved to Gamal about the horrendous violence being perpetrated on his countrywomen.

'Why aren't people out in the streets protesting about *this*?' I cried, knowing I was weighing in on complex cultural and religious issues. 'It's child abuse. It should be *the* number one issue.'

'I agree. It should not be happening,' Gamal said, listening patiently to my objections. 'It is not approved by Islam. It is a tribal custom practised mostly in rural areas which has been going on for centuries. We are dealing with ignorance and ancient traditions as well as illiteracy and poverty. But you have to understand,' he continued with a worn-weary sigh. 'There are more pressing issues facing Egypt at the moment.'

And as he began to elaborate, I shut up and listened. But that night, lying in bed and struggling to fall asleep, I was haunted by the thought that Gamal's mother, surely not his sisters, had undoubtedly undergone the horrific procedure.

✕ ✕ ✕

Now that Egypt was off the co-habitation agenda, Gamal and I needed to think about how to proceed. After twelve stressful and exhausting months of house-sitting, I was over my transient lifestyle. Knowing full well that I wouldn't be able to see Gamal as often, I took out a lease on an apartment in Melbourne. I figured I'd done my bit and now it was up to Gamal to do his.

'I do not know when I will get an attachment to London. I think I should submit the Prospective Marriage Visa application and come to Australia, instead,' he said.

But when I signed onto Skype a few days later, he looked as if he'd been run over by a truck.

'What on earth's happened?' I asked, an icy dread rising in my veins; thinking that his mother had died or something.

'Katherine, I do not know,' he replied, clearly agitated. 'Suddenly I found myself anxious about coming to Australia. I am not a hundred percent sure about it. I think I am having the cold feet.'

I felt sick. But I took a deep breath and asked him to elaborate.

'I am frightened about what I will be like when I come to you,' he blurted. 'What if I cannot find a job? I am worried I will get jealous or homesick and depressed. I will be a burden to you and you will end up hating me. I will not be in control of the situation. I am frightened I will lose you if I come. All these things I am thinking. I cannot eat or sleep. If I arrive in this state I will be a mess and we will not survive,' he said miserably, his tousled head in his hands.

I'd also been worrying about how things could be worked out between us if he came to Australia. I, too, was concerned about his chances of finding employment commensurate with his skills and qualifications, about his transition to Western life and the 'adjustments' I might have to make. He'd be taking a huge risk, committing professional suicide—probably giving up a brilliant career, leaving his family and beloved country; and throwing it all away to come and live with a strong-willed, irreligious woman twice his age in a foreign and, to my mind, xenophobic land. I was apprehensive about my capacity to support him, if it came to that. I felt daunted by an impending weight of responsibility.

By the same token, I was shocked by Gamal's unexpected disclosure. People risked their lives crossing oceans in leaky, overcrowded boats to come to this country. And here he was passing up an opportunity of a lifetime. Not only that, but where was his sense of adventure? He'd spoken with such bravado about doing whatever it took to be together, knowing I'd turned my world upside down and gone to the ends of the earth to maintain our relationship. He claimed he was ready to play his part.

'You will see I love you much more than you love me,' he'd so often declared. Maybe he wasn't as confident or as 'manly' as he portrayed himself to be.

We were on the verge of achieving our goal. Yet after everything we'd been through, everything *I'd* been through, Gamal was having reservations. Evidently, as the time to submit the Prospective Marriage Visa approached and the reality of what he was about to do came into focus, he'd panicked. I understood his concerns, having experienced similar anxieties myself, but amazingly, no doubt foolishly at my age, I was willing to risk everything for love and take a chance on making a life together.

As we continued to talk over the course of that day, however, I began to think that maybe Gamal was right. It could be a disaster if he came to Australia. I knew, too, that unlike him, I didn't have as much to lose. Painful as it was, I respected his foresight and the honesty and courage it took to confess his fears. How could I blame him for having misgivings? For getting anxious about taking such a momentous and possibly catastrophic step. Of course, this was a crucial time in his life. He was treading carefully, leading with his head, not his heart and I wished I'd applied that kind of logic to many of my life's choices.

'Do not say that,' Gamal said when I pointed out the heartache my impulsive 'act first, think later' attitude had created throughout my life. 'You are pure and spontaneous. I love this about you. Please do not ever change.'

After signing off on Skype that day, I rang my mum to tearfully debrief. Thank God she didn't try to jolly me up, assign blame or suggest a solution. She simply listened and at that moment, that was all I needed. Then, curling up on the couch in an all-too-familiar foetal position, I began, like standing back from the chaos of a Jackson Pollock painting, to put things into perspective; realising on reflection that I shouldn't have been surprised by Gamal's sudden change of heart. What's more, I certainly didn't want him turning up on my doorstep unless he was a hundred percent sure it was what he wanted to do.

'I think I need some space from the pressure of submitting the visa,' he said next day, unable to look directly into the lens of the webcam. 'So I can reach a decision about coming to Australia without this…this stress,' he faltered. 'I am so, so sorry I am doing this,' he continued, miserably. 'I do not blame you if you do not want to hear from me again.'

'Do you need some time out?' I asked. 'Maybe we shouldn't contact each other for a while?' I suggested, holding my breath and expecting the worst, my heart gripped in a vice.

'*No, Kathy*! Are you *crazy*?' he exclaimed, his voice rising to a falsetto. 'If you are willing, I want to speak to you every day as usual. And we will see each other again very soon, Insha'Allah.'

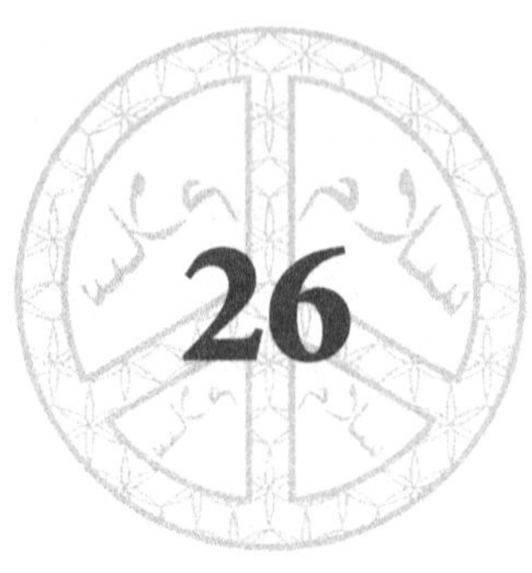

26

Paradise

Every morning Gamal would be waiting online, his dazzling smile radiating across cyberspace.

'I miss you so much,' he'd say.

Then why don't you come to me? I'd have to stop myself from pleading.

But in spite of his request for more time to think, I knew Gamal had made up his mind about coming to Australia.

'Katherine, I want to be with you, you know that. But I am convinced we will fail if we go ahead with this plan,' he said, his mournful expression like a portrait from Picasso's Blue Period.

'It could take twelve months for the marriage visa to be approved. *If* it gets approved. Then it will take years for me to become a permanent resident and be eligible to apply for a job in my field. And how many jobs are there for Egyptian journalists with English as their second language, in your country?' he asked.

'It would be very difficult, not just financially but emotionally, too. It would put so much strain on our relationship. I want to preserve our love, not destroy it. We must find another way to be together,' he concluded.

'If I was rich everything'd be different,' I joked, holding back the tears. 'We could live in a big apartment overlooking Port Phillip Bay and I could support you until you got established.'

'No, Katherine,' Gamal said firmly. 'I do not want that. It is my responsibility to support *you*. But I want you to promise me something,' he said, smiling sheepishly.

'What's that?' I asked.

'I want you to promise that when you die, you will choose to be with me in Paradise.'

'Of course, I'd choose you, you idiot!' I assured him. 'If I ever make it to Paradise, that is,' I added, cheekily.

Besides, I thought, there'd be no choice to make, would there? According to Islam, you have to be Muslim, admit there's no God but Allah and believe that Mohammed was a prophet in order to enter Paradise. Apart from Gamal, I couldn't think of anyone I knew who fitted those particular criteria. Furthermore, I couldn't believe we were having the conversation.

We began to talk about how, where and when we could see each other again, making plans to meet up somewhere between Egypt and Australia as soon as possible. Gamal spoke to his manager about taking his well overdue annual leave, but the political situation in Egypt was rapidly deteriorating so she wasn't going to promise anything. Then once again, on 30th June 2013, the Egyptian people, fourteen million of them this time, took to the streets to rid themselves of yet another tyrant—their Muslim Brotherhood President, Mohamed Morsi. Clashes between opponents and supporters of the twelve-month-old regime erupted all over the country and Gamal's leave was cancelled indefinitely.

The majority of Egyptians were relieved that Morsi had been forced to stand down. In his short reign, he had been a disaster for

Egypt, granting himself unlimited powers, issuing a non-inclusive Islamic-backed draft constitution, persecuting and jailing journalists, demonstrators and members of minority religions whilst crippling the economy with his government's lack of policy. But many Islamists were furious. Describing the party's ousting as a coup, they began a campaign of violent protests all over Egypt, being prepared to die for their cause.

Historically, the Egyptian military hadn't made a habit of opening fire on their own people so at first they tried to disperse the crowds with water cannon and tear gas.

'They are using water cannon to get rid of the Islamists,' Gamal said on Skype one morning. 'But instead of water, they are pumping out raw sewage.'

'Oh God, that's terrible,' I gasped, crinkling my nose in disgust, trying to imagine what the reaction would be if our army did that in Australia.

A couple of days later, he had news about a new type of tear gas the army was trialling.

'You cannot breathe and your body becomes paralysed,' he said.

It sounded like the stories I'd heard about the nerve gas they used in the First World War.

'There is graffiti springing up all over Cairo about it.'

'What does it say?' I asked.

'Dear Army, Please give us back the old gas,' he replied with a chortle.

How on earth do people who've suffered a brutal regime for years, the humiliation of their own army spraying them with excrement and choking them with poisonous gas, manage to retain a sense of humour? I wondered.

Unfortunately, Gamal had been right about the spilling of more blood. The Muslim Brotherhood had reportedly acquired and stockpiled weapons brought into Egypt from Libya after President Gaddafi was killed. The military quickly lost patience with the Islamist protesters who were using not only rocks and petrol bombs to attack them, but guns and grenades as well. They retaliated with brute force: for weeks the streets of Cairo teemed with armed protesters, police and the army. Bombs were exploding, snipers were shooting from rooftops; buildings were stormed and burnt. Unsurprisingly, people became inured to the ongoing violence as evidenced in a YouTube video that Gamal sent me of a man sitting outside a coffee shop smoking sheesha and drinking tea as he watched the police brutally attack a group of peaceful protesters.

'I cannot drive home from work,' he whispered one night into his mobile phone. 'It is too dangerous. We are having to sleep on the floor at the office.'

When he eventually tried to return to his father's apartment, the road was blocked by tanks; it took him hours to negotiate a route.

But in the end, the battle against the might of the Egyptian Army was one the Islamists couldn't win.

'The military have either killed or arrested most of the Muslim Brotherhood and their supporters,' Gamal explained. 'The interim government has declared them a terrorist organisation. There will be some jihadists committing the occasional act of violence but nothing on the scale we have seen,' he said. 'Most Egyptians want the return of a Mubarak-style of government; someone who can rule with an iron fist. At least we will have economic stability and a functioning State.'

The contrast between Gamal's life in Egypt and mine in Australia couldn't have been starker. Like most Australians, I'd never come close to anything that amounted to a civil war and now, through Gamal's eyes, I felt as if I was in the thick of one. As I watched the unfolding events on the media, living and breathing every electrifying moment, I was drawn in—horrified but at the same time, vicariously fascinated.

✕✕✕

Six months passed before Gamal and I saw each other again. They were dark days indeed and we often fell into despair. I kept myself distracted by painting, confiding in friends and family when I needed support. It seemed as though it wasn't our destiny to be together, after all. In fact, events seemed to be conspiring to keep us apart. Gamal's parents' fervent prayers appeared to have found the divine ear. We gave each other permission to call it quits.

'Katherine, I would not blame you, *no one* would blame you, if you chose to end it,' Gamal said one day as he tried to console me during an emotional session on Skype. 'You have struggled so hard for this relationship. I understand if you do not want to continue.'

'It's too much,' I sobbed. 'I miss you. I just want us to be together. Plus, I've only got eighteen months left,' I quipped, as I grabbed another tissue from the box.

'What do you mean?' Gamal asked, visibly alarmed.

'I'll have reached my used-by date by then,' I joked. But even though I was making light of it, I was becoming more and more aware of our age difference—maybe because our separations were increasing in length, and time/gravity waits for no one.

We talked into the night about what we could do; however, one thing became patently clear: neither of us could face the thought of not seeing each other again. Both fighters and loyal to a fault, we agreed we would never give up.

When at long last Gamal was granted leave, we met for ten days in Bali, one of the few destinations where a young Egyptian Muslim male can easily obtain a tourist visa. Flying in from Cairo, Gamal checked into the hotel and waited for my flight to arrive from Melbourne. A few hours later, I was knocking on his door and when he opened it to see me standing there before him, he lifted me clear off the ground, squeezing me so tightly I could barely breathe.

'Oh, Katherine. My Kathy,' he murmured softly, nuzzling my hair.

We didn't do a lot during those two weeks in Seminyak. Mostly, we lounged around the pool or hung out at the beach. In the evenings, we'd eat nasi goreng at an open-air restaurant; afterwards wandering hand-in-hand down to the sea. Lying back on beanbags on the sand, we'd drink our Bintang beer from the bottle and listen to the local reggae band play long into the balmy night.

We were, however, very active in bed. If we weren't making love, sleeping, play fighting, ordering room service or watching movies, we'd lie in each other's arms trying to figure out how we could be together. I couldn't live in Egypt and Gamal couldn't come to Australia—even for a visit. Where in the world could we be? One night, in a touching but also amusing performance, I stood at the foot of the bed and sang for Gamal—a song from *West Side Story* that had stayed with me from the age of nine when my mother took me and Lisa to see the movie at the Palais Theatre in St Kilda on finding Luna Park closed for maintenance:

'There's a place for us. A time and place for us. Hold my hand and we're half way there. Hold my hand and I'll take you there. Somehow. Some day. Somewhere.'

My Egyptian lover had never heard of the musical nor the song about star-crossed lovers, Tony and Maria, and at the end of my heart-rending recital, me laughing and crying all at once, he wrestled me onto the mattress; burying me under his weight as he kissed away my tears.

By the end of our holiday, we agreed that our only option was London. Back in our respective countries, the coldest winter in over a hundred and twenty years descended on Cairo; kids who hadn't seen rain, never mind snow, built snowy pyramids instead of snowmen in the streets, sucking their mittenless fingers to prevent them from turning to ice. A bomb exploded on the roadside outside the shop where we used to buy our spicy sausage sandwiches on the way to Gamal's apartment to make love.

'Was anyone killed?' I asked him.

'Just a cat,' he replied wryly. 'It stepped on the device and set it off. Everyone is joking that the cats of Cairo now have a purpose. We can use them as bomb detonators.'

I laughed, but the situation in Egypt was far from funny. I was so sad for the people of Cairo, and the city with its ancient buildings, steeped in a history that underpinned much of the European story. And then there was Gamal: with bated breath, I prayed for his safety; willing for a miracle to get him out of there.

Every day, he'd check online to see if a post had opened up in the UK. Then one morning, after signing into Skype, I found his flashing white teeth filling the screen.

'Guess what?' he said. 'There is a job for an Arabic-speaking news broadcaster going with my organisation in London. I have applied for it.'

'Oh, My *God*! You're going to be on telly!' was my first reaction.

✕ ✕ ✕

So now it was a matter of waiting, hoping and praying; Gamal was in charge of the praying bit. We knew it would be a prolonged and laborious process involving shortlistings, interviews and screen tests, but as 2014 crept warily into being with his skills, experience, looks and charm, we were quietly optimistic.

Of course, that was a different world; a world before anyone in the West had heard of a terror organisation called Islamic State, or images of the lifeless body of a Syrian toddler washed ashore on a beach in Turkey had flashed around the globe.

With no notion of what lay ahead, I imagined living in London with lover and soulmate; admittedly, sometimes becoming anxious when I thought about uprooting my life again. After all, most unattached women my age had stockpiled their acorns and battened down the hatches for the long, lonely winters ahead. Whereas, here was I throwing open another door like some bright-eyed and bushy-tailed beaver diving head first into uncharted waters. Was I making a big mistake? What was I thinking? How could our relationship possibly work? And for how long? I tried to imagine he and I still together—me seventy, him forty-three. I've been told I have an active imagination, but it was a stretch even for me. And where, oh where, could I buy a copy of *The Mature Woman's Guide to Dating a Man Half Her Age*? But then I'd think about Gamal—about his gorgeous face and tender heart, and knew I couldn't give him up. Not yet, anyway.

27

Mushroom Cloud

As fate, luck or Allah would have it, the London post never eventuated and month by depressing month our optimism and any chance of being together slid slowly but surely away. Wretched and demoralised we began to acknowledge the hopelessness of our situation and tried our hand at breaking up.

It was summer in Australia, winter in Egypt, my morning and Gamal's night, the first time we ended it on Skype. Gamal was huddled under a doona, shivering in his fleecy-striped pyjamas. I was naked, sweating under a sheet.

'We have tried for so long to be together but we are no closer to reaching our goal,' my distraught lover said. And although I'd never seen him cry, knowing full well that for Arab men it's seen as a sign of weakness, he looked as if he was on the verge of tears. 'I love you, Katherine. You have no idea how much I love you, but I cannot have you,' he added desolately.

That break up lasted two months before he weakened and

contacted me again. If he hadn't, knowing me, I would definitely have contacted him.

The next time we split up for a whole five months following an argument about this book. While Gamal was tickled pink when I was writing about him, he saw red when I was writing about my former life with John. With nerves frayed from our intolerable predicament, we'd been arguing about the manuscript on and off for weeks.

'It is like you are reliving your life with him,' he protested bitterly online one day. 'You are thinking about him all the time.'

'I'm writing a memoir, for god's sake. What do you want me to do? Skip thirty years of my life?' I snapped in exasperation, literally tearing at my hair. After everything I'd done to be with him, what further proof did he need of my love and devotion?

'I would not ask you to do this because I know what would happen. You would choose your ex-husband over me,' he said grimly, his face set in stone.

'Writing my life story does *not* mean I'm choosing my ex-husband over you. That's insane,' I shrieked. 'I can't help having a past. My past has made me who I am. If you want someone without a past, go find yourself a fucking virgin.' And with that I hung up. In the heat of the moment I was so pissed off and frustrated, that I determined never to speak to him again.

Then, months down the track I found a publisher. Miserable, missing him and sorry, I emailed Gamal to let him know. He responded immediately and we were on again. Between breaking up and getting back together, we managed to see each other in Thailand.

The year 2015 began and continued with unspeakable evil and horror, the world reeling from one monstrous atrocity to the next— the Charlie Hebdo shooting in Paris, the Boko Haram massacre in Nigeria, the Al Shabaab terrorist attack in Kenya, killings at a beach resort in Tunisia, suicide bombings in Turkey and Beirut, Russian airstrikes in Syria and a second terrorist attack in the French capital; escaping war-torn cities and towns, a dispossessed and desperate river of humanity flowed without end into Europe.

It was Gamal's job to report on these barbarous events and the ongoing conflicts in Afghanistan, Yemen, Iraq, Palestine and just about everywhere else in the Middle East—the beheadings, child crucifixions and mass executions; people buried alive or burnt to death in a cage. He was living in Dante's *Inferno*, encircled by terror, not only in the surrounding region, but with bomb blasts occurring with alarming regularity and violent clashes between supporters of ousted Egyptian President Morsi and riot police rife on the streets of Cairo, in his own backyard as well. Stressed out by the workload and unbearable pressure and disturbed by the heinous content of the stories they were covering, one journalist had collapsed at his desk, while others were seeking counselling. I tried to support Gamal when we spoke on Skype, encouraging him to talk and debrief, but for the most part, he was unforthcoming. He'd had a gutful of horror; he just wanted to hear me rabbit on about the mundane events of my every-day first-world life—like what I'd made for dinner, a conversation I'd had with my mother, a movie I'd seen, the weather etcetera. My inane prattle seemed to relax him. I'd try to make him laugh and tell him that I was proud of him and, in what had become a private joke between us, that I loved him way more than he loved me.

He didn't hesitate though, in his condemnation of ISIS. 'They are not true Muslims,' he said emphatically. 'They have misinterpreted the Qur'an for their own warped agenda. It is terrible. They are destroying the name of Islam.'

And I could see very clearly how the actions of ISIS in Gamal's part of the world, perpetrated in the name of Allah and the Qu'ran, were providing politicians and the media with excuses to make funda-mental changes in our own country to long-held compassionate and welcoming policies towards those fleeing conflict and oppression. Sadly, the public in Australia, as in other Western countries, was turning against the Muslim community in their midst.

In June, Gamal was able to take his annual leave and we met in Phu Quoc, a small island off the coast of the Vietnamese mainland. The first thing I spotted when I caught sight of him at the airport was the sprig of snowy white hair amidst his crop of dark brown curls, despite that fact that he was only thirty-one. He looked older; world-weary; scarred somehow. You could see the burden he'd been carrying in the way he walked; how living where he lived and doing what he did had dragged him down; how he'd been wounded at the very core. His face, although brightening like the sun as usual when he saw me, appeared haggard. Even from a distance, I could detect the sad cast to his eyes. I felt my heart fly through the air to meet him. The idealistic young man I'd met nearly five years ago in Luxor had come to know so much about human evil and suffering; too much, and when I reached his side, falling headlong into his arms, I wished I had the power to erase that horrendous knowledge from his consciousness. We did nothing but eat, sleep, swim and make love during our ten days on the island; and while I couldn't heal what ailed him, for a brief moment I was able to sooth his troubled mind.

Back at work, Gamal couldn't have predicted what happened next. In order to prevent Egyptian men under forty from running off to join ISIS, the government banned them from leaving the country without a security clearance. He lodged an application, which promptly disappeared into some inept and indifferent bureaucratic hole, never to be seen again. Now he was a prisoner in his own land.

✗✗✗

There was a time when I believed that love conquered all, when, as the Beatles told us, love was all you needed. But a month after we'd ended the relationship for good, waking up on the day of the American presidential election to find a dangerous, narcissistic, misogynist, racist bully and buffoon as 'leader of the free world', a long-held belief was shattered. Love hadn't conquered the tyranny of distance between Gamal and I, nor bridged the gap between our conflicting values. We were poles apart, not just geographically and in age but also in our fundamental beliefs. There was no right or wrong and it wasn't for lack of love or endeavour. We simply didn't 'get' one another; he was a creature of his culture, I, a creature of mine.

We'd been limping along for months, contacting each other every day as usual; buoying each other up, calming each other down, hoping in vain for a miracle; both of us avoiding what needed to be done. A year had passed since our holiday in Vietnam and with Gamal still unable to obtain a security clearance it looked unlikely, unless I returned to Egypt, that we'd see each other again. The situation was utterly untenable. One of us had to end it once and for all, and when my insecure and possessive lover had another fit of pique over a text message that I hadn't immediately answered, declaring it was his 'right' to question me, infuriated and up to here with his unnecessary and controlling behaviour, I stepped, albeit metaphorically, like Madame Bovary in front of the train.

'If that's your attitude, there's no way we could live together under the same roof,' I said harshly on Skype, my unruly heart pounding disconcertingly in my throat. 'No wonder you believe it's your right to interrogate me, being raised in an environment where a man's a hero if he kills his wife for cheating on him, and slicing off a girl's clitoris is the norm. You think you're so fucking liberal. Stop kidding yourself,' I blurted angrily, aware I was pressing the nuclear button.

We glared at each other from across the planet for what seemed to me an eternity.

'You know what, Katherine?' Gamal responded matter-of-factly at last. 'I agree with you. We could not live together.' Although I knew they were coming, his cold words were an icy kick in my stomach.

And that was it. Under a mushroom cloud of lost hopes and dreams, the conflict between his East and my West was finally brought to a conclusion. It's better this way I thought after we hung up that day, hugging a pillow to my chest as I wept and wept; stopping myself from calling him to tell him I was sorry and to ask for forgiveness. Angry and indignant, Gamal could move on with his life—find a girl, get married, have babies. God knows how long he would have persisted with our doomed relationship, otherwise.

✕✕✕

As the dust settles, I fluctuate between grief and relief. I don't have to worry about getting into trouble for failing to respond to a text message or committing some other trifling transgression—minor altercations indicative of far bigger issues. The constant and arduous struggle to find a way of being together is over. In many respects, I feel liberated. Although I love him still, I miss being loved by Gamal, even if only from afar. I yearn to see his face, to hear his voice; each morning my heart contracting as I wake up to my life without him. How long before I stop automatically checking the Cairo weather forecast at the end of the nightly news or, despite being unable to understand a word, drop what I'm doing to listen to someone speaking Arabic on TV? When will I forget to calculate the time difference between Egypt and Australia—in my morning, imagining Gamal settling down to sleep; in my evening, picturing him eating breakfast? And when will he cease to inhabit my dreams? Dogged by self-recrimination, I blame myself for my lack of tolerance and understanding, ashamed of my hostility and inability to resolve our differences. If we were unable to work things out, no wonder the rest of the world is tearing itself apart. *Let him go*, a voice whispers inside my head, and I do my best to listen.

For sure it won't be long before Gamal meets and falls in love with a beautiful young woman who'll be everything he wants and deserves. There's so much I could tell her: like that he's partial to stuffed roast pigeon, and chocolate with hazelnuts in it; that he's scared of lizards and not keen on cats and dogs; that he prefers Superman to Batman; that he loves his mother; that despite two years in the military, he has no sense of direction; and doesn't know one end of a screwdriver from the other. I'd let her know that she needn't fret about putting on a few extra kilos because he likes a woman with curves. She might be interested to learn that if she catches him off-guard he's ticklish, that she'll beat him hands down at 'knuckles', but never win in a dog paddling race; that he reads history books and metaphysical fiction; that his favourite colour is blue. She should understand that he'll always choose the side of the bed closest to the front door in order to protect her if someone breaks in; that if she becomes sick he'll get worried and rush out to buy a selection of medicines, snacks and fizzy drinks in the hope they'll make her feel better; that every night he'll hold her in his arms until he assumes she's fallen asleep.

If you added it up, we had scarcely twelve months of physical contact in our five-year long-distance relationship. Not nearly enough time together. But I know I was truly loved by Gamal; loved more than some people are loved in a lifetime—that impossible kind of love that people write poems and songs about. I'm not sorry that he came into my life and, despite the extraordinary trials and trib-ulations, I'm grateful I got the chance to love him in return. I wish nothing but the best for that beautiful and devoted young man and will think of him every day for as long as I live, wondering if he's happy, hoping Insha'Allah, he is; knowing I won't meet anyone like him again.

✕✕✕

'You are in my eyes,' he'd said one day in Cairo.

I guessed what he meant, but in the dim light of his unadorned apartment, the call to prayer filtering through the dusty wooden shutters, I asked him to interpret the traditional Egyptian words of love, to savour them and relish the sound of English spoken with an Arabic accent.

'It means, when I look at the world, I see you before all else,' he said as he smothered my eyelids with butterfly kisses before rolling out of bed and slipping on his gallabiyah.

When you are old and grey and full of sleep,
And nodding by the fire, take down this book,
And slowly read, and dream of the soft look
Your eyes had once, and of their shadows deep;

How many loved your moments of glad grace,
And loved your beauty with love false or true,
But one man loved the pilgrim soul in you,
And loved the sorrows of your changing face;

And bending down beside the glowing bars,
Murmur, a little sadly, how Love fled
And paced upon the mountains overhead
And hid his face amid a crowd of stars.

—William Yeats

Acknowledgements

First and foremost, I want to thank my publisher Catherine Lewis from Wild Dingo Press, without whom this book wouldn't have been possible. Thank you, Cathi, for your guidance, insights and enthusiasm; for pushing me to ever greater heights. What a fabulous team we made and what an incredible experience it has been.

It was also a pleasure collaborating with editor Katia Ariel whose remarkable expertise, sensitivity and respect for the integrity of my work was so appreciated.

Many thanks to Kalinda Ashton from Writer's Victoria for her helpful manuscript appraisal, to Caroline Verge for casting her eagle legal eye over my publishing contract, to Gisela Beer and Mihirini De Zoysa Lewis for their drop-dead gorgeous book cover design and to Fiona Drury from *Write Angle* for her invaluable counsel.

I am gratefully indebted to my family and friends who read, re-read, offered comments, provided emotional support and generally put up with me over the last few years. There are no words to express my gratitude to my mother for her support and encouragement, not just during the writing of this book, but throughout my whole life. Suffice to say—thank you, Mum. I love you.

Finally, thank you, Gamal, for your willingness to share so much about yourself, your country, your culture and faith. Thank you for everything. Live long and prosper, my love.

www.ingramcontent.com/pod-product-compliance
Lightning Source LLC
Chambersburg PA
CBHW071554030726
47593CB00001BA/156